SPIRITUAL COMBAT REVISITED

Jonathan Robinson
of the Oratory

SPIRITUAL COMBAT
Revisited

This is indeed the hardest of all struggles;
for while we strive against self, self is striving against us,
and therefore is the victory here
most glorious and precious in the sight of God.

—Lorenzo Scupoli, *The Spiritual Combat*

IGNATIUS PRESS   SAN FRANCISCO

Cover art: *Crucifix with Christ and Saint Peter*
Master of Saint Francis of Bardi (13th century)
Museo Bandini, Fiesole, Italy
Copyright Scala/Art Resource, New York

Cover design by Roxanne Mei Lum

ISBN 0–89870–930–x
Library of Congress Control Number 2002112863
Printed in the United States of America ∞

To Joseph Pope

In remembrance of his unwearied and generous support of the Toronto Oratory and in gratitude for his many and unsung kindnesses to all of us in St. Philip's House.

J. R.

January 2002

CONTENTS

Spiritual Combat Today

> The function of grace, according to Augustine, is not to drag us kicking and screaming to salvation, but to allow us to want and to do the things that are right and in every sense desirable. For no one is just against his will. We shall want to do the right if we love the right, so that once we are "prepared" to love well, we shall need no manipulation, but simply God's support to keep us going.
>
> —John M. Rist, *Augustine: Ancient Thought Baptized*

It is a part of the unvarying tradition of the Church that there must be a continuing effort to bring the way we live into harmony with the demands of our faith. This effort involves a struggle with ourselves because we are divided creatures; we are pulled toward what is good, and we lean to what is evil. No one has ever written with more accuracy and pathos than Newman about our fallen human condition:

> Oh, what a dreadful state, to have our desires one way, and our knowledge and conscience another; to have our life, our breath and food, upon the earth, and our eyes upon Him who died once and now liveth; to look upon Him who once was pierced, yet not to rise with Him and live with Him; to feel that a holy life is our only happiness, yet to have no heart to pursue it; to be certain that the wages of sin is death,

yet to practise sin; to confess that the Angels alone are perfectly happy, for they do God's will perfectly, yet to prepare
ourselves for nothing else but the company of devils.[1]

The struggle, or combat, to overcome these deep divisions in
our nature and to bring our lives into harmony with the demands of our faith is called asceticism, and asceticism is an essential element of Christianity. Our desires must gradually be
reordered so that we learn to want what Christ wants of us and
to loathe in ourselves whatever stands in the way of our being
united to his will. "In its most general sense asceticism can be
said to represent all those elements of the spiritual life that involve an organized campaign against the sinful aspects of the
self, and against exterior temptation, as well as positive efforts
directed toward the perfection of our own spiritual activities."[2] This use of the word asceticism is broader than one that
identifies the word with external and physical austerity, as, for
example, when it is defined as "complete abstinence or re-
striction in the use of food, drink, sleep, dress, and property,
and especially continence in sexual matters".[3]

This book is about the theory and the practice of spiritual
combat, or ascetical life, understood as the ordered effort to
imitate "Christ Jesus, and him crucified" (1 Cor 2:2), and

1. "Love of Religion, a New Nature," sermon 13 in vol. 7 of *Parochial and
Plain Sermons* (San Francisco: Ignatius Press, 1997), p. 1524.

2. "Nous prendrons les mots ascèse et ascétisme dans leur sense plus com-
préhensif comme représentant tout ce qui dans la vie spirituelle est exercice,
effort, lutte contre soi et contre les tentations extérieures, travail positif de
perfectionnement de nos activités spirituelles" (J. de Guibert, "La Notion
d'ascèse, d'ascétisme," in *Dictionnaire de spiritualité*, ed. Marcel Viller, S.J. [Par-
is: G. Beauchesne et ses fils, 1932–], vol. 1, col. 938).

3. Cited by Pierre Hadot, *Philosophy as a Way of Life: Spiritual Exercises from
Socrates to Foucault*, ed. Arnold Davidson, trans. Michael Chase (Oxford: Blackwell, 1999), p. 128.

what the reader will find here is a discussion of asceticism as understood in the light of a tradition that stretches from the New Testament to our own day. The discussion has been undertaken within the theological framework of the Second Vatican Council and the *Catechism of the Catholic Church*. The fundamental lines of this tradition are constant: Asceticism is essential, but by itself it is not enough.

It may indeed have been the case that sometimes in the past the theory and practice of asceticism were badly understood, and imperfectly practiced, and this has provoked a reaction in favor of a less structured, less "law-orientated" Christianity. That is not to say that those who are unhappy about the way the ascetical life was taught and was practiced are advocating a sinful life-style or saying that the virtues do not matter. Nonetheless, they do want to contend that the ascetical life in the past had come to dominate most people's conception of Christianity in a way that deformed the very notion of what being a Christian meant. They argue that the horizons of Christianity were reduced to a sort of unattractive, and largely irrelevant, obstacle race in which those who stayed the course without knocking over too many hurdles were assured of a prize in some future state. This misreading of the place of asceticism, they maintain, had especially deleterious effects in the life of prayer.[4]

This perception, that the ascetical life had come to dominate the thinking and the practice of many Catholics to a disproportionate degree, is so widespread that it cannot be ignored. Nonetheless, however imperfectly understood or practiced, the conviction that Christianity demanded an effort to fight personal sin and to develop virtues such as kindness,

4. See below, chap. 7.

patience, truth-telling, and chastity was and remains a valid one. It is true that spiritual combat is not an end in itself but is undertaken to work for perfection, purity of heart, or charity, and to lose sight of this is to have a deformed picture of the Christian life. On the other hand, it does not follow from this that authentic Christianity can, or should try to, forget about the tradition of asceticism.

In order to provide the reader with a short and coherent statement of the elements of this tradition, I have followed the structure of one of the classics of ascetical theology, *The Spiritual Combat*, by Lorenzo Scupoli (1530–1610).[5] *The Spiritual Combat* is a short, uncompromising statement of the theory and practice of the ascetical life, and Scupoli's pithy, laconic style leaves no room for ambiguity. It is a book that was the fruit of the author's own great personal anguish and still retains a quiet but unmistakable authority. Scupoli wrote of what he knew by first-hand experience.[6] On the other hand, his book is extremely condensed and presupposes a theological and moral outlook that today has to be sketched in if the contemporary reader is to benefit from its teaching. My own book spells out the elements of these moral and theological presuppositions.

Spiritual Combat Revisited should be understood, first of all, as an invitation to every reader to recognize the necessity of a spiritual combat in serious Christian living as well as a discussion of the weapons to be used in this warfare. At the same time, I would also like to think that my work might help to revive interest in one of the great spiritual classics of the ascetical life, that is, in Scupoli's own book, *The Spiritual Combat*.

---

5. Lorenzo Scupoli, *Spiritual Combat, Together with The Treatise of Inward Peace* (London: Burns & Oates, 1963), hereafter cited as SC. See "Scupoli", in *Dictionnaire de spiritualité*, vol.14, cols. 467–84.

6. See below, pp. 15–16.

PART ONE

SPIRITUAL COMBAT

O let not your foot slip, or your eye be false, or your ear dull, or your attention flagging! Be not dispirited; be not afraid; keep a good heart; be bold; draw not back;—you will be carried through. Whatever troubles come on you, of mind, body, or estate; from within or from without; from chance or from intent; from friends or foes;— whatever your trouble be, though you be lonely, O children of a heavenly Father, be not afraid! quit you like men in your day; and when it is over, Christ will receive you to Himself, and your heart shall rejoice, and your joy no man taketh from you.

—J. H. Newman, "Warfare the Condition of Victory,"
Parochial and Plain Sermons

In this part of *Spiritual Combat Revisited* the reader will find an analysis of the structure and some of the main arguments of Scupoli's book. Before beginning this analysis, however, we should know something about the author himself and the circumstances under which *The Spiritual Combat* was written. In addition to this information, I have added a few lines on the sources of Scupoli's work and on his influence.

Scupoli was born in Otranto (Italy) about 1530, and at the age of thirty-nine he was admitted to the Theatine Order, a community that was dedicated to the cultivation of the spiritual life, to preaching and teaching, and to the care of the sick and of prisoners. Scupoli, who had St. Andrew Avellino as his novice master for part of his novitiate, took his vows, was ordained a priest in 1577, and worked in Milan in a

house of his order and then in Genoa. He was strict in the
observance of his rule, constant in prayer, and "a lover of
solitude and silence".[1] In 1585 there began a harsh ordeal
and a long humiliation. By order of the general chapter of
his order, he was sent to prison, deprived of the sacraments
for a year, and reduced to the status of a lay brother. There is
no evidence as to what he had done to merit this severe
judgment, as, after a reconsideration of the verdict a year
later, all the papers concerning the trial were burned. Whatever the cause may have been, Scupoli made no appeal, and
it was not until April 1610, the year of his death, that he was
once again allowed to take up his priestly ministry.

Scupoli accepted the harsh judgment against himself with
such resignation and humility that, from the beginning of
his life as a lay brother, he acquired the reputation of a man
of great virtue. He maintained a strict silence and made no
appeal against his sentence. It was out of his suffering and his
resignation that *The Spiritual Combat* was born. It is a small
book, written in Italian, which has had an enormous influence since it was first published in 1589. By the time of the
author's death there had been at least sixty different editions,
including translations into many different languages.[2] Since
then it has gone through hundreds of editions and has provided strength and counsel to numberless Christians who
have wanted to live a deeper spiritual life.

---

[1] H. A. Hodges, introduction, sec. 5, to *Unseen Warfare: The Spiritual Combat
and Path to Paradise of Lorenzo Scupoli*, ed. Nicodemus of the Holy Mountain
and rev. by Theophan the Recluse; trans. E. Kadloubovsky and G. E. H. Palmer
(London: Mowbrays, 1978), p. 37.

[2] There was a German translation in 1590, Latin in 1591, French in 1595
and 1610, English in 1598, and Castilian and Catalan both in 1608. It is reck-
oned that by the middle of the twentieth century there had been more than
six hundred different editions in various languages, including Polish, Croatian,
Armenian, Arabic, Greek, and Russian.

Scupoli's doctrine is rooted in the Fathers of the Church, in Cassian, St. Augustine, and St. Thomas Aquinas.[3] I have used Cassian to illustrate the influence of earlier thinkers on his work. It was John Cassian who recorded much of what was best in Eastern monasticism and then gave it to the West. St. Benedict used Cassian's work in his *Rule* and cites him more often than any authority other than the Bible.[4] He presents a sane if austere doctrine that is firmly based on human nature as it is. The main lines of classical asceticism are already to be found in Cassian's work.

In dealing with the influence of Scupoli on others, I have concentrated on St. Francis de Sales and Newman, and I have used both of these thinkers to illustrate Scupoli's work. St. Francis de Sales was given a copy of an early version of the book, possibly by the author himself, while Francis was studying in Padua in 1590.

One day I asked François who his Spiritual Director was? His answer was to take the *Spiritual Combat* from his pocket and say: "You see my Director in this little book which has taught me, with the help of God, things concerning the interior life since my youth. When I was a student in Padua, a Theatine Father instructed me in it, and since then all has gone well with me in following its directions."[5]

---

[3] See "Scupoli", in *Dictionnaire de spiritualité*, ed. Marcel Viller, S.J. [Paris: G. Beauchesne et ses fils, 1932–], vol. 14, cols. 477–79.

[4] See Owen Chadwick, *John Cassian: A Study in Primitive Monasticism*, 2d ed. (Cambridge: Cambridge Univ. Press, 1968), and Columba Stewart, *Cassian the Monk* (New York: Oxford Univ. Press, 1998). Cassian wrote the *Institutes* for Castor Bishop of Apt (north of Marseilles) to describe Eastern monasticism. He also wrote the *Conferences*, which purport to be summaries or reports of discussions or discourses at which he was present while visiting the monks of the desert in Egypt.

[5] Jean Pierre Camus, *The Spirit of St. François de Sales* (New York: Harper, 1952), p. 236.

All the early biographers of St. Francis recognized the profound influence Scupoli's book had on the saint's spiritual development. In 1610 St. Francis himself wrote that it was "my dear book, which I have carried in my pocket for the last eighteen years and which I never reread without profit".[6] He read a passage every day, and the entire book once a month. He translated the book into French and only withdrew his translation when he found another translation was already on the point of being published.[7]

The Spiritual Combat was also of great importance for Newman at the end of his Anglican days and throughout his life as a Catholic. In 1843 he wrote to a friend: "Do you know the little book called "spiritual combat"? it will bear reading again and again. . . . Think of the very title 'Spiritual Combat'—how much it implies."[8] When he wrote this letter, Newman had retired to Littlemore and was, as he himself put it, "on my death-bed, as regards my membership with the Anglican Church".[9] Yet he saw clearly that dissatisfaction with Anglicanism was not a sufficient reason to become a Roman Catholic. Although attracted to the Church of Rome, he had to reconcile himself with what he had come to think of as the Tridentine Church. One aspect of this coming to grips with Tridentine Rome, and the only one that concerns us here, was his investigation of the spiritual works of the Post-Reformation Church, and Scupoli's was among these. He made careful use of it during the Advent of 1842, and most particularly from Lent

---

[6] André J.-M. Hamon, *Vie de St. François de Sales* (Paris: Gabalda, 1920), p. 8.

[7] *Dictionnaire de spiritualité*, vol. 14, col. 480.

[8] From an unpublished letter to Emily Bowles. Kindness of the Birmingham Oratory.

[9] J. H. Newman, *Apologia pro vita sua*, sec. 6 (New York: Doubleday [Image Books], 1956), p. 247.

1843 onward.[10] It was not, of course, the only such book he used. The *Spiritual Exercises of St. Ignatius of Loyola* had pride of place; they are repeatedly referred to, and he used them as a vehicle for personal analyses and memoranda. Newman found in these practical, ascetical works the reality of a living and real spiritual tradition. The Church of Rome was not a paper church or a theory but had carried into his own time a doctrine and a discipline about the soul's approach to God. It was a doctrine and a discipline that crystallized into a coherent framework much of what he had thought and taught.

This is not a book about St. Francis de Sales or Newman, or even about Scupoli's influence on these great masters of the spiritual life. But St. Francis used and expanded on Scupoli's work, and Newman found in *The Spiritual Combat* a matter-of-fact, concise, but powerful statement of much of the scriptural Christianity he had always preached. He never repudiated either the *Parochial and Plain*, or the *University Sermons*; in fact he republished them as a Catholic in later years.[11] He continued to use Scupoli's book as a Catholic[12] and to recommend it to others.[13]

---

[10] I owe this information to the generous assistance of Mr. Gerard Tracey, the archivist of the Birmingham Oratory.

[11] In fact, he even used to read them when he preached as an aged cardinal. "He took to reading some of his Parochial Sermons from MS.—touched up, I suppose, a little bit—and very nice it was for those who had never heard him *read* in his younger days" (introduction to *Sermon Notes of John Henry Cardinal Newman 1849–1878*, ed. Fathers of the Birmingham Oratory [London: Longmans, Green, 1913–1914], p. vi).

[12] "Please ask William to send me a copy of Scupoli's Christian Warrior. I have not the title quite right" (J. H. Newman, letter of October 12, 1862, in *The Letters and Diaries of John Henry Newman* [Edinburgh: Thomas Nelson, and Oxford: Clarendon Press, 1978–], 20:298).

[13] "Put away your scientific books. Keep to the New Testament, the Imitation of Christ, the Spiritual Combat and some book of meditations" (letter to Eddie Froude, July 28, 1864, in *Letters and Diaries*, 21:172–73).

In sum, both St. Francis de Sales and Newman were influenced by Scupoli's work, and from this it follows, at very least, that where there is an identity of subject matter and of the treatment of this subject matter, the works of both thinkers may be legitimately and usefully used to illustrate Scupoli's work. And this is what I have done.

The Spiritual Combat is a work directed toward the practice of the ascetical life and does not contain a theoretical discussion about the necessity and nature of asceticism.[14] The practical thrust of Scupoli's work, however, is firmly grounded in scriptural and theological principles to which he refers but for which he does not argue. Scupoli assumed that we were created for beatitude and that we have to play our part if we are to achieve our final destiny; but we have divided hearts, and following the way of Christ is going to involve a warfare against everything in our nature that pulls us away from the happiness for which we were created.

Scupoli used these basic Christian truths to illuminate his own painful trials. His humble acceptance of injustice and misunderstanding enabled him to write in a way that carries conviction. It is not that what he says is particularly new, but like St. Paul, he could have said "I believed, and so I spoke" (2 Cor 4:13). Scupoli lived what he wrote about, and so his writing carries with it the authenticity of Christian truth.

---

[14] E. B. Pusey, in a translation of Scupoli's work with introduction, says his work was intended "For the Use of Members of the English Church", and he was especially struck by this aspect of Scupoli's book: "[The book] is eminently, what [St. Francis de Sales] terms it, 'all practice'. Nowhere, perhaps, in the same space of human books, is there the same fullness and explicitness of rules, *how* to live holily. It seems the experience of a life condensed" (*The Spiritual Combat and The Path of Paradise*, 2d ed. [London, n.p.,1849], Notice, pp. xii–xiii).

If we were to categorize Scupoli's work in somewhat anachronistic terms, we could say he teaches a form of what today is called virtue ethics, but it is a virtue ethics based on theological principles. He is concerned with the building up of good habits and the effort to eradicate bad ones. On the other hand, he is quite clear that he is dealing with human beings and not dogs being trained to jump through a hoop. He is remarkably sensitive to failure and setbacks in the moral life, and his discussions of virtue and vice have to be seen in the perspective of the Christian faith. We are born in sin; we are saved by Christ; we must live in hope; and we can do no good without God's grace. There is no suggestion in his work that we are saved by building up a bank account consisting of repeated acts of virtue.[15] The virtues help to overcome the divisions in the self and open the way to Christian perfection and purity of heart. These virtues are essential for salvation, but they are not sufficient in themselves. We engage in the spiritual combat because we desire beatitude. We look forward to what has been promised us. In this Scupoli echoes the words of St. Paul to the Philippians: "Forgetting what lies behind and straining forward to what lies ahead, I press on toward the goal for the prize of the upward call of God in Christ Jesus" (Phil 3:13–14).

On the other hand, looking forward is going to involve us in a struggle with everything that interferes with our obtaining this prize. Scupoli teaches how sinful, even if redeemed, creatures such as ourselves are prepared for union with God;

---

[15] St. Thomas firmly rejects the possibility that the virtue of charity increases by addition: "Charity grows, not by one charity being added to another, but by its being intensified in its subject, which is to say that it increases as to its essence" (*Summa Theologiae* 2a 2ae, 24, 5; hereafter abbreviated as ST).

his teaching reaches right down into the murky, hidden, sinful aspects of our nature and points toward the heights of a mystical union with God, a union that is more absorbing and more powerful than any other human experience. The light of faith illuminates and makes demands on every facet of human nature and human conduct, and it does this to show us that the whole of our nature must be recognized, trained, and developed so that the whole man, and every aspect of his experience, may be fashioned into a fitting instrument for God's purposes for us.

The reader will find an outline of Scupoli's teaching in a chapter called "First Principles", (chapter 1). These principles are designed to show the perspective from which Scupoli approaches the spiritual life, and I have illustrated his teaching with texts from the Bible. The next six chapters deal with the four weapons of the spiritual combat.

The first weapon is humility and self-distrust (chapter 2). By humility, Scupoli means the virtue by which man attributes to God all the good he possesses, and by self-distrust he intends a serious assent to the truth that we are human beings wounded by original sin and liable to do bad things.

The second weapon is the practice of the virtue of hope and confidence in God (chapter 3). What we should hope for is eternal happiness, and we should be confident that God will provide us with the means to attain that happiness.

The third weapon is what he calls spiritual exercises (chapters 4, 5, and 6). By spiritual exercises he means the systematic efforts we undertake to cooperate with God's grace to build up the Christian virtues, such as patience and charity, and to root out vices, such as sloth and unchastity.

The fourth weapon is the practice of prayer, which ought to be at the center of our lives (chapter 7). St. Thomas teaches that the goal or end of our prayer is to be united with God in a union of love.[16] In prayer we draw nearer to the Lord, and in prayer Christ draws us closer to himself. It is from the living contact with God through Christ that we find and are given the desire and the strength to go on with the struggle both to gain our own sanctification and to make the Lord better known and better loved.

[16] ST 2a, 2ae, 83.

First Principles

It is easy to have vague ideas of what perfection is, which serve well enough to talk about, when we do not intend to aim at it; but as soon as a person really desires and sets about seeking it himself, he is dissatisfied with anything but what is tangible and clear, and constitutes some sort of direction towards the practice of it.

—J. H. Newman, "A Short Road to Perfection",
Meditations and Devotions

Scupoli teaches an asceticism of love. He wants us to be clear that we are bound by our Christianity to fight the vices and develop the virtues. At the same time, however, he reminds us that the goal of spiritual combat is an ever more intimate union in love between the individual and Christ. This is clear from the opening words of his book: "Wouldst thou attain in Christ the height of perfection, and by a nearer and nearer approach to thy God become one spirit with him?" From the form of the question we can see that perfection and becoming one spirit in Christ are not exactly the same thing and stand in a relation of means to end. That is, working for perfection is the means or the way we become united with God, and being united with God is what gives sense and purpose to the ascetical life.

The notion of perfection does not sit well with contemporary Catholics. Whether this is so because we tend to distrust large claims about human perfectibility or because we have been taught to accept ourselves as we are, in either case perfection seems to many people to be an unreal or empty concept when applied to human beings. On the other hand, the spirituality of the Church has always employed the concept, which is a scriptural one,[1] and it was used by the Second Vatican Council. Newman gives a simple version of the traditional doctrine, and one that is adequate for our purposes at this point, when he writes:

> By perfect we mean that which has no flaw in it, that which is complete, that which is consistent, that which is sound—we mean the opposite to imperfect. As we know well what *im*-perfection in religious service means, we know by the contrast what is meant by perfection.[2]

Spiritual combat is directed toward perfection, and it really is a combat. Our religious service, to use Newman's expression, is clearly very imperfect, and it is more difficult to change than we at first think. True holiness and spirituality do not consist, Scupoli insists, in "exercises which are pleasing to us and conformable to our nature", but only in those that "nail that nature with all its works to the cross" and that, "by renewing the whole man by the practice of the evangelical virtues, unite him to his crucified Saviour and Creator".[3]

---

[1] Mt 5:48: "You, therefore, must be perfect, as your heavenly Father is perfect."

[2] J. H. Newman, "A Short Road to Perfection", in *Meditations and Devotions*, in *Prayers, Verses, and Devotions: The Devotions of Bishop Andrewes, Meditations and Devotions, Verses on Various Occasions* (San Francisco: Ignatius Press, 2000), pp. 328–29; here, p. 328.

[3] SC 13, pp. 33–34.

Spirituality is a word that is often heard today. On the face of it this might seem to be a good thing. That is, the interest in spirituality seems to show that there is a growing concern for the things of the spirit and a serious distaste with materialism and consumerism. Yet somehow this does not seem to be the case, and all too often spirituality means techniques for obtaining peace of soul that have little to do with either Christianity or morality. In 1920 Abbot Chapman wrote that "Bad people love Mysticism, because they think it is occultism or magic. Good people dislike it for almost the same reason!",[4] and while the abbot was perhaps hard on the dabblers in mysticism, his point is still true and important. It is true because more than techniques for the enhancement of consciousness is required to make a Christian, and it is important, because much of what is paraded today as spirituality is in fact indifferent, when it is not hostile, to Christian living. The abbot's "good people" today distrust much contemporary spirituality because instinctively they perceive it is neither Christian nor allied to the law of Christ.

In the face of this neglect, or ignorance, of the first principles of the spiritual life, we have to restate what should be at the basis of any spirituality that claims to be Christian. Scupoli says that the spiritual life consists in:

1. "the knowledge of the goodness and the greatness of God, and of our nothingness and inclination to all evil";

2. "the love of him and the hatred of ourselves";

3. "subjection, not to him alone, but, for love of him, to all his creatures";

4. "entire renunciation of all will of our own, and absolute resignation to all his divine pleasure";

[4] John Chapman, letter 93, in *Spiritual Letters* (London: Sheed & Ward, 1935), p. 269.

5. "willing and doing all this purely for the glory of God and solely to please him, and because he so wills and merits thus to be loved and served".[5]

We see that none of the first principles is, at first sight, particularly attractive. If we are to accept them as the basis for the realignment of our lives, then we will have to begin by understanding what they mean. In the first place, we are told that the spiritual life consists in knowledge about God and ourselves; then, secondly, that we are to love God and hate ourselves; thirdly, subjection, not to him alone, but, for love of him, to all his creatures; fourthly, that our love for God must show itself in uniting ourselves to him by trying to do what he wants us to do; and, finally, the motive for doing all this is for the glory of God and because God, just because he is who he is, deserves to be so loved and served.

How do we use these first principles in such a way that they will serve as a basis for our spiritual lives and affect our practice? Well, we have to consider them attentively, or meditate on them; that is, we have to think and ponder on these truths of our faith and try to see how they could affect us personally. I do not think it matters whether we call these considerations or this meditation prayer or a preparation for prayer. The important thing is actually to consider and meditate on the first principles and to do so in a regular way. We should be actively engaged, actually using our heads, and not sitting around trying to make the mind a blank in the hope of receiving some ill-defined and comforting illumination.

In what follows I have illustrated the first principles of the spiritual life with texts from the Bible. These texts are meant to be used as a basis for meditation on the truths they con-

[5] SC I, p. 4.

tain; they are not to be thought of as arguments or proofs of the particular truth being considered.

1. Knowledge about God and about Ourselves

The Knowledge of the Goodness and Greatness of God

We are to think first of all on the goodness and greatness of God. There are four points upon which we should reflect. In the first place, God *is*; that is, he exists altogether apart from what we may believe or not believe about him. Secondly, God is totally other than his creation, which depends on him but upon which he is in no way dependent. Thirdly, God directs all creation, including our own interior lives, through his providence. Finally, the God who is, and who rules all things, is also the God who wills what is best for us in this life and who has destined us for a life of blessedness and completion at the end of our existence here.

God exists.   In the Book of Exodus, God reveals to Moses that he, God, is the one who has existed and still exists.

> Then Moses said to God, "If I come to the people of Israel and say to them, 'The God of your fathers has sent me to you,' and they ask me, 'What is his name?' what shall I say to them?" God said to Moses, "I AM WHO I AM." And he said, "Say this to the people of Israel, 'I AM has sent me to you.'"
> (Ex 3:13–14)

We all tend to feel, even if do not actually think or say it, that God's existence somehow or other depends on ourselves. We must remind ourselves that whether we acknowledge God or deny he exists, whether we remember him or try to forget him, whether we obey him or try to live our lives without him, all this is irrelevant to the existence of God. God *is*, that is the first thing we have to begin to make real to ourselves. "And without faith it is impossible to please him. For whoever would draw near to God must believe that he exists and that he rewards those who seek him" (Heb 11:6).

God is Creator, other, and mysterious.   God exists and is beyond anything we can conceive or imagine. St. Thomas says that God is beyond, or outside, the order of all existing things.[6] Furthermore, he created everything there is freely and not because he needed to. The act of creation makes no difference to who, or what, God is. All creation depends on him, but he in no way depends on what he has created. God is not subject to our thoughts or theories as to how he should act. This means that even after he reveals himself, God remains a mystery beyond words.[7]

> For my thoughts are not your thoughts,
>   neither are your ways my ways, says the LORD.
> For as the heavens are higher than the earth,
>   so are my ways higher than your ways
>   and my thoughts than your thoughts. (Is 55:8–9)

> "Can you find out the deep things of God?
>   Can you find out the limit of the Almighty?
> It is higher than heaven—what can you do?
>   Deeper than Sheol—what can you know?" (Job 11: 7–8)

---

[6] "Extra ordinem entium existens", cited in Herbert McCabe, O.P., *God Matters* (1987; reprinted, London and New York: Mowbray, 2000), p. 45.
[7] See CCC 230.

To whom then will you compare me,
  that I should be like him? says the Holy One.
Lift up your eyes on high and see:
  who created these?
He who brings out their host by number,
  calling them all by name;
by the greatness of his might,
  and because he is strong in power
not one is missing. (Is 40:25–26)

O the depth of the riches and wisdom and knowledge of God! How unsearchable are his judgments and how inscrutable his ways!

  "For who has known the mind of the Lord,
    or who has been his counselor?" (Rom 11:33–34)

God is everywhere and directs all things by his providence. God is wholly transcendent, or other, than his creation, but creation itself depends upon the creative power of God for its existence and for its ability to act. God sustains and directs the whole of his creation, including the lives of human beings and their free actions, and this is what we mean by God's providence. God is involved with his creation; he cares for all things, from the very least to the greatest, and through his wisdom and power he directs all creation.

    Whither shall I go from thy Spirit?
      Or whither shall I flee from thy presence?
    If I ascend to heaven, thou art there!
      If I make my bed in Sheol, thou art there!
    If I take the wings of the morning
      and dwell in the uttermost parts of the sea,
    even there thy hand shall lead me,
      and thy right hand shall hold me.

If I say "Let only darkness cover me,
    and the light about me be night,"
even the darkness is not dark to thee,
    the night is bright as the day;
    for darkness is as light with thee. (Ps 139:7–12)

Many are the plans in the mind of a man,
    but it is the purpose of the LORD that will be established. (Prov
19:21)

Our God is in the heavens;
    he does whatever he pleases. (Ps 115:3)

Are not two sparrows sold for a penny? And not one of them
will fall to the ground without your Father's will. But even
the hairs of your head are all numbered. (Mt 10:29–30)

God is good, and only God is good.   The God who is, who
creates and who directs all things by his providence, is a good
God whose loving wisdom directs our lives and human history so that his creation may share in his wisdom, beauty,
and goodness. The reality of evil and suffering in the world
has tempted some people to deny God's goodness, but our
faith teaches that God is good and merciful. We must pray
for a serene and serious acceptance that everything that happens to us is directly or indirectly from the hand of God for
our own good.

And now arise, O LORD God, and go to thy resting place,
    thou and the ark of thy might.
Let thy priests, O LORD God, be clothed with salvation,
    and let thy saints rejoice in thy goodness. (2 Chron 6:41)

Thou art good and doest good. (Ps 119:68)

Thou hast granted me life and steadfast love;
    and thy care has preserved my spirit. (Job 10:12)

No one is good but God alone. (Lk 18:19)

Be merciful, even as your Father is merciful. (Lk 6:36)

The God of love and peace. (2 Cor 13:11)

The Knowledge of Our Own Nothingness and Inclination to All Evil

We have to base our spiritual life not only on what is true about God but on what is true about ourselves and what is true about the way we should try to live. Even though it is the case that, absolutely speaking, God is the foundation and source of the Christian life, nonetheless, what is more immediate to ourselves, those actually living the spiritual life, is our condition and our own nature. In addition to a knowledge of the goodness and the greatness of God, we must add a clear awareness of our own nothingness and inclination to all evil. This is Scupoli's formulation, and I think it requires some reflection before we can both understand it properly and assent to it.

Man is physically nothing. In the first place, what is meant by a knowledge of our own nothingness? Obviously, in one sense, we must be something or I would not be writing this book and you would not be reading it. One way of understanding our own nothingness is to reflect on the fact that while it is quite true that we are here now, nonetheless, there was a long time before now when we did not exist in this world, and there will be a long time afterward when we will have ceased to exist—at least so far as this world is concerned. Whatever being we have is contingent; it is given to us from outside ourselves, and it has no necessity about it. So, there is a perfectly acceptable meaning to the phrase "our own nothingness", and this is the metaphysical understanding, as distinct from the moral one, that of ourselves we are nothing.

Abraham answered, "Behold, I have taken upon myself to speak to the Lord, I who am but dust and ashes." (Gen 18:27)

As for man, his days are like grass;
   he flourishes like a flower of the field;
for the wind passes over it, and it is gone,
   and its place knows it no more. (Ps 103:15–16)

Man is morally weak.   In addition to this natural understanding of our own nothingness, there is also the teaching of both experience and our faith that, left to ourselves and our wounded human nature, we turn to sinful ways and wrongdoing.

Behold, even the moon is not bright
   and the stars are not clean in his sight;
how much less man, who is a maggot,
   and the son of man, who is a worm! (Job 25:5–6)

For the imagination of man's heart is evil from his youth. (Gen 8:21)

Behold, I was brought forth in iniquity,
   and in sin did my mother conceive me. (Ps 51:5)

For behold, every one of you follows his stubborn evil will, refusing to listen to me. (Jer 16:12)

For out of the heart come evil thoughts, murder, adultery, fornication, theft, false witness, slander. (Mt 15:19)

Man is dependent on God's grace.   Without grace we can do nothing to merit our salvation. This does not mean that natural talent is nonexistent, nor does it mean that there are no genuine efforts to live moral lives. But, difficult as it may be for us to accept, we have to try to realize that whatever is good in us is God's gift and that without this gift we cannot merit salvation. Left to ourselves we cannot please God and so inherit eternal life. All this is a blow to our pride, and it goes against much modern thought, but our faith teaches us that all the good in us that works toward our salvation is God's gift and that to trust in our own talents and endowments is to set out on the road to spiritual self-destruction.

> I say to the LORD, "Thou art my Lord;
> I have no good apart from thee." (Ps 16:2)

When the disciples heard this they were greatly astonished, saying, "Who then can be saved?" But Jesus looked at them and said to them, "With men this is impossible, but with God all things are possible." (Mt 19:25–26)

So neither he who plants nor he who waters is anything, but only God who gives the growth. (1 Cor 3:7)

Every good endowment and every perfect gift is from above, coming down from the Father of lights with whom there is no variation of shadow due to change. (Jas 1:17)

2. The Love of God and Hatred of Ourselves

The Love of God

God's truth is received by the intellect and is understood, insofar as it is understood, by the ordinary workings of the human mind. What God gives to us in faith is far beyond anything we can understand completely, but insofar as we do understand it, we understand it by using ordinary human thinking. Thinking is motivated by trying to find out what is true about a situation or a problem. Furthermore, no matter how sublime or how ordinary the object of our thought may be, we understand, and search for an answer, by using the same fundamental constitution of the human mind in our efforts to grasp the way things really are.

There is, however, another attitude we take up toward things, and this is to desire or to love them or to be repelled by them. If we are moved positively by something, then we are said to love it; if we experience it as repellent, then we are said to hate it. Loving or hating are not concerned fundamentally with trying to understand, but with trying to appropriate, get for ourselves, the object of our desires, or reject whatever interferes with our desires.[8]

The difference between thinking and loving is easy enough to understand at one level.[9] A worker in a brewery will be interested in the composition of a particular beer he is making. His interest in the beer is similar to that of a chemist in a laboratory; he is interested in the composition of the beer and in what temperatures and what length of time will produce a particular result. The brewer can do all this without any interest in drinking beer. But take the case of a man on a hot day who is thirsty and wants a bottle of beer. He is

---

[8] A distinguished modern philosopher illustrates this aspect of moving toward the thing desired in the following way: "The primitive sign of wanting is *trying to get*; in saying this, we describe the movement of an animal in terms that reach beyond what the animal is now doing. When a dog smells a piece of meat that lies the other side of the door, his trying to get it will be his snuffling around the bottom of it and so on. Thus there are two features present in wanting; movement towards a thing and knowledge (or at least opinion) that the thing is there" (G. E. M. Anscombe, *Intention* [Oxford: Basil Blackwell, 1957], p. 68).

[9] There are, of course, a great many levels of analysis of this fundamental and difficult matter. For a modern and sophisticated treatment of willing and action, the reader should consult Stephen L. Brock, *Action and Conduct* (Edinburgh: T&T Clark, 1998), especially chap. 4, "The Agency of the Will".

interested in satisfying his thirst by somehow or other obtaining the bottle of beer and then slaking his thirst by actually drinking the beer.

In the tradition with which Scupoli is working, the slaking of the man's thirst has three aspects. The thirsty man, let us call him Tom Jones, is struck, in the first place, by an experience that is partly intellectual and partly emotional, in that he badly wants a glass of beer; for the time being anyway, there exists a natural affinity between Tom Jones, who is thirsty, and the glass of beer. He is apt to say: "I would love a glass of beer." So St. Thomas says that the first effect produced in Tom Jones is love, "which is simply a feeling of an object's attractiveness".[10] This experience gives rise to a movement toward the object that we call desire. The desire is not for an idea of the beer, but for a real drink, and so Tom has actually to get hold of the beer. Perhaps he only has to go to the refrigerator; perhaps he has to go to a nearby town; but in any case he has to go out toward the beer in the real world. As St. Thomas puts it: The desire moves toward the object "with the purpose of actually possessing it".[11] Finally, he slakes his thirst by drinking the beer, by actually uniting himself with what he desired, and so the desire finally "comes to rest in joy".[12]

We have then three aspects or stages: Tom is struck, sometimes very sharply and in an overwhelming way, with the fact that a drink of beer is what he wants; this deep awareness, or the "experiencing of a natural affinity",[13] as Gilson

---

[10] ST 1a, 2ae, 26, 2.

[11] Ibid.

[12] Ibid.

[13] Étienne Gilson, *The Christian Philosophy of St. Thomas Aquinas* (New York: Random House, 1956), p. 272.

puts it, leads him to say he would love a glass of beer, and he shows he is serious about this love by actually taking steps to obtain the beer; finally he is united to the object of his love, in this case, the beer, by actually drinking it.

The love of God, even when all the proper qualifications and distinctions are made, follows this model. "Love" in the traditional usage is "fundamentally the modification of the human appetite by some desirable object" [14] but is then extended to cover the experience of willing to possess any sort of good. "Wherever the appetite moves toward a good there is love, but its nature varies according to the nature of the object desired." [15] In a mysterious yet profound way we are moved to love God. We hardly know what the words mean, and there are any number of ways that this love first impresses itself on us. But love once awakened in us leads to the desire for God, and the desire for God will not be satisfied until we are united with him.

> You shall love the Lord your God with all your heart, and with all your soul, and with all your mind. This is the great and first commandment. (Mt 22:37–38)

> Beloved, let us love one another; for love is of God, and he who loves is born of God and knows God. (1 Jn 4:7)

> God's love has been poured into our hearts through the Holy Spirit which has been given to us. (Rom 5:5)

> May the Lord direct your hearts to the love of God and to the steadfastness of Christ. (2 Thess 3:5)

[14] Ibid.
[15] Ibid., pp. 272–73.

The Hatred of Self

If we really want our glass of beer, then we are going to dislike anything that gets in the way of obtaining it. We will, in a more robust language than we use nowadays, hate whatever it is that gets in our way. The use of the word "hate" has, no doubt, its dangers, but it does point up the deadly seriousness of the spiritual combat. Furthermore, it is the language of St. Thomas, and his usage here is instructive. He asks whether the sinner ought to be loved out of charity, and of course he wants to say yes, but his argument will not please everyone today. We should love the sinner according to his nature, which he has from God and which is capable of eternal happiness. On the other hand, we can consider his sin and recognize that because it is opposed to God it is an obstacle to eternal happiness. Hence, he says, "sin makes men God's enemies, and so we must hate all sinners without exception, even our own father or mother or near ones."

> It was the wicked, as such, that the Prophet hated, the object of his hatred being their wickedness, the evil that afflicted them. This is a holy hatred, and he himself says of it, *I hated them with a perfect hatred*. Now hating what is bad for someone and loving what is good for him amount to the same thing. Hence even this perfect hatred belongs to charity.[16]

We are only concerned here with making some sense of Scupoli's statement that one of the foundations of the spiritual life is hatred of ourselves. He means we have to detest whatever in us is at enmity with obtaining God, who is the

---

[16] ST 2a, 2ae, 25, 6.

treasure of our heart. Hate is not too strong a word, if we have any notion of the value of the treasure.

> I had heard of thee by the hearing of the ear,
> but now my eye sees thee;
> therefore I despise myself,
> and repent in dust and ashes. (Job 42:5–6)

If any one comes to me and does not hate his own father and mother and wife and children and brothers and sisters, yes, and even his own life, he cannot be my disciple. (Lk 14:26)

He who loves his life loses it, and he who hates his life in this world will keep it for eternal life. (Jn 12:25)

3. Subjection to God and His Creatures

A friendship that is truly human in the deepest sense involves, not only pleasure and usefulness, but a giving of self to the other person. It makes sense to say I would love a glass of beer, but it makes no sense to say I am in love with beer. The beer cannot return my desire to be united with itself, while another person can and must return my love if it is to be a fully human relationship. A friendship is not unrequited love, but involves a mutual giving of self. When this self-giving is real, it will involve helping the other person in any number of different ways. We look with some suspicion on a man who says he loves his wife but makes no effort to help her or who is consistently unfaithful and contributes nothing to her upkeep. Love that is serious involves at least an effort to serve, to be faithful, and to nurture the other person.

When we come to apply this model to the love of God, it does not at first sight appear to work very well. We can and do love God because we find it attractive and useful, but how can we *give* anything to God? How can we be said to strengthen in God those aspects of his nature that are attractive? Or what sense does it make to talk about deepening God's hold on what is good, noble, and true? Well, it makes no sense at all, but what we can retain from the model is that we, at our end of the relationship, have to try to strengthen our grasp on what is good, noble, and true. We begin to love God, to desire God, and to possess God in a deeper way by becoming more the sort of people who are capable of giving a love that is unselfish and that does not always put our own interests first. St. Francis de Sales puts it this way: "We have two principal exercises of our love towards God, the one affective, the other effective, or, as St. Bernard calls it, active." [17] Affective love means being pleased and satisfied with God and the things he loves, while effective love is serving God and doing what he commands; "[affective love] joins us to God's goodness, [while effective love leads us to] execute his will." [18]

To develop effective love we have to learn to operate in the real world in a way more conformable to the will of God. Perhaps this may involve thinking in a new way, but the basic reform is one that concerns the will. If we are going to be united with God, then we must first of all subject ourselves to the law of Christ in action as well as in intention.

> Thy kingdom come,
> Thy will be done,
> On earth as it is in heaven. (Mt 6:10)

[17] St. Francis de Sales, *Treatise on the Love of God*, bk. 6, chap. 1, trans. Henry Benedict Mackey (Westminster, Md.: Newman Press, 1953), p. 231.
[18] Ibid.

Besides this, we have had earthly fathers to discipline us and we respected them. Shall we not much more be subject to the Father of spirits and live? (Heb 12:9)

Humble yourselves therefore under the mighty hand of God, that in due time he may exalt you. (1 Pet 5:6)

And he went down with them and came to Nazareth, and was obedient to them. (Lk 2:51)

Be subject to one another out of reverence for Christ. (Eph 5:21)

4. Renunciation of Our Own Will and Resignation to the Will of God

We must renounce the self-direction of our lives in the sense of determining for ourselves the moral standards and the goals by which we are to live. Self-renunciation means a determined effort to live a Christian life by Christian standards in every circumstance of our lives, and this will in all likelihood mean giving up on cherished ambitions and dreams.

> Teach me to do thy will,
>   for thou art my God!
> Let thy good spirit lead me
>   on a level path! (Ps 143:10)

Thus says the LORD: "Cursed is the man who trusts in man
   and makes flesh his arm,
   whose heart turns away from the LORD." (Jer 17:5)

"Behold, happy is the man whom God reproves;
   therefore despise not the chastening of the Almighty." (Job 5:17)

Again, for the second time, he went away and prayed, "My Father, if this cannot pass unless I drink it, thy will be done." (Mt 26:42)

Love does not insist on its own way. (1 Cor 13:5)

Resignation to the Will of God

Finally, we have to accept God's providence for us willingly. That is, we have not only to try to do what God wants in every circumstance of our lives, but we have to try to will what God wants of us. Behind this willingness is our belief in God's providence, but often this abdication of our own will turns into a dark and painful business. Yet our willing must be modeled on the words attributed to Pope Clement XI, and our prayer will have to be:

> Volo quidquid vis, Volo quia vis,
> Volo quomodo vis,
> Volo quamdiu vis.
>
> I will whatever you will, because you will it,
> I will it in the way you will it,
> I will it for as long as you will it.[19]

> I delight to do thy will, O my God;
>   thy law is within my heart. (Ps 40:8)

> Trouble and anguish have come upon me,
>   but thy commandments are my delight. (Ps 119:143)

Jesus said to them, "My food is to do the will of him who sent me, and to accomplish his work." (Jn 4:34)

---

[19] Thanksgiving after Mass in the Roman Missal. This prayer is readily accessible in *Handbook of Prayers* (Princeton, N.J.: Scepter Publishers, 1995), p. 288.

5. To Will and to Do All for the Glory of God

To Will and to Do All for the Glory of God

Ultimately the spiritual life is about God and the way he deals with us; that is, it is not concerned in the first place with *our* striving and *our* prayer, but with God, who is a reality that endures and who will be our happiness both now and in eternity. To remind ourselves of this will help to avoid a self-centeredness that is an ever-present danger in the thinking and practice of the ascetical life.

> Ascribe to the LORD the glory due his name;
>   bring an offering, and come before him!
> Worship the LORD in holy array. (1 Chron 16:29)

> Let them praise the name of the LORD,
>   for his name alone is exalted;
>   his glory is above earth and heaven. (Ps 148:13)

Welcome one another, therefore, as Christ has welcomed you, for the glory of God. (Rom 15:7)

For it is the God who said, "Let light shine out of darkness," who has shone in our hearts to give the light of the knowledge of the glory of God in the face of Christ. (2 Corin 4:6)

[Let] every tongue confess that Jesus Christ is Lord, to the glory of God the Father. (Phil 2:11)

Acting to Please God

Our progress in the love of God begins with a recognition that it is pleasant and useful to believe in God. In our life of prayer we move toward a realization that there is more to God than our experience of him. We begin to understand in a real way that he is lovable in himself and that our service of him and our efforts to obey the commandments and to love our neighbor are based on a deepening perception that in submitting to his will, in renouncing our own plans for our salvation, and in actually trying to will what his providence provides in our daily lives we are uniting ourselves to God in the fullest and truest way possible in this life.

> Teach me to do thy will,
>   for thou art my God!
> Let thy good spirit lead me
>   on a level path. (Ps 143:10)

So whether we are at home or away, we make it our aim to please him. (2 Cor 5:9)

And try to learn what is pleasing to the Lord. (Eph 5:10)

Finally, brethren, we beseech and exhort you in the Lord Jesus, that as you learned from us how you ought to live and to please God, just as you are doing, you do so more and more. (1 Thess 4:1)

God's Worthiness of This Service

The more we try to please God, the more we become aware that God merits to be served and worshipped for what he is. If we persevere, we begin to realize that our love and service of God are based in the most fundamental way neither on pleasure nor on usefulness, but on the goodness of the good God.[20]

---

[20] It is important to recognize, however, that the gradual realization of the overwhelming importance of the love of God as a motive does not exclude the reality and lawfulness of other motives. This was the mistake of the Quietists. De Caussade discusses this in *On Prayer* (London: Burns, Oates & Washbourne), bk 1, dialogue 9, "On Perfect Love of God, Which Does Not Exclude the Hope of Reward".

I call upon the Lord, who is worthy to be praised,
and I am saved from my enemies. (2 Sam 22:4)

Every one who is called by my name,
whom I created for my glory,
whom I formed and made. (Is 43:7)

For my own sake, for my own sake, I do it,
for how should my name be profaned?
My glory I will not give to another. (Is 48:11)

To lead a life worthy of the Lord, fully pleasing to him, bearing fruit in every good work and increasing in the knowledge of God. (Col 1:10)

Yet Jesus has been counted worthy of as much more glory than Moses as the builder of a house has more honor than the house. (Heb 3:3)

We should meditate on these five first principles of the spiritual life in a quiet and realistic way. The love and service of God has to be disentangled from other loves and other duties, and this will take time and prayer. We must not force ourselves into false attitudes or pretend that things are other than they are with us, under the illusion that this represents progress in the spiritual life.

The love and service of God is sometimes presented to us as something that must exclude all other loves, or else as something so immediate and so engrossing that everything else seems second-rate and finally useless. Such a view must be wrong because, first of all, it falsifies what seems to be the example of the saints, who love people in this life in a way that does seem overwhelming and appears to be at least as immediate as their love for God. When we think about St. Philip Neri's love for his penitents, or St. Peter Claver's love for his slaves, it is surely wrong to say that these loves were second-rate or the dregs of another love left over from the love of God. Secondly, whether it means to or not, the view that any human love is somehow second-rate denigrates all the human and gracious aspects of life that make it worth living. It seems to imply that married love, the love of friendship, and the whole network of trust and support that can, and often does, exist between human beings is somehow shoddy and in competition with the love of God.[21] The second great commandment is that we are to love our neighbor as ourselves; and this commandment is presented to us as being like the first, not as being in competition with the love of God. And so we find that the great doctor of the love of God, St. Francis de Sales, teaches explicitly that the love of God is one love among many and that the fact that we love other people and other things is not displeasing to God.

> Man gives himself wholly by love, and gives himself as much as he loves. He is therefore in a sovereign manner given to God when he loves the divine goodness sovereignly. And having once made this donation of himself, he is to love nothing that can remove his heart from God. Now never does any love take our hearts from God, save that which is contrary unto him. . . . The divine goodness is not offended by seeing in us other loves besides his, so long as we preserve for him the reverence and submission due to him.[22]

In fact, as we all know, the love of God is learned through loving other people. Our awareness of the God whom we are learning to love is usually built up through a long

---

[21] St. Augustine as a convert had to learn to take the second commandment (to love our neighbor) seriously. The development of his thought is traced with authority and insight by John M. Rist in *Augustine: Ancient Thought Baptized* (Cambridge: Cambridge Univ. Press, 1994), chap. 5, "Will, Love and Right Action", in a way that illuminates not only St. Augustine but the whole question of the love of God and the love of neighbor.

[22] St. Francis de Sales, *Treatise on the Love of God*, bk. 10, chap. 3, p. 415.

experience of trying to pray seriously and to obey the commandments. We are human beings, and human beings move from what they perceive, from what they see, hear, smell, and touch, to what they cannot see, to what they cannot hear and smell, to what they cannot touch. Our senses are stepping stones to take us from our ordinary ways of looking at things and to bring us closer to the reality of the spiritual world. We do not leave our senses behind, but they become the medium or the instrument by which we grasp the great hidden mysteries of our faith. Through our senses we enter into the most mysterious and most important reality of all, for through our senses we move to the existence, to the greatness, and to the goodness of the almighty God who not only created us but loved us enough to be born and to die for us.

CHAPTER TWO

SELF-DISTRUST AND HUMILITY

But we are engaged in considering the actual state of man, as found in this world; and I say, considering what he is, any standard of duty, which does not convict him of real and multiplied sins, and of incapacity to please God of his own strength, is untrue; and any rule of life, which leaves him contented with himself, without fear, without anxiety, without humiliation, is deceptive; it is the blind leading the blind: yet such, in one shape or other, is the religion of the whole earth, beyond the pale of the Church.

—J. H. Newman, "The Religion of the Pharisee, the Religion of Mankind," *Sermons Preached on Various Occasions*

The first weapon in the spiritual combat is mistrust of self and humility. This, on the face of it, is an unpromising start for a rich and vigorous spiritual life. Scupoli's principle seems to be part and parcel of a dark and defeatist view of the human condition that modern theological developments have been at pains to correct. It seems to be felt in many quarters, and felt very strongly, that we are standing on the threshold of a new age when humanity will have remade itself, if not into Nietzsche's superman, then at least into members of a rational, progressive, and caring society.

Scupoli does not argue against this sort of rosy view of the human condition. His concern is to teach us what it is we should actually do in order to achieve our destiny. That is, he is not arguing for the coherence or plausibility of the Catholic faith at a theoretical level, but he does want to show us how to use this faith in our own personal struggle to achieve union with God. This first weapon of self-distrust and humility is meant to be a practical, or real, attitude that must affect our conduct.

Faith teaches us that we are creatures wounded by original sin and therefore pulled toward sinful behavior. Furthermore, the escape from this fact about the human condition is only possible through the acceptance of the grace of Christ. Finally, our own experience shows us that without God's help we are unable to keep clear from mortal sin for an extended period of time.[1] Scupoli's aim is to show us how to use these principles in a constructive way.

God "desires and loves to see in us a frank and true recognition of this most certain truth, that all the virtue and grace which is within us is derived from him alone, who is the fountain of all good, and that nothing good can proceed from us, no, not even a thought which can find acceptance in his sight".[2]

Although both God and we play a role in attaining to this self-distrust, we ourselves have to do our part in obtaining it, and Scupoli gives four methods by which, in dependence always on divine grace, we may acquire this gift:

1. We are to consider or meditate on the truth of our own radical incapacity to merit our salvation.

---

[1] Cf. CCC 385–419.
[2] SC 2, pp. 6–7.

2. We should pray to obtain the gift of a real and personal assent to this truth about our own nature.

3. We should distrust our own judgments about ourselves and realize it is hard to be truthful about ourselves.

4. When we sin we should look more deeply into ourselves and feel more keenly our absolute and utter weakness.

Meditating on the Human Condition

From faith we learn about the existence of original sin and that we are fallen creatures. By ourselves, left to our own resources, we cannot save ourselves. We are dependent on God for the life of grace and for the hope of heaven. This truth about our condition is the basis of the practice of the virtue of humility and distrust of ourselves. We are wounded creatures given to sin, and humility helps to get rid of a false pride and confidence and makes us submissive and ready to receive divine favor.

The fact that we are wounded creatures is reaffirmed with great vigor in the *Catechism of the Catholic Church*:

> The doctrine of original sin, closely connected with that of redemption by Christ, provides lucid discernment of man's situation and activity in the world. By our first parents' sin, the devil has acquired a certain domination over man, even though man remains free. Original sin entails "captivity under the power of him who thenceforth had the power of death, that is, the devil" (Council of Trent (1546): DS 1511; cf. *Heb* 2:14). Ignorance of the fact that man has a wounded nature inclined to evil gives rise to serious errors in the areas of education, politics, social action (cf. John Paul II, *Centesimus annus* 25), and morals.[3]

---

[3] CCC 407.

From the doctrine of original sin, secondly, there follows the teaching of our faith that without grace we can do nothing to merit our salvation. In the Letter of St. James we are taught that "Every good endowment and every perfect gift is from above, coming down from the Father of lights with whom there is no variation or shadow due to change" (Jas 1:17). The Church understands this to mean that left to ourselves we cannot please God and inherit eternal life. As the Council of Trent says: "If anyone says that man can be justified before God by his own works, whether done by his own natural powers or through the teaching of the law, without divine grace through Jesus Christ, let him be anathema." [4]

Of course, what we do matters, and in the traditional language, we are justified by both faith and works. But good works that help us on the road to salvation issue from God's gift of faith and accompany God's gift of faith. They are also, I suppose, in the case of the saints anyway, the evidence of the presence of God's gift of faith.

There is a third reason for self-distrust, and this is the fact that we are all sinners. Sin, says St. Augustine, is "any transgression in deed, or word, or desire, of the eternal law". [5] Sin in this sense, as something each one of us does, may be called personal sin as distinct from original sin. [6] The *Catechism of the Catholic Church* refers us to *Gaudium et Spes* of the Second Vatican Council where we read:

---

[4] *Canons and Decrees of the Council of Trent*, sess. 6, can. 1 (Rockford, Ill.: Tan Books, 1978), p. 42.

[5] St. Augustine, *Contra Faustum*, bk. 22, no. 27.

[6] Original sin describes the human condition as it is now and from out of which our own personal sins arise. Original sin is proper to each individual, although it does not have the character of a personal fault—we inherited it in virtue of our humanity. We are people who are weakened and inclined to evil. Our condition quickly leads to personal sins for which we are responsible.

> What Revelation makes known to us is confirmed by our
> own experience. For when man looks into his own heart he
> finds that he is drawn toward what is wrong and sunk in
> many evils which cannot come from his good creator.[7]

We are drawn to do the wrong things by our fallen nature,
and, as often as not, we follow the promptings of our nature
and commit sin. The *Catechism of the Catholic Church* reminds us that sin is present in human history; any attempt to
ignore it or to give to "this dark reality other names would
be futile".[8] In the light of revelation we see that sin is more
than "a developmental flaw, a psychological weakness, a mistake, or the necessary consequence of an inadequate social
structure"[9]—or anything like that: "[S]in is an abuse of the
freedom that God gives to created persons",[10] a freedom that
was supposed to have been used to love God and our fellow
men.

Assenting to These Truths

These truths, at least for some people, are easier to accept at
a theoretical level than they are in practice. This is not surprising as they are distinctly unpalatable, and deep in our
hearts we tend to believe that they do not really apply very
adequately to us. I do not say we are consistent about this
conceptually, yet there is a real block somewhere in our nature

---

[7] Pastoral Constitution on the Church in the Modern World, *Gaudium et
Spes* (December 7, 1965), no. 13, § 1, in *Vatican Council II*, vol. 1: *The Conciliar
and Postconciliar Documents*, ed. Austin Flannery, new rev. ed. (New York: Costello Pub. Co., 1996), p. 914.

[8] CCC 386.

[9] CCC 387.

[10] Ibid.

to accepting them. Here I think we should notice that so long as we do not lie to ourselves, this does not matter very much if the block shows itself only as a feeling or as a reluctance to accept an unpalatable truth. There are lots of things in life we have to face that we do not want to face, such as having a serious operation, say, or being forced to stay in and work on a beautiful day. Our system rebels against the operation or having to do the work, but, so long as we do not really imagine that not liking the facts is going to drive them away, we are still living in the truth.

A similar observation obtains with the recognition that we are not capable of saving ourselves. So long as we admit the truth of the teaching of our faith and pray that we may learn to understand it more deeply, then we have enough for a solid beginning. The important thing is that there should be no denial of truth or deliberate falseness about ourselves. We must not try to force ourselves into a false feeling either of inferiority and wickedness or, on the other hand, of superiority and holiness. Gradually, as we go on with life, and with our prayer, the truth of our incapacity for good when left to ourselves, as well as the strength of bad habits and of the forces of evil arrayed against us, become ever more apparent to us.

Distrusting Ourselves

The earliest tradition concerning the ascetical life insisted on the importance of living with other people for the development of the virtues. Solitude not only preserves but intensifies the faults of those who are not subject to the correction that is brought to bear on the individual by living with others. Like a mirror, a community holds up the faults of its members, and without the reflector it is easy to obtain a distorted view of ourselves.

Living with others is not, however, enough to guarantee accurate self-knowledge. Nor is avoiding self-deception enough to guarantee living in the truth. Although, certainly, however we are to explain this strange capacity we have for misleading ourselves, this is one element in the situation. The root cause of a justified self-distrust is that we do not know ourselves very well, nor have we any certainty as to how we will act in the future. In the *Confessions* Augustine makes this very clear, and what he wrote at the end of the fourth century is still as accurate and as succinct an expression of the human situation as can be found. He refers to the text in the First Letter to the Corinthians that asks "what person knows a man's thoughts except the spirit of the man which is in him?" (1 Cor 2:11). He then goes on to say that there still remains an area in ourselves that we do not know: "Yet there is something of the human person which is unknown even to the 'spirit of man which is in him' ".[11] Proper integration into a community and an honest effort to understand ourselves do not bring full self-knowledge. That is the fact of the matter, and then the saint goes on to draw the conclusion that he cannot be sure how he will behave in the face of future temptations:

> I know that you cannot be subjected to violence, whereas I do not know which temptations I can resist and which I cannot. There is hope because "you are faithful and do not allow us to be tempted beyond what we can bear, but with the temptation make also a way of escape so that we can bear it" (1 Cor. 10:13). Accordingly, let me confess what I know of myself. Let me confess too what I do not know of myself. For what I know of myself I know because you grant me

---

[11] St. Augustine, *Confessions*, bk. 10, chap. 5, no. 7, trans. Henry Chadwick (Oxford and New York: Oxford Univ. Press, 1992), p. 182.

light, and what I do not know of myself, I do not know until
such time as my darkness becomes "like noonday" before
your face (Isa. 58:10).[12]

Through his faith Augustine knows something about himself: "You Lord know everything about the human person;
for you made humanity",[13] and in that knowledge given by
God to Augustine, he knows that the good in him is from
God and that the evil is from himself. There is a tendency
we all have to claim our good actions as our own and the
bad things we do as not pertaining to ourselves in the same
way. The truth is the reverse: The good things we do are the
result of God's grace and mercy, and the evil things we do
are the sign of what we really are. This theological truth is
behind Scupoli's insistence that we must learn to distrust ourselves when it comes to the foundations of the spiritual life.
Scupoli writes that our corrupt nature too easily inclines us
to a false estimate of ourselves: "so that, being really nothing, we account ourselves to be something, and presume without the slightest foundation, upon our own strength." [14]

The good in us is God's, and the evil in us is our own.
However much this may go against contemporary modes of
thought, this unpleasant truth is the lesson of Scripture and
the teaching of the Church. But it is not just contemporary
modes of thought that find the truth repellent—it is we ourselves. Somewhere, buried not all that deep in ourselves, is a
conviction that we are not really all that bad. Here we have
to learn to pray for the humility to see and accept this fundamental lesson of the Gospel about the human condition.

[12] Ibid.
[13] Ibid.
[14] SC 2, p. 6.

Acknowledging Our Weakness

With experience comes a deepening in the practice of humility. Humility is a large subject and has been much written about and analyzed. St. Benedict, for example, dealt with twelve degrees of humility, which indicates the importance that traditional spirituality attached to this virtue.[15] Humility in its primary sense has to do with moderating an exaggerated feeling of hopefulness about something that is difficult to obtain. Leading our lives in such a way that we will not only end with the Blessed Vision of God, but also begin to live in the presence of God now is just such a difficult goal. All too often we approach our spiritual lives as though sanctification and salvation were really easy to obtain; or even worse, that we do not really have to try at all in order to lead a perfectly satisfactory Christian life. We may not quite say all this, but our actions show we think there is little urgency about the law of God and its application to our own existence here; and we say, at least to ourselves: Let us not get into a sweat; let us take it easy, and it will all come out in the wash. If we had a better developed sense of reality, and that is at least part of what is being talked about here, if we began to practice the virtue of humility, then we might begin to get rid of this terrible complacency. St. Thomas puts it this way:

> The chief reason for repressing presumptuous feelings of hopefulness . . . lies in the reverence you bear towards God, which prevents you from claiming more than is due to you according to your divinely apportioned lot. Humility implies most of all man's subjection to God.[16]

---

[15] *The Rule of St. Benedict,* ed. and trans. Abbot Justin McCann (London: Sheed & Ward, 1972), chap. 7.

[16] ST 2a, 2ae, 161, 3.

It is very hard for us to accept this. We give lip service to the fact we need God, but we think, in a confused way, that some aspect, some quality of ourselves is good in and of itself without God's grace. That is, we seem to believe that this aspect or quality is good through our own nature and our own doing and that this aspect or quality merits, that is, is entitled to, the commendation of God. Well, it is hard to take, and it is a blow to our pride, and it does go against much modern thought, but our faith teaches us that all the good in us that works toward our salvation is based on God's gift and that left to ourselves and our own endowments we are on the road to spiritual self-destruction.

Self-distrust and humility are the first weapons of the spiritual combat. Until we have some sense of our own nothingness, and some realization that we are unable to save ourselves without God's grace, there will be no serious understanding of our faith. And, such a serious understanding of our faith is required if we are to be capable of both deepening our relationship with God as well as changing the way we behave.

CHAPTER THREE

Hope in God

Why do we not obey as we ought? Many people will answer that we have a fallen nature, which hinders us; that we cannot help it, though we ought to be very sorry for it; that this is the reason of our shortcomings. Not so: we can help it; we are not hindered; what we want is the will; and it is our own fault that we have it not. We have all things granted to us; God has abounded in His mercies to us; we have a depth of power and strength lodged in us; but we have not the heart, we have not the will, we have not the love to use it.

> —J. H. Newman, "The Power of the Will,"
> *Parochial and Plain Sermons*

The second weapon in the spiritual combat is hope in God. From faith we learn the truth that we are fallen creatures, and we also know that we have a history of sinful actions that predisposes us to further sin. All this is true, but if it were the only truth we would be justified in giving way to despair. However, a fallen human nature and our own sins are not the whole of the truth, and from faith we also learn that God loves us, that he is rich in mercy, and that through baptism and the forgiveness of sins Christians have been given the power to live as God wants them to live:

As seeds have life in them, which seem lifeless, so the Body of Christ had life in itself, when it was dead; and so also, though not in a similar way, we too, sinners as we are, have a spiritual principle in us, if we did but exert it, so great, so wondrous, that all the powers in the visible world, all the conceivable forces and appetites of matter, all the physical miracles which are at this day in process of discovery, almost superseding time and space, dispensing with numbers, and rivalling mind, all these powers of nature are nothing to this gift within us.[1]

"Unless we would be put to flight and remain helpless and vanquished in the hands of our enemies, we must add to it [that is, self-distrust] a perfect trust in God, and expect from him alone succour and victory".[2] Coupled, that is, with mistrust of ourselves, there must be joined a great confidence in God. Otherwise, we will give way to despair and give up the fight almost from the beginning.

There are four means to acquire a real confidence in God and in his power to help us:

1. We must ask it of God.

2. We must try to deepen our faith in the power of God, who wants to help us.

3. We should recall the truth that no one who trusted in God has ever been confounded—that is, overthrown or defeated.

4. We should develop hope in our daily lives. When any duty presents itself, or any struggle with self is at hand, we should reflect on our own weakness and then on the power and the goodness of God. This will help to obtain both self-distrust and confidence in God.

---

[1] J. H. Newman, "The Power of the Will", sermon 24 in vol. 5 of *Parochial and Plain Sermons* (San Francisco: Ignatius Press, 1997), p. 1177.
[2] SC 3, p. 9.

Finally, Scupoli gives us a test to see whether or not we have really developed self-distrust and confidence in God.

Asking God for Hope

We do not pray often enough for a deeper hold on the truths of our faith. Our grasp of the truths given to us is not like understanding an object of our ordinary experience. There are a lot of things we can understand completely, at least in principle. The more we grasp the truths of faith, however, the more mysterious they become. Yet the effort to understand what can be understood of the truths of faith leads to a process by which they take an ever firmer hold on us. We can compare the truths of faith with each other or with our own experience, and if we do this in a spirit of obedience and prayer gradually we are given a loving knowledge of God that is quite different from speculative knowledge. This sense of the mysteries, which, St. Thomas says, is a living connaturality with divine things, becomes ever more important to us, and we begin to live with a real assent to the truths of God's help and care for us.[3]

Hope, says the *Catechism of the Catholic Church*, "is the theological virtue by which we desire the kingdom of heaven and eternal life as our happiness, placing our trust in Christ's promises and relying not on our own strength, but on the help of the grace of the Holy Spirit".[4]

---

[3] This gift is the gift of wisdom, which St. Thomas discussed in 2a, 2ae, 45. "The Gift of Wisdom ... does not add a superior reason to the natural superior reason, but it causes reason, in its investigation of the divine, to feel as it were at home therein, instinctively sensing what is true long before grasping its demonstration" (É. Gilson, *The Christian Philosophy of St. Thomas Aquinas* [New York: Random House, 1956], p. 348).

[4] CCC 1817.

There are two points in this definition that are important for us. In the first place, what we hope for, the object of the theological virtue of hope, is eternal happiness. Of course, we can legitimately hope for other things, but that is not hope in the sense we mean when we say "faith, hope, and charity". Hoping in the deepest Christian sense means wanting what God has promised us: and what he has promised us is an eternity of bliss and completion in the vision of the Blessed Trinity. Secondly, the capacity to practice the virtue of hope comes from God, not from us. This is Scupoli's second point.

Deepening Our Faith

The second of these four means deals with considerations to help us in seeking to acquire confidence in God.

> [We should gaze] with the eye of faith at the infinite wisdom and omnipotence of God, to which nothing is impossible or difficult, and [confide] ourselves to his unbounded mercy and willingness to give, hour by hour and moment by moment, all things needful for the spiritual life, and perfect victory over ourselves, if only we will throw ourselves with confidence into his arms.[5]

It is all very well to say that the object of hope is beatitude, but there remains the question of how we are able to hope in any very serious way and for any length of time for something we do not see and for something that exceeds all our powers to grasp. We know the object of hope is eternal happiness, but what are the means by which we will be able to hope for what we do not see and cannot touch? It does seem

[5] SC 3, p. 9.

to be the case that left to ourselves we cannot persevere in wanting and trusting in an unseen God. The *Catechism of the Catholic Church*, as we have just seen, says that we must place our trust in Christ's promises and not rely on our own strength, but on the help of the grace of the Holy Spirit. It is this reliance on the work of the Holy Spirit that St. Thomas takes up and develops in a serious way. "The hope of which we are now speaking", St. Thomas says, "attains God by *leaning on his help in order to obtain the hoped for good*".[6] It belongs to an infinite power, that is God, to lead us to an infinite good. The infinite good in question here is eternal happiness, which consists in the enjoyment of God himself; and we obtain this infinite good by being helped by the infinite power of God.

> The hope of which we speak now, attains God by leaning on his help in order to obtain the hoped for good. Now an effect must be proportionate to its cause. Wherefore the good which we ought to hope for from God properly and chiefly is the infinite good, which is proportionate to the power of our divine helper, since it belongs to an infinite power to lead anyone to an infinite good.[7]

Under the dry, matter-of-fact tone of St. Thomas' prose there is this wonderful truth that it is the power of the Holy Spirit that fuels our hope, that makes us persevere in hope, that is the bridge from *believing* there is a God to actually wanting him above everything else. We lean on God's help so that we will not give way to discouragement and despair when life is difficult. Perhaps we are tempted to say that if I cannot merit my salvation if left to myself, and if I am a creature so prone

[6] ST 2a, 2ae, 17, 1.
[7] ST 2a, 2ae, 17, 2.

to sin that I cannot even keep the moral law for any length of time, then what is the use of trying? But God's gift of hope to us gives us the strength to go on hoping when things seem bleak and cold and the attractions of this world seem to be so much more immediate and important than the hope of heaven.

Recalling that No One Who Trusts in God Has Ever Been Confounded

This third point is really a continuation of the second, but it is so important that it deserves to be considered separately. It is relatively easy to deduce this truth from a belief in God's providence. If God is good and governs all things, it follows that whatever happens to those who trust in him must be for their good. Experience, though, often suggests a very different conclusion, and it requires a deep faith in providence and in the goodness of God, not only to accept, but also to will what his providence ordains for us in the actual course of our lives. We must, therefore, develop the idea of providence that we have already met in the chapter on "First Principles".[8]

It is part of our faith that God created the world according to his wisdom. The *Catechism of the Catholic Church* says:

[The world] is not the product of any necessity whatever, nor of blind fate or chance. We believe that it proceeds from God's free will; he wanted to make his creatures share in his being, wisdom, and goodness: "For you created all things, and by your will they existed and were created" (*Rev* 4:11). Therefore the Psalmist exclaims: "O LORD, how manifold

---

[8] See above, pp. 31–32.

are your works! In wisdom you have made them all"; and
"The LORD is good to all, and his compassion is over all that
he has made" (*Ps* 104:24, 145:9).[9]

God created everything there is, not because he had to, but
for his own glory.[10] He did not, however, just create the
world, then set it going (as it were) and leave it to its own
devices. An eighteenth-century idea of God was that he is
like a great watchmaker. This cool, detached God was thought
to have created a finely tuned mechanism that then ran itself without God's interest, much less his intervention. But
this is not just an eighteenth-century theory; it also lies
behind the contemporary attitude that is prepared to admit
the reality of some sort of a God but is unwilling to admit
he acts in any significant way. People who are anxious to
avoid anthropomorphism in thinking about God all too
often tend to talk about God as substance in an unhelpful
way. Thinking about God as substance often becomes a sub-
stitute for watchmaker talk, because the idea of substance
being used is so bland there is no danger it would actually do
anything.

The watchmaker image is a very inadequate idea for two
reasons. In the first place, "with creation, God does not abandon his creatures to themselves. He not only gives them being and existence, but also, and at every moment, upholds
and sustains them in being, enables them to act and brings
them to their final end".[11] In other words, God never retires
from the scene; he is always actively involved in maintaining
his creation in existence.

[9] CCC 295.
[10] See CCC 293–94.
[11] CCC 301.

Secondly, however, the universe was created " 'in a state of journeying' (*in statu viae*) toward an ultimate perfection yet to be attained, to which God has destined it".[12] Now on this journey to perfection God takes an active and the most important part. God's activity in bringing about the perfection of his creatures is called *providence*. The *Catechism of the Catholic Church* says: "We call 'divine providence' the dispositions by which God guides his creation toward this perfection".[13]

The word "disposition" here does not mean a mood or a state of mind, but has the sense of arranging and controlling or directing. We say, for example, that a person *disposes* of his property and money in his last will and testament. By that we mean that he directs how the money and property are to be used and to whom it is to go. We even talk about the *dispositions* of a person's will. So when we talk about providence being the dispositions by which God guides his creation toward perfection, we mean the controlling arrangements through which he brings about what he wants to bring about:

> The witness of Scripture is unanimous that the solicitude of divine providence is *concrete* and *immediate*; God cares for all, from the least things to the great events of the world and its history. The sacred books powerfully affirm God's absolute sovereignty over the course of events: "Our God is in the heavens; he does whatever he pleases" (*Ps* 115:3). And so it is with Christ, "who opens and no one shall shut, who shuts and no one opens" (*Rev* 3:7). As the book of Proverbs states: "Many are the plans in the mind of a man, but it is the purpose of the Lord that will be established" (*Prov* 19:21).[14]

---

[12] CCC 302.
[13] Ibid.
[14] CCC 303.

This is what Catholics believe, or are supposed to believe, about God's creation and his providence. But belief is supposed to provide the basis of our spiritual life. We have to learn to grasp the truth in such a way that it will affect the way we approach God, the way we face life, as well as help to change the way we act. We have to try to develop a deep-seated realization that the will of God is behind everything that happens to us and that, furthermore, this providence of God is his loving disposition for our own happiness and perfection. We have to try to allow this truth of faith to take hold of us: we have to try to give serious assent to the truth that everything that happens in the world, with the exception of sin, happens only because God wills it.

We will probably find that, as we meditate about God's providence and our own lives, we have an instinctive revulsion against regarding the troubles life brings us as manifestations of God's love and favor. So the first thing is to be firm with ourselves, refuse to be guided by this instinctive reaction, and then pray for an increase in the strength to persevere, which is one aspect of the gift of the virtue of hope.

Developing Hope in Daily Life

The fourth means for developing trust in God consists in turning the truths we have been trying to acquire, concerning our own radical incapacity to merit heaven and our confidence in God, into a technique for dealing with the actual situations of life as they arise. If we try to apply distrust of self and confidence in God to our daily lives, this attempt itself helps us to realize their truth. When a duty presents itself to be done, any struggle with self to be made, any victory over self to be attempted, before proposing or deciding to do it, "think first upon thine own weakness; next turn,

full of self-distrust, to the wisdom, the power, and the goodness of God; and in reliance on these, resolve to fight generously." [15] The practice of the truths, that is, helps us to
grasp their reality more deeply.

The order to be observed is, first, distrust of self and, then,
an act of confidence in God. Scupoli believes that if we begin with confidence in God, we are all too liable to leave out
the unpleasant part of the equation, which is self-distrust.
Next, there is a point to be made about the relation between
the two. Humility and hope have somehow to become, both
of them together, aspects of our attitude toward God, toward each other, and toward the world. That is, Scupoli is
not teaching that we are to be humble one minute and then
full of hope the next in an uneasy see-saw movement of con-
trasting attitudes. On the contrary, we have to try to develop
a permanent attitude that combines sorrow for sin with a
living hope in the possibility of doing better.

The experience of being sick at heart for something we
realize we have done and for what we are, while, at the same
time, desiring something better, is what the early Fathers of
the Church called *compunction*. It is not a word we use much
nowadays, and the Oxford Dictionary concentrates on the
first half of the condition: "A pricking or stinging of the
conscience or heart; uneasiness of mind consequent on wrong
doing; remorse or contrition". In the second chapter of Acts
there is an account of Peter's address to the Jews in Jerusa-
lem. The sermon ends with the words "Let all the house of
Israel therefore know assuredly that God has made him both
Lord and Christ, this Jesus whom you crucified" (Acts 2:36).

The reaction of the Jews is described in the next verse:
"Now when they heard this they were cut to the heart, and

[15] SC 3, p. 10.

said to Peter and the rest of the apostles 'Brethren, what shall we do?'" Peter then consoles them and tells them: "For the promise is to you and to your children and to all that are far off, every one whom the Lord our God calls to him" (Acts 2:39).

The Venerable Guigo, the fifth prior of the Grande Chartreuse (d. 1188), wrote that the books the Carthusians wrote made them (the Carthusians) "heralds of the truth ... and thus we may hope that God will reward us for all those who are saved from their errors or make progress in the Catholic truth by means of our books, or are pierced to the heart for their sins and vices, or are fired with longing for their heavenly home." [16] This is a wonderful statement of compunction, which in the tradition has two sides: that is, a piercing sorrow for sin, which is accompanied at the same time with longing for our heavenly home.

The words of the Jews on hearing Peter's sermon reflect a complex experience of remorse, fear, and astonishment, but also of confidence. We can use this experience in our prayer during those times when things seem very gray and we are unable to focus our minds on God and the things of God.

In a quiet but sincere way, we should acknowledge our own sinfulness. It is not a question so much of dwelling on past sins in particular, but being able to say with the Psalmist, "Out of the depths I cry to thee, O LORD! Lord, hear my voice!" (Ps 130:1–2); "For I know my transgressions, and my sin is ever before me" (Ps 50:3). The depths are our own condition—the wounds of original sin, our blurred vision of

---

[16] Guigo I, *Consuetudines*, PL 153:695: "Quot enim libros scribimus, tot nobis veritatis praecones facere videmur, sperantes a Domino mercedem pro omnibus, qui per eos, vel ab errore correcti fuerint, vel in catholicae veritate profecerint, pro cunctis etiam qui vel de suis peccatis et vitiis compuncti, vel ad desiderium fuerint patriae coelestis accensi."

God's truth, our weakness in doing good, and our inability to keep God's law for very long without his grace. The depths are this sinful condition, but they are also, in addition to this, the actual sins we may have committed, the broken resolutions, and all the times we have left unanswered God's call to try to do just a little better.

I think today that people have too little sense of the reality of original sin and of the awfulness of sin. We have had so many exhortations to be positive and to have a good image of ourselves that we are in danger of leaving sin out altogether. A positive image may not always be an accurate reflection of what we are. A deep sense of our own sinfulness is a grace, and there is much profit to be gained from meditating quietly on the truth of our sinfulness even if we do not feel it very deeply.

Secondly, however, we must use this realization of our own sinfulness to hope more firmly in God and to pray "to be fired with longing for our heavenly home". How many of us, I wonder, have ever prayed for an increase of hope? To be actually fired with longing for our heavenly home is a great grace that we cannot count on receiving. On the other hand, we most certainly can pray for a deeper realization of the reality of God's promises. And nothing will lead us to this deeper realization more quickly than a sense that it is, in truth, from out of the depths that God has called us to be his sons.

This analysis of compunction should be used in times of stress or when we are overcome with a deep and bitter remorse. Rather than drowning in a psychological sea of self-pity or self-hatred, we should use those experiences as ways of educating ourselves in compunction. Pray that the sense of our own wickedness will be used by God to pierce us to the heart so that we may really hope in his forgiveness and base our lives on his promises. All our experience, even that of which we may quite properly be ashamed, can be used in our journey to God.

Testing Our Self-Distrust and Confidence

We can examine whether we have developed genuine self-distrust or not by observing the effect made upon us when we sin. "If thou art so saddened and disquieted thereby as to be tempted to despair of making progress or doing good, it is a sure sign that thy trust is in self and not in God." [17] We make a resolution, for example, to be patient, and we fail; or we make a resolution to avoid an occasion of sexual sin and then enter into the occasion and perhaps fall. In both cases there is often a disproportionate sense of failure and of grief. How could this possibly happen to me? What's the use of trying? The whole thing is unrealistic; I'll never be any good anyway.

This reaction shows we have been depending too much on our own efforts. If we really mistrusted ourselves, we would not be surprised when we fall, nor would we give way to despondency and bitterness. We would recognize that our sin flows quite naturally from the sort of people we are and that our reaction is occasioned as much by hurt pride as by sorrow at having offended God.

A fall should teach us to recognize our own weakness and to become more distrustful of what we can do when left to our own resources. A fall should make us detest the fault "and the unruly passions which have occasioned it".[18] That is, rather than allowing ourselves to be overcome with

[17] SC 4, p. 11.
[18] Ibid., p. 12.

emotions of self-disgust or anger at ourselves, we should direct our dislike onto the fault itself and the disorganization in our nature that has led us into sin. Too much attention to the fact that it is *we* who have failed may very well deflect us away from *what* it is we have done. The sin itself is, as it were, left unscathed and its attraction really unaltered, because our energy has not been directed against it itself.

Scupoli says that a fault should leave us more distrustful of self and more humbly confident in God: "detesting above all things his fault and the unruly passions which have occasioned it, and mourning with a quiet, deep, and patient sorrow over his offence against God." [19] "Mourning with a quiet, deep, and patient sorrow": There must be real contrition, but the energy generated by our reaction to the fall—if I may put it this way—must be spent on hating the sin and resolving to fight it more effectively in the future.

There is a clear application of all this to the use of the sacrament of penance. St. Thomas teaches that the proximate, or immediate, matter of this sacrament is the penitent's contrition, his grief, over the sins he has committed. The remote matter is the sins over which he grieves. There has to be an element of real sorrow over what we have done, either because we have offended God or, less perfectly, because we are afraid of hell, before the proper dispositions for confession exist. Sometimes people run to confession more to disassociate themselves from the sin than because they are sorry for what they have done. This is especially true of sexual sin. People sometimes go to confession (which in itself, of course, is a good thing) after a sexual lapse more from a sense of ritual, or external, uncleanness and a general sense

[19] Ibid.

of unease than because they think that they, themselves, are the sort of person who needs forgiveness and healing in this area. Confession thus becomes a kind of therapy that makes them feel better for a while but leaves the predisposition to sin untouched. Scupoli says the following:

> I would that these things were well considered by certain persons so called spiritual, who cannot and will not be at rest when they have fallen into any fault. They rush to their spiritual father, rather to get rid of the anxiety and uneasiness which spring from the wounded self-love than for the purpose which should be their chief end in seeking him, to purify themselves from the stain of sin, and to fortify themselves against its power by means of the most holy sacrament of penance.[20]

---

[20] Ibid.

CHAPTER FOUR

Spiritual Exercises

It is the opinion of a large class of religious people, that
faith being granted, works follow as a matter of course,
without our own trouble.

—J. H. Newman, "Human Responsibility,
as Independent of Circumstances,"
*Fifteen Sermons Preached before the University
of Oxford between* A.D. *1826 and 1843*

In addition to self-distrust and confidence in God we must
also practice *spiritual exercises.*

If in this warfare we are provided with no weapons except
self-distrust and trust in God, needful as both these are, we
shall not only fail to gain the victory over ourselves, but shall
fall into many evils.[1]

Spiritual exercises involve using ordinary human means, accompanied of course by prayer and the sacraments, to see to
it that our thinking, our acting, and our desiring are centered on Christ so that gradually we may be remade in his
image. In a quiet and unemotional way we have to look at
the way we actually live and then try to root out what is evil

---

[1] SC 7, p. 14.

in our lives as well as develop what is good. These efforts to grow in the knowledge and love of Christ will use both the understanding and the will, and they will involve suffering that often seems to make little sense.

The idea of spiritual exercises has a long history that pre-dates Christianity, but it is one of those ideas that have all but disappeared from the contemporary Christian conscious-ness. This means we have to begin with a statement of what the tradition meant by the term.

In the First Letter to Timothy, St. Paul writes:

> Train yourselves in godliness; for while bodily training is of some value, godliness is of value in every way, as it holds promise for the present life and also for the life to come (1 Tim 4:7–8).

This text, which has had a great influence in the develop-ment of Christian spirituality,[2] tells us three things. First of all, we are to train, or exercise, ourselves in godliness. Sec-ondly, this training, while it bears some resemblance to bodily training, is more than bodily training and has to do with acquiring what St. Paul calls *godliness* (*eusebia*). Thirdly, we are told that this godliness is useful, or holds out a promise, both for this life and for the life to come.

In chapter 1 we outlined Scupoli's first principles of the spiritual life.[3] These principles were about God and our

---

[2] See "Exercises spirituels", in *Dictionnaire de spiritualité*, ed. Marcel Viller, S.J. [Paris: G. Beauchesne et ses fils, 1932–], vol. 4, cols. 1903–33.

[3] These principles were: (1) knowledge of the goodness and the greatness of God and of our nothingness and inclination to all evil; (2) the love of him and the hatred of ourselves; (3) subjection, not to him alone, but, for love of him, to all his creatures; (4) entire renunciation of all will of our own and absolute resignation to all his divine pleasure; (5) willing and doing all this purely for the glory of God and solely to please him and because he so wills and merits thus to be loved and served.

relation to him and provide us with guidelines as to how we are to think and act if we are to be united with God and so find that happiness which the Gospel promises to the faithful Christian. But the principles are for action and must be put into practice. Furthermore, putting the principles into practice is going to involve a struggle, and we are going to have to use or *exercise* them because the intellectual stance and the moral imperatives of Christianity run counter to the demands of our wounded human nature. The organized campaign to exercise the virtues and eradicate the vices is one aspect of what Scupoli calls spiritual exercises.

There is, however, more to the idea of spiritual exercises than trying to build up a series of virtues that are externally linked together like a number of beads on a string. Spiritual exercises are directed toward a new orientation of our whole being. When St. Paul said "Put on the Lord Jesus Christ" (Rom 13:14), he was telling his converts that spiritual progress tends to an ever more intimate union with Christ. Furthermore, this union will be the result not only of the call of God, but of our own freedom as well.[4] Growth into Jesus Christ extends beyond both intellect and will to the very self, so that in the case of the saints they can say with St. Paul:

> I have been crucified with Christ; it is no longer I who live, but Christ who lives in me; and the life I now live in the flesh I live by faith in the Son of God, who loved me and gave himself for me. (Gal 2:20)

Spiritual exercises only make sense for a Christian within this Pauline framework. Whatever we are going to understand by them, and however we are going to put them into

---

[4] See "Christian Holiness", in CCC 2012–16.

practice, they have to be seen as one of the ways we answer to the call of Christ.

Pierre Hadot in *Philosophy as a Way of Life* has shown how much of the theory and practice of spiritual exercises is rooted in Hellenistic and Roman schools of philosophy. These exercises were designed:

> to raise the individual from an inauthentic condition of life, darkened by unconsciousness and harried by worry, to an authentic state of life in which he attains self-consciousness, an exact vision of the world, inner peace, and freedom.[5]

It is difficult to read these words without a sense of excitement and a feeling that this is exactly what the modern world needs. To achieve "an authentic state of life" seems like an ideal that is both human and noble, and Christianity can be viewed as playing a part in the achievement of this ideal. However, it will not do as a description of Catholic spiritual exercises, because the focus is wrong. The purpose of Christian spiritual exercises is union with God through the knowledge and imitation of Christ, and Christ is not a means to anything else.

Imitating Christ involves more than trying to achieve "self-consciousness, an exact vision of the world, inner peace, and freedom". An authentic Christian spirituality must deal with the reality and the "ordinariness" of everyday existence, and over everyday existence there hangs the shadow of the cross, of sin, and of suffering. These realities have to be recognized and dealt with, not as realities that unfortunately interfere from time to time with "an authentic way of life", but as

---

[5] Pierre Hadot, *Philosophy as a Way of Life: Spiritual Exercises from Socrates to Foucault*, ed. Arnold Davidson, trans. Michael Chase (Oxford: Blackwell, 1999), p. 83.

part and parcel of real life in the world. For Scupoli, and for
Newman, it is in and through these hard and painful times
that Christ is found and imitated. "Indeed I count everything as loss", said St. Paul, "because of the surpassing worth
of knowing Christ Jesus my Lord" (Phil 3:8). Newman wrote
in the same vein:

> And be sure of this: that if He has any love for you, if He sees
> aught of good in your soul, *He* will afflict you, if you will
> not afflict yourselves. He will not let you escape. He has ten
> thousand ways of purging those whom He has chosen, from
> the dross and alloy with which the fine gold is defaced. . . .
> Let us judge ourselves, that we be not judged. Let us afflict
> ourselves, that God may not afflict us. Let us come before
> Him with our best offerings, that He may forgive us.[6]

There is more to imitating Christ than the cross, sin, and
suffering. St. Paul tells us that we are to think on "whatever
is just, whatever is pure, whatever is lovely, whatever is gracious" (Phil 4:8), and to deny the beauty and goodness of
God's creation is not part of Catholicism. But, at the same
time, we will think well of these things only if we have tried
to imitate Christ and have followed St. Paul, who forgot what
lay behind and strained forward to what lay ahead (see Phil
3:13–14).

The basic difficulty for contemporary readers with Scupoli's discussion of spiritual exercises is not so much what he
actually says but that he bothers to say anything at all. The
notion, that is, of an organized campaign to fight sin and to
practice doing good actions is at total variance with how
people today think about the spiritual life.

---

[6] J. H. Newman, "Life the Season of Repentance", sermon 2 in vol. 6 of
Plain and Parochial Sermons (San Francisco: Ignatius Press, 1997), pp. 1200–1201.

The source of this mistrust may be based on theological arguments that lead to the neglect of ascetical practices and the failure to recognize what Newman called the duty of self-denial.[7] Often today this failure of recognition is expressed not so much in an explicit denial as in a failure to put it into practice. But whether expressed or not, it is clear that a refusal to admit the duty of self-denial results in a deep scepticism with regard to any talk about spiritual exercises.

There is, however, another source of discomfort with the concept of spiritual exercises that has more weight. It is a perennial criticism of ascetical practices that, although they are supposed to be based on the duty of self-denial, they are in fact a not so skillfully designed exercise in self-will and manifest an unedifying (and unconvincing) preoccupation with self. Fasting, disciplines, hair shirts, abstaining from various pleasures, and the whole range of ascetical practices are nothing but a spiritual obstacle race, so it is said, whose motivation is pride and spiritual self-aggrandizement. The practices themselves are undertaken, so it is claimed, for self-improvement in a way that suggests that beatitude and the love of God and neighbor have been largely forgotten.[8]

The argument in itself is a serious one, although it does not carry much conviction when presented by those who in fact deny there is any need for asceticism and at a period of history when self-denial is looked on as in itself unhealthy. On the other hand, St. John of the Cross and many others in

---

[7] "The Duty of Self-Denial", sermon 7 in vol. 7 of *Parochial and Plain Sermons*, pp. 1470–78.

[8] "I agree with you that there was a good deal of 'Stoicism' in the desert, and that their mortifications were very like modern record breaking—a kind of sport" (John Chapman, letter 24, in *Spiritual Letters* (London: Sheed & Ward, 1935), p. 81.

more recent times have warned against this abuse of asceticism, and the warning should be taken seriously.

The core of this argument against asceticism is that, because ascetical practices are chosen, this shows they are just one more exercise in self-will. The reply to this objection is twofold. In the first place, physical penance, and this is what people are usually talking about when they oppose asceticism, is only to be undertaken in obedience to a legitimate authority, and, secondly, the ordinary circumstances of life, properly used, will provide an asceticism that is more than adequate for most people most of the time.

If the purpose of physical penance is to help destroy self-will, it is clear that it ought not to be an exercise in self-will. One of the great achievements of the sixteenth-century masters of the spiritual life, such as St. Philip Neri, St. Ignatius of Loyola, and later St. Francis de Sales, was to teach people that corporal penance in itself was not an automatic passport to sanctity. St. Philip said that sanctity consisted in the mortification of the *razionale*, that is, in firmly saying no to the thinking, judging, willing aspect of human nature, and he imposed this mortification ruthlessly on all who came to him for direction in the ways of holiness. He once gave permission to a young nobleman to wear a hair shirt, but then told him he had to wear it over his fashionable clothes. To be badly dressed, and to look a fool in the eyes of the young man's world, was, St. Philip thought, much more of an exercise in mortification than the physical discomfort the hair shirt would have caused. The purpose of the command was to help the youth destroy the self-will and vanity that stood in the way of his progress toward purity of heart and, finally, beatitude.

The prayer of St. Ignatius of Loyola in which he offers up his freedom, his memory, his understanding, and his will in order to be governed by the will of Christ is a clear state-

ment of an asceticism of love, an asceticism based on hand-
ing over to God what is most intimate, most precious, and
most personal in order that Christ may live in him.

> Lord Jesus Christ, take all my freedom,
> my memory, my understanding, and my will.
> All that I have and cherish you have given me.
> I surrender it all to be governed by your will.
> Your grace and your love
> are wealth enough for me.
> Give me these, Lord Jesus,
> and I ask for nothing more.[9]

The danger today with this asceticism based on interior mortification is that it is taken as an excuse for no corporal penance whatsoever. St. Philip Neri, who did so much to move
the emphasis from exterior to interior mortification,[10] nonetheless held that "outward mortifications are a great help towards the acquisition of interior mortification and the other
virtues",[11] and St. Vincent de Paul taught that he who has
no use for corporal penance shows he does not understand
interior mortification.[12] This must be true. Human beings
are not pure spirit, and the notion of disincarnate experience that is purely interior is difficult to understand, much
less to accept. Mortification is the experience of a human

---

[9] *The Spiritual Exercises*, reprinted in *Handbook of Prayers* (Princeton, N.J.:
Scepter Publishers, 1995), p. 286.

[10] "Those who pay a moderate attention to the mortification of their bod-
ies and direct their main intention to mortify the will and understanding, even
in matter of the slightest moment, are more to be esteemed than they who
give themselves up exclusively to corporal penances and macerations" (St. Philip
Neri, maxim for February 20, in *Maxims and Counsels*, arr. Fr. Faber [1890;
reprint, Toronto: The Oratory, 1995]).

[11] Ibid., maxim for February 16.

[12] St. Vincent de Paul, cited in Jordan Aumann, *Spiritual Theology* (London:
Sheed & Ward, 1980), p. 180.

being, that is, of a body with a soul, and what the body is, and what is done to the body, is indispensable for the very existence of the experience.[13] Certainly, St. Philip, St. Ignatius, and St. Francis de Sales, who were the architects of a more personal and interior spirituality, all allowed and imposed penances in a way that would be unthinkable today, and Scupoli takes these practices for granted. I conclude from this that, although the forms and amount of physical penance may vary, St. Philip and St. Vincent de Paul are right; that is to say, exterior mortification must not be left out of account.

The second response to the contention that asceticism is an exercise in self-will is that the opportunities for asceticism are forced on us by circumstances whether we will them or not. Although Scupoli does not use the expression *the sacrament of the present moment*, the notion that we find the will of God for us in the actual circumstances of our daily lives is a central theme in his spirituality. That is, the demands of our fallen, wounded human nature are constantly at odds with the law of God, and this conflict, properly understood and properly used, is the way that in fact we take our cross and follow Christ, so that where he is we may be also.

Scupoli warns us that there is no escape from the spiritual combat, for either we struggle, or we are overcome by sin, despair, and death,[14] and implicit in his discussion is the further point that the warfare between the flesh and the spirit is

---

[13] This is not to say we do not have a direct access to our present mental states that no one else possesses, and it is the case that only I can feel my mortification and self-sacrifices. But this first-person awareness does not show that my experience of being mortified is a purely mental or interior one.

[14] "That thou fail not to fight courageously bear in mind that this is a conflict whence there is no escape; and that he who will not fight must needs be captured or slain" (SC 15, p. 39).

of benefit to us if we use it in the right way. This point is an old one and goes back at least to Cassian. In discussing the reasons why our prayer is often dry and difficult, Cassian says that one cause is the "Lord's design and trial".[15] God shows us how pitifully weak and inadequate we are by leaving us with nothing but a sense of our own weakness and of our own distractions. He compares this to the way God left Israel's enemies to test them and toughen them up and quotes the book of Judges:

> Now these are the nations which the LORD left, to test Israel by them. . . . They were for the testing of Israel, to know whether Israel would obey the commandments of the LORD, which he commanded their fathers by Moses. (Judg 3:1, 4)

God reserved this conflict for Israel, Cassian goes on to say, in order to teach them the need of God's help in every circumstance and so that they would continue to struggle to do God's will. "For frequently", he says, "security and prosperity have brought low those whom adversities cannot overcome."[16] When our prayer ceases to be easy for us, and when we are distracted and dry, we become particularly exposed to temptations of the flesh; like the Jews who were attacked by the five lords of the Philistines (Judg 3:3), we are suddenly made aware of the demands of the flesh as well as the call of the spirit. Cassian begins his treatment of this warfare

[15] John Cassian, conference 4, of Abbot Daniel, chap. 3, in *The Conferences*, trans. Boniface Ramsey, O.P. (New York: Paulist Press, 1997), p. 156.

[16] Ibid., chap. 6, no. 4, p. 158. In no. 5 of the same chapter, he says that "God did not begrudge Israel their peace nor look with malice upon them, but he planned this conflict in the knowledge that it would be beneficial. Thus, constantly oppressed by the onslaught of the nations, they would never feel that they did not need the Lord's help. Hence they would always meditate on him and cry out to him, and they would neither lapse into sluggish inactivity nor lose their ability to fight and their training in virtue" (p. 158).

with the famous text from Galatians: "For the flesh lusteth against the spirit, and the spirit against the flesh. But these two are opposed to each other so that ye should not do what ye would"; or, in another translation, "For the desires of the flesh are against the Spirit and the desires of the Spirit are against the flesh; for these are opposed to each other, to prevent you from doing what you would" (Gal 5:17).

The reason for the conflict is "that ye should not do what ye would". We are prevented from doing what we want to do by the conflict. Cassian does not say that it is either the flesh or the spirit in itself that prevents us from fulfilling what we want to do. It is the reality of the conflict itself that gets in the way of giving ourselves over wholly to what we might want to do at any given time. For example, I might be tempted to overeat, but I also remember that I will not be able to pray afterward, and so a conflict ensues because I really do want to do both things. This conflict is implanted in us by arrangement of the Creator, and so, in the present dispensation (after the Fall) it is natural, as it were, and good for us. But how? The answer is that the struggle calls and urges us on to a higher state; and if it ceased, most surely there would ensue a peace that is fraught with danger. Either, that is, to use the example of overeating and praying, I would give way to the desire to overeat and not pray, or I might go to such excesses to satisfy the desire to pray that I do not eat properly. In both cases a false peace would be achieved, but not one that would last. If I am going to achieve a higher and more balanced state, in which the lawful needs of both the flesh and the spirit are recognized, then I must exercise control over them both. In other words, the higher state is not going to be brought about by yielding to the promptings of either of them as they first present themselves to us, but to some sort of higher reconciliation brought about by the conflict. Let us try to unpack this answer.

Cassian points out that there seem to be three factors involved: first, the flesh against the spirit; second, the spirit against the flesh; and finally, our own free will, which seems to be placed between the two.

The word flesh is not always used in the same way in the Scriptures. St. Paul, Cassian says, is using the word here, in Galatians, to mean the carnal will and evil desires. The spirit means the good and spiritual desires of the soul. Flesh and spirit are realities that in one and the same man struggle for domination either at the same time or separately, with the shifting and changing of circumstances. The warfare is misdescribed if we look on it as a struggle between what is physical and material (and therefore bad), on the one hand, and what is immaterial and unworldly (and therefore good), on the other. Giving way to either the flesh or the spirit as they first present themselves will end in disaster, because both, in their own way, are totalitarian and incomplete. The lust of the flesh rushes blindly toward sin and revels in those delights that are connected with ease. That is perhaps simple enough to see. On the other hand, the desire of the spirit is opposed to these, but it wishes to be entirely absorbed in spiritual efforts, so that it actually wants to be rid of even the necessary uses of the flesh and longs to be so constantly taken up with spiritual things as to desire to have no share or anxiety about the weakness of the flesh. *The flesh delights in luxuries and pleasure, but the spirit does not give in even to natural desires.*[17]

The will stands in an intermediate position between the demands of the flesh and the demands of the spirit, and it is somewhat worthy of blame.[18] It is worthy of blame because "it neither delights in the disgrace of sin nor agrees to the hardship of virtue." [19] It is anxious to pursue future blessings in such a way as not to lose present ones. Free will wants to have it both ways. It wants to shuttle back and forth between the demands of the flesh and those of the spirit, and this uneasy and often frenetic effort at conciliation can never lead to the attainment of true perfection. Free will dithers and is in danger of plunging us into a most miserable condition of lukewarmness, making us like those who were rebuked by our Lord—neither hot, nor cold so I will spew thee out of my mouth (see Rev 3:15–16).

Gradually, however, things begin to change. The elements in the struggle remain constant, but the fact that the warfare goes on begins to teach us about ourselves. The flesh and the spirit are moderated, as it were, but they are only incompletely synthesized; we go slack, and the desires of the flesh begin to stir and "drag us to that chilling path of pleasure which horrifies us and which is full of briars".[20] On the other hand, if we have been inflamed with spiritual fervor, we want "to extinguish the works of the flesh regardless of human frailty".[21] So the will does not like to give itself completely to either, and this daily struggle begins to strengthen it and teaches us the limits of flesh and spirit more accurately.

While this conflict is stirred up within us every day to our benefit, we are salutarily driven to that fourth condition, which we do not want, in order to acquire purity of heart not at leisure or at ease but with constant toil and a contrite spirit. . . . The proper equilibrium which results from the struggle of these two opens up the healthy and temperate

[19] Cassian, conference 4, chap. 12, no. 1, p. 161.
[20] Ibid., no, 2, p. 162.
[21] Ibid.

path of virtue between the both of them and teaches the soldier of Christ always to proceed along the royal road. [22]

The struggle between the flesh and the spirit forces us to follow "the royal road of Christ". But if we are to follow this road, we must know where to find it and then know how to stay on it. Scupoli's third weapon of the spiritual combat is for precisely that purpose. Spiritual exercises, as we saw above,[23] will use both the understanding and the will.

1. *We begin first with the understanding.* We should remember that trying to live a Christian life involves using our head as well as our will. We have to know something about God and what he wants for us if we are to please him; and we also have to know something about ourselves and how we act and react in particular circumstances. In what concerns the understanding, we have to guard against ignorance and the wrong kind of curiosity.

2. *Next we must train the will.* We have to practice not only desiring what God wants us to desire, and refusing the things he does not want us to desire; we also have to strive after wanting and not wanting them precisely because this is God's will for us.

Spiritual Exercises concerning the Understanding

Scupoli says that the first set of spiritual exercises is concerned with the understanding. We have first of all to do away with ignorance about spiritual realities and also to avoid the sort of curiosity that leads to unnecessary detours that would take us off the road.[24] Our world presents us with all

[22] Ibid., no. 4, p. 162.
[23] See above, p. 75.
[24] Exercises against ignorance: SC 7–9, pp. 14–19.

sorts of different ways to live our lives, and even people who are trying to be serious about their faith are confused as to what should be accepted and what rejected. If we are to find the Way, then we must know how to find it hidden as it is under a mass of conflicting theories about life and how it should be lived. In order to be successful in our search, we will have to have some standard for rejecting false views that lead away from Christ to destruction as well as possess enough knowledge to keep on the right way. Ignorance and curiosity have to be fought if we are to find and to stay on what Cassian calls the royal road. Ignorance darkens the understanding and prevents it from seeing the truth, while unrestrained curiosity leads us away from the truth once we have begun to grasp it.

The general principle that without truth we cannot really live as we should is of fundamental importance. In St. Matthew we read:

> The eye is the lamp of the body. So, if your eye is sound, your whole body will be full of light; but if your eye is not sound, your whole body will be full of darkness. If then the light in you is darkness, how great is the darkness! (Mt 6:22–23)

This light is the knowledge faith gives us, and we have seen that our understanding of who we are, of how we are to behave, and of our destiny comes from the revelation of God in Christ.[25] A personal encounter with the Lord must be based on, and supplemented by, this objectivity of faith if it is to endure. This knowledge provides the essential framework, or backbone, of a life centered on God. We do not all have to be theologians in any technical sense, but we do

[25] See above, p. 50.

have to have an understanding of our faith based on authoritative teaching as found, for example, in the *Catechism of the
Catholic Church.* This understanding must be thought over
and applied to ourselves as outlined in the five first principles of the spiritual life, and they will become "a lamp to my
feet and a light to my path" (Ps 119:105).

The Old Testament attests that *God is the source of all truth.*
His Word is truth. His Law is truth. His "faithfulness endures to all generations" (*Ps* 119:90; cf. *Prov* 8:7; *2 Sam* 7:28;
Ps 119:142; *Lk* 1:50). Since God is "true," the members of
his people are called to live in truth (*Rom* 3:4, cf. *Ps* 119:30).

"The members of his people are called to live in truth."

> In Jesus Christ, the whole of God's truth has been made
> manifest. "Full of grace and truth," he came as the "light of
> the world," he *is the Truth* (Jn 1:14; 8:12; cf. 14:6).[26]

These words remind us that the effort to accept the truth so
that it determines the way we behave has an inescapably personal element. It has a personal element in two different ways.
In the first place, it is personal because it is a specific individual who believes, and faith is a "personal adherence of
the whole man to God who reveals himself";[27] and it is personal because the demands of faith for Christian living must
be applied by each one to himself.

Faith, insofar as it is our act, "believes an informant amid
doubt, yet accepts his information without doubt";[28] that
is, the believer accepts God's revelation in Christ as the
truth, even though he may be surrounded by obscurity and

[26] CCC 2465 and 2466.
[27] CCC 176.
[28] J. H. Newman, "Wisdom as Contrasted with Faith and with Bigotry",
sermon 14, sec. 34, in *Fifteen Sermons Preached before the University of Oxford
between A.D. 1826 and 1843* (London: Longmans, Green, 1900), p. 298.

perplexity. If faith is to become, and then remain, a living principle in our lives, we have to prepare to receive it, and to keep it, with "a preparation of heart".[29] Carelessness, lack of respect for its sacred character, is the mark of "gross eyes" that see not and "heavy ears" that hear not. "In the schools of the world the ways towards Truth are considered high roads open to all men, however disposed, at all times. Truth is to be approached without homage."[30] Gross eyes and heavy ears may characterize the schools of the world, but we too have to be careful we do not share in this heaviness and the carelessness of those who:

> will enter upon the most sacred points of Faith at the moment, at their pleasure,—if it so happen, in a careless frame of mind, in their hours of recreation, over the wine cup. Is it wonderful that they so frequently end in becoming indifferentists, and conclude that Religious Truth is but a name, that all men are right and all wrong, from witnessing externally the multitude of sects and parties, and from the clear consciousness they possess within, that their own inquiries end in darkness?[31]

We must be careful and humble before the gift of our faith, and in this sense it is an intensely personal concern. Secondly, faith is personal because it must be put into practice by the individual. Faith, Newman insists, is a *practical principle* and has to guide the thoughts and actions of the individual person.

> It judges and decides because it cannot help doing so, for the sake of the man himself, who exercises it—not in the way of opinions, not as aiming at mere abstract truth, not as teach-

[29] J. H. Newman, "Faith and Reason Contrasted as Habits of Mind", in ibid., sermon 10, sec. 43, p. 198.

[30] Ibid.

[31] Ibid, pp. 198–99.

ing some theory or view. It is an act of the mind feeling that it is its duty any how, under its particular circumstances, to judge and to act, whether its light be greater or less, and wishing to make the most of that light and acting for the best.[32]

This light that faith sheds on how we practice our Christianity is, to use Newman's word, defective. It is defective in the sense that it has to be used in the ordinary wear and tear of life and does not provide us with a series of answers that follow inevitably from clearly established principles. But although this knowledge provided by faith is defective, it is sufficient for our purposes.

> The servant who hid his Lord's money was punished; and we, since we did not make our circumstances, but were placed in them, shall be judged, not by them, but by our use of them.[33]

To act in a Christian way is to act with a sense of personal responsibility. That is, faith is given to us so that we can behave as followers of Christ, not to regulate the affairs of those around us. It is of course the case that Christians have to take stands on public issues, but it must be clear that bigotry and dogmatism will be an ever-present danger[34] and that our first battle is against the self we all carry about with us, the self that is constantly trying to pull us away from living in the charity of Christ.

[32] Newman, "Wisdom", sermon 14, sec. 35, p. 298.

[33] Ibid., p. 299.

[34] Ibid., sec. 36, p. 299. "It is when our presumptions take a wide range, when they affect to be systematical and philosophical, when they are indulged in matters of speculation, not of conduct, not in reference to self, but to others, then it is that they deserve the name of bigotry and dogmatism. For in that case we make a wrong use of such light as is given us and mistake what is a 'lantern unto our feet' for the sun in the heavens."

To live in this love, to find the Way, and to build up the virtues and fight the vices require an understanding that is illumined by faith so that we may be able to see and discern plainly what we have to do. The light may be obtained first of all by praying for it and then by using our heads to weigh up the good and the bad in situations.

First of all, we must pray the Holy Spirit to pour light into our hearts and minds so that we will *see* clearly. The prayer of the Psalmist: "Give me understanding, that I may keep thy law" (Ps 119:34) should be ever in our hearts and on our lips, and especially when we are in confusion or doubt or discouragement.

Secondly, we have to practice trying to see, and to judge, the things life presents us with, and to see them and to judge them *as God wants us to see and judge them*. We must begin to evaluate the circumstances of our lives, and how we are to deal with them, according to the teachings of the Holy Spirit and not according to their outward appearances. In Newman's words, we have to see the Cross as the measure of this world. In one of his *Parochial and Plain Sermons* Newman says that reflective people want to have standards about how they are to evaluate things and to know "what is given by revelation to estimate and measure this world by".[35]

Newman's answer to his question is not an easy one to accept, but it is, nonetheless, the Christian answer:

---

[35] J. H. Newman, "The Cross of Christ the Measure of the World", sermon 7 in vol. 6 of *Parochial and Plain Sermons*, pp. 1239–40: "*How* are we to look at things? this is the question which all persons of observation ask themselves, and answer each in his own way. They wish to think by rule; by something within them, which may harmonise and adjust what is without them. Such is the need felt by reflective minds. Now, let me ask, what *is* the real key, what is the Christian interpretation of this world? What is given us by revelation to estimate and measure this world by?"

It is the death of the Eternal Word of God made flesh, which is our great lesson how to think and how to speak of this world. His Cross has put its due value upon every thing which we see, upon all fortunes, all advantages, all ranks, all dignities, all pleasures; upon the lust of the flesh, and the lust of the eyes, and the pride of life.[36]

The Psalmist's prayer for understanding had been answered by the Cross of Christ. To use the Cross in a serious and reflective way as our standard for judging is the way to combat that ignorance which hides the royal road from our sight.

The second thing from which the understanding must be protected is *curiosity*. St. Augustine taught that *curiositas*—idle curiosity—was the desire to know "what should not be known" and that this curiosity should be fought.[37] Clearly such a position runs counter to the modern stance that anything is a suitable object for human curiosity. To adopt this position shows a marked insensitivity to the enormities committed by some scientists and medical practitioners.[38] No

[36] Ibid., p. 1240. Newman continues: "[The Cross] has set a price upon the excitements, the rivalries, the hopes, the fears, the desires, the efforts, the triumphs of mortal man. It has given a meaning to the various, shifting course, the trials, the temptations, the sufferings, of his earthly state. It has brought together and made consistent all that seemed discordant and aimless. It has taught us how to live, how to use this world, what to expect, what to desire, what to hope. It is the tone into which all the strains of this world's music are ultimately to be resolved."

[37] See John M. Rist, "Idle Curiosity", in *Augustine: Ancient Thought Baptized* (Cambridge: Cambridge Univ. Press, 1994), pp. 140–45.

[38] "Unheeding advocates of this sort of 'progress' rarely pause—at least when attempting an evaluation of the past—to consider whether it really is not idle curiosity, for example, to want to know exactly the degree of pain felt by a tortured animal (or human), or whether such knowledge, even if hitherto unrecorded, should always be a licensed subject for research. The force of such examples can show us that Augustine (and his predecessors both Christian and pagan) were right to suppose that there is such a thing as idle curiosity" (ibid., p. 141).

doubt the subject is a complex one, and no one wants to stand in the way of serious and responsible enquiry. The only point I wish to make here is that one does not show a line of enquiry is in fact serious and responsible by calling it research. Idle curiosity exists and often has serious social consequences.

Our primary concern here, however, is not the social or political order, but the struggle for purity of heart, and Scupoli assumes with St. Augustine that there is such a thing as idle curiosity and that it has baleful consequences. This is a truth that has never been so obvious as it is today. On the other hand, there has probably never been a time in Christian history when it has been so ignored. Newman in the 1830s gave a clear analysis of what is and was a temptation, even though it may now have come to be seen as almost a virtue:

> One chief cause of the wickedness . . . in the world, and in which, alas! each of us has more or less his share, is our curiosity to have some fellowship with darkness, some experience of sin, to know what the pleasures of sin are like. I believe it is even thought unmanly by many persons (though they may not like to say so in plain words), unmanly and a thing to be ashamed of, to have no knowledge of sin by experience, as if it argued a strange seclusion from the world, a childish ignorance of life, a simpleness and narrowness of mind, and a superstitious, slavish fear.[39]

Curiosity leads us into sin, but we consent with the provision, so we tell ourselves, that we can always go back to a Christian way of life once we have deepened our experi-

[39] J. H. Newman, "Curiosity a Temptation to Sin", sermon 5 in vol. 8 of *Parochial and Plain Sermons*, p. 1603.

ence. We think, as Newman says, that we can "return to our duty, and continue where we left off; merely going aside a moment to shake ourselves, as Samson did, and with an ignorance like his, that our true heavenly strength is departed from us".[40] But once we have begun to sin in one way or the other it becomes increasingly difficult to return to the royal road.

There is, however, more to be said than this about curiosity. The danger goes something like this: When we fill up our minds with a lot of useless material, we weaken our capacity to put first things first. Our understanding may have become clear enough to see the road, but if we are not careful we may lose sight of it and lose track of where we are going. Unrestrained, or uncritical, curiosity inhibits our capacity to discriminate or judge what is really important in a situation.

We are not talking here about a serious effort to master a subject that we may be required to learn. What we are talking about is the desire to satisfy our curiosity on any and every conceivable subject that catches our fancy. Again and again people find the Way but lose it again by running down every blind alley that presents itself. In the *Idea of a University* there is a passage where Newman warns us that "you must be above your knowledge, not under it, or it will oppress you; and the more you have of it, the greater will be the load."[41] Unrestricted curiosity fills up the memory, and the memory, Newman warns us, can tyrannize as well as the imagination, and sometimes seem to paralyse the capacity for controlled thought to the point of madness:

---

[40] Ibid., p. 1604.
[41] J. H. Newman, *The Idea of a University*, discourse 6, sec. 7 (New York: Doubleday & Co. [Image Books], 1959), p. 162.

Derangement, I believe, has been considered as a loss of control over the sequence of ideas. The mind, once set in motion, is henceforth deprived of the power of initiation, and becomes the victim of a train of associations, one thought suggesting another, in the way of cause and effect, as if by a mechanical process, or some physical necessity.[42]

Of course, curiosity understood as an impediment to progress in the spiritual life is not always so pronounced as to lead to madness, but the extreme case points up the danger. Curiosity unchecked leads to a reluctance to focus on what is important. Even when there is a dim realization that the claims of God are being neglected, the attention span has become so weakened and so limited that nothing is done to put first things first.

There is, however, a still further point to be made. If we never say no to our desire to know, then we will never do anything, or refrain from doing anything, unless we see why we should or should not do it. This leads to a false confidence in our own judgment, or at least to the inability really to listen to anyone else. In the end, it inhibits us from listening even to the promptings of the Holy Spirit. Scupoli puts it this way: "Being already accustomed to have recourse in all circumstances to their own judgement, they come gradually and imperceptibly to believe that they have no need of advice or control from others."[43] This unwillingness to listen to others is often accompanied by a stubbornness that reinforces the blindness and the tyranny of the memory, and

[42] Ibid. Newman continues: "No one who has had experience of men of studious habits but must recognize the existence of a parallel phenomenon in the case of those who have overstimulated the memory. In such persons reason acts almost as feebly and as impotently as in the madman; once fairly started on any subject whatever, they have no power of self-control."

[43] SC 9, p. 19.

the dead weight of the memory only increases the stubbornness and unwillingness to listen to others.

It is often people who are being serious about their spiritual lives who sometimes fall into this defect; and, as we are talking about what is the best thing for each one of us to do in order to inherit eternal life, it is clear this is an important point. St. Philip Neri used to say that sanctity lies in the space of three fingers: he would hold up three fingers to his forehead and say that the key to sanctity lay in saying no to useless speculation, or what he called the *mortificazione razionale*. Deliberately mortifying our curiosity, for example, deliberately saying no to gossiping about ecclesiastical politics, is a most useful way of helping to ensure we do not begin to judge the whole Church exclusively from our own point of view and then forget that it is our own sanctification that should be our primary aim. Scupoli gives a warning that we should think about:

> [The Devil] often infuses lofty and curious speculations into the minds [of those who are aiming at the spiritual life], especially if they be of an acute and intellectual order, and easily inflated with pride; and he does this in order that they may busy themselves in the enjoyment and discussion of such subjects, wherein as they falsely persuade themselves, they enjoy God, and meanwhile neglect to purify their hearts and to apply themselves to self-knowledge and true mortification. So, falling into the snare of pride, they make an idol their own understanding.[44]

So, "blunt the acuteness of thine intellect, willingly submit thine own opinion to that of others, become a fool for the love of God, and thou shalt be wiser than Solomon."[45]

[44] Ibid.
[45] Ibid., p. 20.

We have seen that spiritual exercises concerning the intellect involve fighting the ignorance that blinds us to the practical demands of faith and building up a Christian evaluation of life. Then we have to avoid the wrong kind of curiosity and try to focus our lives on the truths of our faith.

Spiritual Exercises concerning the Will

In addition to the intellect, the will also can lead us astray. We have to learn to regulate or control it so that it may learn to desire what God wants for us. It is easy to make too sharp a distinction between understanding and willing and forget that it is the same person who does the thinking and desiring. Yet there is a difference, as we have seen,[46] between the attitude taken up by the intellect as it tries to understand something and the will, which wants either to possess the object for itself or to distance itself from it. Once we are aware of whatever it is our experience presents us with, we almost automatically adopt an attitude of love or of hatred toward it.

We can, though, evaluate this attitude and then try to act in accordance with this evaluation. We may have a strong desire to dive into what looks like a deep pond on a hot summer's day, but if we do not know the water, we do well to get in quietly and discover whether there are hidden rocks or fallen tree trunks below the surface. The example shows that we are not forced actually to act on what the will finds attractive at first sight, and sometimes saying no to ourselves is nothing but common sense.

We all know that it is difficult to say no to ourselves: if we are thirsty and want a drink, it requires a struggle to finish what we should be doing before we go off and get a

---

[46] Chap. 1, "First Principles", pp. 25–48.

glass of water. That is obvious, but because it is obvious it does not follow that it is unimportant. Saying no to ourselves is an essential moment in the spiritual life because what we want is often in fact unhelpful to purity of heart when it is not actively hostile to it. We may, that is, desire things that it is natural to desire, that are not in themselves sinful, but from which we should distance ourselves. We say no to them because we are aware of our own weakness and tendency to sin, and never to deny ourselves in these legitimate matters is to deprive ourselves of the power to say no to ourselves when the object of our desire is in fact sinful. But this is only half the story, because we have also to train ourselves in the warfare against our attraction to what is sinful in itself. "Self-denial", says Newman, "of some kind or other is involved, as is evident, in the very notion of renewal and holy obedience." [47]

The element of struggle with self, then, is not restricted to trying to deny ourselves things bad in themselves; it also concerns self-denial about anything that tends to make us spiritually soft. The analogy with physical training for a game is still an apt one. If we never exercise, our muscles go slack, our heart goes fatty, our breathing becomes erratic, and our reactions slow down. The desire of physical comfort leads us to underestimate the exercise that is really needed to play the particular game we want to play. The desire for comfort is the great obstacle to physical well-being, and the desire for comfort is one of the most dangerous enemies of spiritual health.

> Nothing is so likely to corrupt our hearts, and to seduce us from God, as to surround ourselves with comforts,—to have things our own way,—to be the centre of a sort of world,

[47] Newman, "The Duty of Self-Denial", *Parochial and Plain Sermons*, p. 1470.

whether of things animate or inanimate, which minister to us.[48]

Comfort is dangerous because it leads us to become dependent upon what pleases us. This is true even of our life of prayer, because it is unhappily the case that we can desire even what is holy and spiritual in a way that is little more than the satisfaction of our own desires. "As soon, therefore, as they are presented to us we look wistfully on them, and desire them, not because such is the will of God, nor with the sole view to please him, but for the sake of the satisfaction and benefit to be derived from willing those things which God wills".[49]

The writer of the *Cloud of Unknowing* says that we are not to snatch at spiritual consolations like greedy greyhounds,[50] and that is exactly what Scupoli is talking about. The minute we find some consolation in prayer, or the satisfaction we experience in doing a good action, we want more of the same. If we are not careful, we end up praying because we find it enjoyable and doing good actions because we find them pleasant. In itself the error may be hard to discern and is often in fact an imperfection rather than a sin. On the other hand, it is a very inadequate way of doing the will of God, and experience shows that if the only motive for praying or doing good actions is pleasure, the minute we cease to find prayer pleasing or doing good actions pleasant, we stop doing them.

[48] Ibid., p. 1476.

[49] SC 10, p. 20, begins Scupoli's discussion of exercises of the will, that is, in fighting sins and developing virtue, which continues through to the end of chap. 43, p. 113.

[50] *The Cloud of Unknowing, Together with The Epistle of Privy Counsel*, chap. 46, ed. Abbot Justin McCann (London: Burns & Oates, 1952), p. 64: "And abide courteously and meekly the will of our Lord, and snatch not over-hastily, as it were a greedy greyhound, though thou hunger never so sore."

In this way, if we are not careful, we may give up prayer and trying to be good altogether. "The Christian", Newman says,

> denies himself in things lawful because he is aware of his own weakness and liability to sin; he dares not walk on the edge of a precipice; instead of going to the extreme of what is allowable, he keeps at a distance from evil, that he may be safe. He abstains lest he should not be temperate; he fasts lest he should eat and drink with the drunken.[51]

Self-denial in those things that are not in themselves harmful but that may be harmful for us involves reining in the will and evaluating what it is we desire. Giving in to our desire for comfort in the extended sense of self-satisfaction is the great enemy to watch out for. One way of avoiding this danger is to try quite consciously to weigh up the good things that life presents us with and ask something like this: Does God, here and now, want me to pray or to give this money to the poor man, or whatever else it may be. In both cases the things are good in themselves, but (a) they may not be what is required here and now: for example, perhaps I should be writing an essay or saving my money to buy something for my family; and (b) we have to try to learn to do even the right things here and now because God wants us to. This exercise of waiting and asking will help us to do the right thing both at the right time and for the right reason.

> Let thy will, then, being thus moved and attracted by his, be impelled to will it because he wills it, and solely to please him and honour him.[52]

---

[51] Newman, "The Duty of Self-Denial", p. 1474.
[52] SC 10, p. 21.

CHAPTER FIVE

WORKING FOR HOLINESS

To make sinful creatures holy was the great end which
our Lord had in view in taking upon Him our nature,
and thus none but the holy will be accepted for His sake
at the last day. The whole history of redemption, the cov-
enant of mercy in all its parts and provisions, attests the
necessity of holiness in order to salvation; as indeed even
our natural conscience bears witness also.

—J. H. Newman, "Holiness Necessary for Future
Blessedness", *Parochial and Plain Sermons*

Spiritual exercises, as we have seen, are one of the weapons
of spiritual combat. In the last chapter we examined spiritual
exercises mainly from the standpoint of the mortification of
the intellect and the will. We must always remember, though,
that the goal of this mortification is an ever more intimate
union in love between the individual and Christ. Spiritual
exercises are undertaken in order that our thinking, our desiring, and our acting may lead to a deeper and firmer identification with Christ and our life be "rooted and grounded
in love" (Eph 3:17). We have to try both to root out the evil
in our lives and to develop what is good. It is a mistake to
look on spiritual combat as entirely negative, because the
goal of mortification is to become more Christlike, and this

requires the development of all those aspects of our nature that lead to union with Christ in love.

The Spiritual Combat is a very down-to-earth book, and Scupoli is not content to leave us with general principles, however true and inspiring these may be. He is interested in providing us with practical advice for fighting vice and developing virtue, and in this chapter we are to look at three practices, in addition to the mortifications discussed in the last chapter, that will help in working for holiness. These practices are the use of considerations, the examination of conscience, and patience with our own sinfulness.

Considerations

Spiritual exercises, as we have seen, involve both reflection and planning if they are to be effective. Progress in the knowledge and love of God requires an awareness of the law of Christ and of how we fall short of it in our own lives as well as a project or scheme to rectify this disorder and strengthen what is good in ourselves. One of the ways we put our awareness of Christ's law, as well as what we perceive must be done in our own particular case, into practice is by the use of considerations. Scupoli discusses considerations in relation to what he calls the regulation of the senses, and sense experience is an integral part of living that cannot be suppressed. It is our whole nature that has to be trained to love and serve God, and not merely, as a modern English philosopher put it, "a ghost in a machine";[1] and so the senses must be used and integrated into this love and service. One way

---

[1] Gilbert Ryle, *The Concept of Mind* (Watford, Herts.: William Brendon and Son, 1949). Ryle calls the "official doctrine" of mind "the ghost in the machine" (p. 15).

of doing this is to use what the senses present us with and consciously or explicitly to relate these sense experiences to the reality of God and of his demands on us. In other words, we are to consider, or turn over in our minds, the objects of our awareness and connect them to our striving after union with Christ.

It is easy to overlook this positive side of the ascetical life and to present its teaching as having no room for beauty and the natural goods of life. St. John of the Cross taught an austere and even frightening doctrine of the ascetical life, but we should not forget he is one of the greatest of Spanish poets and that when he became novice master of his province he obtained a house in the country where the young men could learn to love God through the beauties of nature.[2] Properly used or regulated, Scupoli teaches, the senses need not "remain in a miserable captivity to empty pleasure" but can "gather a noble spoil from each passing object".[3]

We all have a tendency to limit our spiritual life to specific times of prayer and reflection. Such periods of retirement are essential, but living with God and trying to do his will require practicing our relationship with God outside of fixed times specifically devoted to him. We need to be reminded both of the reality of God and the truth of the Incarnation in our daily lives. After all, it is in the circumstances of everyday existence that we make most of the choices for or

[2] "But, attracted as he was by 'silent music', the dominant interest of St John of the Cross on the earthly plane appears to have been his love of Nature. Of this his poems alone, and commentaries upon them, furnish sufficient proof, but it is confirmed and reinforced by external evidence, which becomes so much more definite and abundant, as his life proceeds, that it would seem as if his love of Nature deepened with the years" (E. Allison Peers, *Spirit of Flame* [London: S.C.M. Press, 1943], p. 98).

[3] SC 21, p. 55.

against God. If we are going to put into practice the resolutions made at times of formal prayer, then we have to have
a continuing sense of the reality of God and of the Incarnation. For example, during our time of formal prayer we may
determine to do a specific act of kindness for someone we
dislike, but faced, later on, with the reality of having to do
the act, we need something to support our resolution. What
we need is not only the *memory* of having decided to be
patient with X, we also require, here and now, a reminder of
the reality of the God for whose sake we first determined to
be more patient. The principle behind this practice is a simple one:

> When any object is presented before one of thine exterior
> senses, separate in thy mind from the material thing the prin-
> ciple which is in it; and reflect that of itself it possesses noth-
> ing of all that which it appears to have, but that all is the
> work of God who endows it invisibly by his Spirit with the
> being, beauty, goodness, or whatever virtue belongs to it.[4]

Scupoli then lays out in an ordered way the different sorts of
sense experience that can lead us to renew our awareness of
the existence of God. He starts with the awareness of "grand
and noble objects", let us say, the sight of high mountains on
a fine day, and then says that we are to

> reduce the creature mentally to its own nothingness; fixing
> the mind's eye on the great Creator therein present, who
> gave it that great and noble being, and delighting himself in
> Him alone, say: "O Divine Essence, and above all things to
> be desired, how greatly do I rejoice that thou alone art the
> infinite Principle of every created thing." [5]

[4] Ibid.
[5] Ibid.

He then goes on to repeat the exercise by moving through plants that should lead us to think of the living God, animals who move to the First Mover, through beauty of body and then of mind, to remind us of the beauty of God, through hearing and tasting to the God who contains the perfection of the particular object of sense we are experiencing.

We can also use these sorts of ordinary sense experiences to remind us of the Incarnation.[6] Because Christ entered into the visible world of space and time, it is particularly appropriate that we draw nearer to him through that same visible nature. "All things in the universe may serve to this end", says Scupoli. Consider that God gave them their "being, beauty and excellence". Then remind yourself "how great, how immeasurable" is Christ's love for us—Christ, who, although he is the Lord of all creation, became incarnate, suffered, and died for man, "permitting the very works of his hands to arm themselves against him, and to crucify him".

> Many objects will then bring these holy mysteries before thy mind's eyes, such as weapons, cords, scourges, pillars, thorns, reeds, nails, hammers, and other instruments of his Passion.[7]

Then Scupoli expands his treatment and shows how sense experience can be used to help us meditate on the reality of other fundamental Christian truths as applied to our own lives. He gives a number of examples of what he is talking about, but he is clear we should only take what is useful to us and not try to follow everything he suggests.[8]

----

[6] SC 22, p. 58.

[7] Ibid.

[8] "As the tastes of souls are many and various, so also may be their nourishment" (SC 23, p. 59).

> When looking upon the sun, consider that thy soul is brighter
> and more beautiful if it be in thy Creator's favour; if not, that
> it is blacker and more hateful than the darkness of hell.[9]

A person may be tempted to sin, or more generally he may
be wondering whether or not it is really worthwhile going
on with the spiritual combat. He then can make a "mini-
meditation" such as Scupoli suggests and use the sun to remind himself that grace is light and life and that to forget
this is to condemn oneself to darkness. The notion of an
exercise includes the idea of repetition, and gradually, if the
meditation is repeated, the sun shining on a bright day will
almost automatically reinforce the connection between it and
the life of grace.

Then perhaps we may in fact be trying to live as though
we were never going to die and to compromise our Christianity in any number of ways; what we need is an effective
reminder that death is a reality that cannot be avoided;

> When walking, remember that every step brings thee nearer
> to death. Let the flight of birds and the flowing of water re-
> mind thee that thy life is hastening far more swiftly to its close.[10]

Once again we are to use ordinary occurrences to establish
habitual responses. In this case what we are trying to build
up is a real assent to the truth that I am not going to live
forever and then to judge what I am going to do, as well as
my more long-term attitudes, in the light of this truth.

Again, there is a lesson in how to practice what Fr. de
Caussade was later to call *the sacrament of the present moment*.[11]

[9] Ibid., p. 60.

[10] Ibid., p. 61.

[11] See Jean-Pierre de Caussade, *Abandonment to Divine Providence* (Garden
City, N.Y.: Doubleday, 1975), p. 24.

The sacrament of the present moment involves trying to accept what we cannot change as being an aspect of God's providential care for us. Often enough, this is a difficult lesson, but we can prepare ourselves for the more difficult times by practicing trying to see his providence in the most ordinary circumstances of our lives.

> In the variety of accidents which may befall thee, exercise thyself thus: When, for instance, thou art oppressed by sadness or melancholy, or sufferest heat, cold, or the like, lift up thy heart to the eternal will, which for thine own good willeth that at such a time and in such a measure thou shouldst endure this discomfort.[12]

The practice of seeing the will of God in the immediate circumstances of our lives demands, as we have seen, a belief in God's providence, and God's providence is *concrete* and *immediate*.[13] This belief is strengthened and made real in our lives by the effort actually to live by it in our daily lives. Furthermore, we will not have learned to practice it until we at least attempt to give thanks to God even for the difficult things that come our way. The last citation from Scupoli continues:

> Then, rejoicing in the love thus shown thee by thy God, and at the opportunity of serving him in the way he is pleased to appoint, say in thine heart, "Behold in me the divine will fulfilled, which from all eternity has lovingly appointed that I should now endure this trial. All praise be to thee for the same, my most gracious Lord."[14]

[12] SC 23, pp. 61.
[13] See above, p. 66.
[14] SC 23, pp. 61–62.

The Examination of Conscience

One way in which self-knowledge and humility are gained is through the examination of conscience. But if we are not, as St. Teresa says, to "stay in our own little plot of ground and tie ourselves down to it completely",[15] then this examination will have to be properly understood.

The argument for the necessity of the examination of conscience is clear. If we are to follow Christ by imitating him, then we have to fight the vices and build up the virtues. Vices and virtues are habits that move us to perform bad or good actions. Now because we begin with a disordered human nature with habitual patterns that incline us to sin, the spiritual combat is, in the first place, directed "mainly to withdrawing from sin and resisting the appetites, which drive [the Christian] in the opposite direction to charity".[16] If we are to fight the vices in our own nature, we have first to recognize them, admit they are vices, and try to do something about eradicating them. This recognition or discernment of our spiritual condition involves the practice of examining our conscience.

The argument for the necessity of the examination of conscience is clear. There are, however, difficulties with it in practice, because the examination of conscience involves self-knowledge, and self-knowledge is hard to come by. All too easily the examination of conscience can lead to a false assessment of our sins, seeing sin where there is no sin, and this results in scruples and anxiety. Or, again, the examination can also lead to an exaggerated and overly emotional

---

[15] St. Teresa of Avila, *Interior Castle*, mansion 1, chap. 2, trans. E. Allison Peers (Garden City, N.Y.: Doubleday [Image Books], 1961), p. 38.
[16] ST 2, 2ae, 24, 9.

reaction to what is in fact real sin. Finally, the examination may be so badly done that even serious sins are passed over unrecognized. True discernment, the recognition of what really moves us, and the avoidance of scruples, of overemotional reactions, and of a failure to recognize real sins all require time and patience as we go on with the slow business of eradicating the vices and beginning the first unsure steps of establishing the virtues.

St. Francis de Sales says that "As to the examination of conscience . . . everyone knows how it is to be performed." [17] Those words may have been true when he wrote them at the beginning of the seventeenth century, but they are certainly not true today, so it is worth restating what the expression means. A standard book on confession by Benedict Baur, O.S.B.,[18] which has recently been reissued, begins by pointing out that there are slightly different reasons for practicing examination of conscience.

> It can have as its aim the discovery of those venial sins—we prescind here from mortal sin—that are fully deliberate. Or it may aim at the discovery of our less deliberate or barely deliberate sins of frailty. Or, finally, it may try to find out how we could and ought to correspond better with God's graces. It is clear in any case that we can make our examination of conscience well and fruitfully only with the help of divine grace.[19]

The author distinguishes different types of examination of conscience: (1) *general*, (2) *particular*, and (3) *habitual*. It is

---

[17] St. Francis de Sales, *Introduction to the Devout Life*, pt. 2, chap. 11, trans. and ed. John K. Ryan (New York: Harper & Brothers, 1950), p. 53.

[18] Benedict Baur, O.S.B., *Frequent Confession, Its Place in the Spiritual Life*, trans. Patrick C Barry, S.J. (Dublin: Four Courts Press, 1984).

[19] Ibid., p. 52.

worth getting the distinctions straight, as the meaning of the expressions used, while clear enough when understood, is not intuitively obvious.

"The general examination of conscience passes under review all the happenings of the day that has gone by: thought, feelings, words, deeds."[20] When this examination of conscience is made regularly, it is not very difficult because the person making the examination gets to know himself well and has a clear idea of where he is liable to fail. If there is an unusual sort of lapse, it will stand out clearly to a person striving to fight sin and acquire virtue. It should be noticed that "general" here means only the sins committed during the course of the day; it is not the sort of examination that would precede a general confession of all the sins of one's past life.

Next there is the particular examination of conscience. "Particular" here means that the examination is related to a particular vice one is trying to get rid of or a particular virtue after which one is striving. In other words, although the expression "particular examination" might seem to indicate a more focused examination of the same period that the general examination took as its object, this is not the case. The particular examination is concerned with a particular sin or virtue over an extended period of time.

Finally there is the "habitual examination". It is important to explore our interior attitudes and dispositions. These interior attitudes and dispositions are not in themselves either sinful or virtuous, but can incline us to either vice or virtue. As set out by Baur, "habitual" refers both to the act of examining our conscience and to those "attitudes and dispositions" that the examination reveals:

[20] Ibid.

"Where is my heart?" What is the prevailing disposition that
determines its attitude, the real mainspring that keeps all the
rest of its movement going? It may, perhaps, be some long-
existing tendency: some attachment or bitterness or aver-
sion. It may be just a momentary impression: but so deep
and strong that it has affected the heart for long afterwards.
In the "habitual" examination of conscience we ask ourselves: "Where is my heart?" And thus, often during the day,
we uncover the disposition and inclination of our heart at
the moment and so penetrate to its central core, from which
our various words and deeds and activities issue. We discover
the chief wellsprings of good and evil within ourselves.[21]

Scupoli has no doubt about the importance of this "habitual" examination. On the other hand, he is quite clear that
the habitual refers, not to the frequency of the activity, but
to what is discovered. Spiritual exercises have to do with
overcoming particular sins and establishing the contrary virtues, and so it is of great importance, Scupoli says, that we
should know how to observe "a due order in this combat,
lest, as too many do to their own great injury, we should
fight in a casual or desultory manner".[22] The order should
be as follows:

Look well into thine heart, and search diligently till thou
hast discovered by what thoughts and affections it is surrounded, and by what passion it is most tyrannously swayed;
and against this first take up arms and direct thine attack.[23]

We can see from this quotation that the "habitual examination" is of the greatest importance for Scupoli. Be clear, he

[21] Ibid., p. 54.
[22] SC 17, p. 41.
[23] Ibid., p. 42.

is telling us, about the sins that are most powerful in your own particular case in drawing you away from God, and then take up the warfare against them. But what does this mean in practice? What does Scupoli actually recommend we do?

First of all, we should notice that he devotes relatively little space explicitly to the examination of conscience. There is one short chapter, which is found, not in the section on spiritual exercises, but in the part of the *Spiritual Combat* dealing with prayer. On the other hand, he has some useful and original things to say about how to use the results of the habitual examination in chapter 16, entitled "In What Manner the Soldier of Christ Should Take the Field in the Morning". The thrust of this chapter is that we are to use the result of the habitual examination to prepare us to make good use of the day ahead, rather than regret what may have happened in the past. There is a *prospective* aspect, rather than a backward looking or retrospective note, to his treatment of the principal fault. That is not to say that contrition has no place in Scupoli's teaching, but it is contrition closely allied to doing better. We are to use our particular weaknesses to show us where we have to do better in the day just begun.

In his discussion, Scupoli uses the imagery of St. Ignatius' famous meditation on the two standards,[24] in which we picture to ourselves Christ, the angels, and the saints, on one side, and the devil and the legion of devils, on the other, and resolve to fight under the banner of Christ. The imagery is used, however, for a more restricted purpose than in St. Ignatius. Scupoli uses it in connection with fighting the leading fault, not with making a decision designed to reinforce a decision to follow Christ. St. Francis de Sales in the

---

[24] *The Spiritual Exercises of St. Ignatius of Loyola*, ed. by Louis J. Puhl, S.J. (Chicago: Loyola Univ. Press, 1951), pp. 136–48.

Introduction to the Devout Life, follows Scupoli's prospective attitude in his chapter "The Morning Exercise":

> Foresee what business, what affairs, and what situations for serving God you will encounter on this day and to what temptations of offending Him you will be exposed, either by anger, by vanity, or by any other irregularity. By a holy resolution prepare yourself to make the best use of those means which shall be offered you to serve and to advance in devotion. On the other hand, dispose yourself carefully to avoid, resist, and overcome whatever may present itself that is prejudicial to your salvation and the glory of God. It is not sufficient to make this resolution unless you also prepare the means of putting it into practice.[25]

Patience with Our Own Sinfulness

The examination of conscience can become an activity that discourages us from going on trying and can sometimes lead to scruples or an exaggerated (and paralyzing) sense of sin that is close to despair. All this is true; but it sometimes happens that we do in fact sin, and sometimes sin mortally. The temptation is then to give up. It is easy to say we should not despair, but (in Scupoli's words) "What should we do when we are wounded?"[26] He answers that when "thou feelest thyself wounded from having weakly, or it may be even wilfully and deliberately, fallen into some sin, be not over fearful or over-anxious, but turn instantly to God",[27] and then:

1. Admit frankly to God that it was really you yourself who sinned, and not someone else. Then humble yourself before God, and "be full of indignation against thy evil pas-

---

[25] *Introduction to the Devout Life*, pt. 2, chap. 10, p. 51.
[26] SC 26, p. 70.
[27] Ibid.

sions, especially that which has occasioned thy fall." The sin, that is, is yours, and do not try to shift the blame onto someone or something else. On the other hand, realize that the sin does not define your nature, and try to distance yourself from it.

2. Thank God that the fall was not any worse than it was. "Not even here, Lord, should I have stopped, if thy goodness had not withheld me." God still loves you; turn to him in thanksgiving for his patience and mercy.

3. Lastly, humbly ask for his forgiveness with a deep trust in his compassion. "Forgive me, Lord, for thine own sake; suffer me not to depart from thee, nor to be separated from thee, nor evermore to offend thee."

> And if after any fault thou feel uneasy, distrustful, and confused in mind, the first thing to be done is, to recover thy peace and quietness of mind, and with it thy confidence in God. Armed with these, turn again to thy Lord; for thy uneasiness on account of thy sin arises not from the consideration of the offence against God, but of the injury to thyself.[28]

Scupoli is here teaching a lesson that St. Francis de Sales was later to inculcate with such suavity and force, that patience and gentleness with ourselves is a prerequisite if we are to conquer our own sins and to deal patiently with others. This leads naturally to saying something about patience itself.

In the Letter of St. James we read:

> Be patient, therefore, brethren, until the coming of the Lord. Behold, the farmer waits for the precious fruit of the earth, being patient over it until it receives the early and the late rain. You also be patient. Establish your hearts, for the coming of the Lord is at hand. (Jas 5:7–8)

[28] Ibid., p. 72.

We are told to wait for the Lord patiently, but what are we to understand about this patience?

St. Thomas says that patience helps us to bear hardship and protects the good of reason against dejection.[29] What he means is something like this. We tend to become sorrowful when things do not work out the way we want them to and when we want them to. Perhaps today we would tend to say we become frustrated when things go wrong or when our own timetable and plans are upset. And so St. Augustine writes that "human patience is what enables us to bear hardship with tranquillity (that is without being troubled by dejection), so that we do not abandon, through mental unbalance, the goods by which we may attain a better state." [30] St. Gregory says that patience enables us to endure with tranquillity the evils inflicted on us by others.[31]

We are to wait patiently for the Lord, but things as they in fact are make us sad. We seem a long way away from the goods promised us by our faith; the world seems gray, and we are fed up both with ourselves and with other people. The temptation is to sink into a slough of despond and allow our reason to be overwhelmed by our emotions. We forget that we should be living in hope, patiently waiting for the coming of Christ. If we are not careful, our whole outlook on life will be dominated by what other people do to us, or what we think they are doing to us. The dejection and dreariness that giving way to frustration brings have to be prevented by establishing the virtue of patience in ourselves.

The matter is not a question of temperament. Some people are naturally given to irritation while other people are

[29] ST 2a, 2ae, 136, 1.
[30] Cited by St. Thomas, ST 2a, 2ae, 136, 1.
[31] Cited by St. Thomas, ST 2a, 2ae, 136, 4.

phlegmatic. The virtue of patience is something deeper and of greater importance than temperament. The Book of Proverbs says that "he who is slow to anger is better than the mighty, and he who rules his spirit than he who takes a city" (Prov 16:32), and Christ tells us that "In your patience you shall possess your souls" (Lk 21:19; Douay Rheims). We have to wait obediently for the coming of Christ, and this patience involves both the courage not to give way before the hardships life so often brings and perseverance if we are to be ready to meet Christ when he comes again.

Without patience we are in danger of becoming like corks bobbing up and down on the sea with no direction, no constancy, and making no progress in our spiritual lives. Patience helps to keep us pointed in the right direction, steady in our journey to meet the Lord, and through this very singleness of purpose and steadiness of direction we bear witness to the truth of what we believe. So "let us run with patience the race that is set before us" (Heb 12:1). But there is a positive side to all this, a side of which Scupoli and St. Francis de Sales are the great teachers. It is this: Even our sins can be used in our effort to imitate Christ if we use them to humble ourselves and to give us a clear idea of our smallness and lack of generosity. Without a clear view of ourselves, as we are in our sins and weakness, we miss an essential element in any growth in the knowledge and love of Christ. God allows people who are really trying to imitate him, especially if they are full of presumption and self-righteousness, to fall, often daily, into any number of sins, precisely so that their humiliation will serve as a remedy for their pride. We all tend to take credit for our good acts and reject the fact that it is we ourselves who sin and that our sins tell us as much about ourselves as do our virtues. When we begin to be truly sorry for our sins, as *our sins*, as *my own sin*, it is then that we begin to build a solid foundation for the imitation of Christ.

So sin, Scupoli says over and over again, is not a reason for despair, but it is what God permits to lead us into a true recognition of the sort of people we are. St. Philip Neri said "My Jesus, if you do not keep your hand on Philip this day, he is sure to betray you." No doubt, when we first hear these words we may be tempted to say that a person as holy and as lovable as St. Philip was exaggerating—but Philip meant what he was saying. Great sanctity recognizes evil and the ever-present possibility of sin. It was just because St. Philip was a saint that he could say in all truthfulness that without God's grace he, Philip, would certainly betray Christ.

Most of us, however, are a long way away from St. Philip's habitual consciousness of his own sinfulness, and we have, again and again, to learn humility from our falls. A serious knowledge of our nothingness and continuing capacity to sin is the foundation of the whole spiritual edifice.

> And the deeper we dig into this knowledge, the higher will the building rise. And in proportion as we clear away the earth of our own misery, the divine architect will bring solid stones for its completion.[32]

So, we require patience in the face of our falls, but also the humility to recognize that we do in fact sin. This recognition is hard to come by, especially if we tend to think we have made more progress than in fact we have, and "thoughts of self-exaltation will still molest us and make an impression on our hearts".[33] These experiences of self-satisfaction should be used as warnings as to how little "we have advanced in

[32] SC 32, p. 88.
[33] Ibid., p. 89.

the spiritual life and true self-knowledge", but not as an excuse for giving up. Once again, we have an example of Scupoli's constructive attitude toward sin and evil tendencies;
they must be fought; but setbacks and temporary failure are
to be used to teach us patience and humility:

> So shall we extract honey from the poison and healing from
> the wound.[34]

[34] Ibid., p. 90.

CHAPTER SIX

Spiritual Exercises
and Chastity

But if a man is in earnest in wishing to get at the depths of his own heart, to expel the evil, to purify the good, and to gain power over himself, so as to do as well as know the Truth, what is the difficulty?—a matter of time indeed, but not of uncertainty is the recovery of such a man. So simple is the rule which he must follow, and so trite, that at first he will be surprised to hear it. God does great things by plain methods; and men start from them through pride, *because* they are plain. This was the conduct of Naaman the Syrian.

—J. H. Newman, "Knowledge of God's Will without
Obedience," *Parochial and Plain Sermons*

When the first enthusiasm of our conversion has begun to fade, we seem to be surrounded by such a welter of sins that we hardly know which way to turn. We may be discouraged by the very fact that a struggle is still imposed on us after all the difficulties we have experienced in answering the call of Christ. We have begun to live a life in the grace of God, but it is the reality of our old life, and of past sins, that seems to cloud our consciousness. St. Teresa said that living in mortal sin was "living with reptiles",[1] but a good many of the reptiles manage to stay around as we begin our efforts to live in a state of grace. Yet the awareness of a struggle should be an encouragement rather than a discouragement. The fact that a person is trying to do better, that he has not acquiesced entirely in the pull of his past sinful behavior, is a sign that God's grace is still being offered to him and that he is cooperating with it.

At the beginning of a serious spiritual life, however, there are certain sorts of obvious temptations that seem to afflict most people: lust, anger, sloth, impatience, calumny, and detraction are obvious examples. In fact, Scupoli begins with a discussion of chastity, and we will follow his example. The discussion of the virtue of chastity, and of the vices opposed to it, will also serve as an example of what Scupoli means by spiritual exercises as an organized campaign of fighting sinful behavior and doing good actions.

One of the main difficulties in writing about chastity today is that the Christian understanding of the expression of sexuality is actively controverted even in the Church. This means that we have to start with the first exercise concerning the intellect, which is to clear the rubbish away so we can see the truth. Sex education from this perspective should be a statement of what sex is for, not of how to do it in the safest possible way.

The Catholic teaching on sexuality has been clearly stated in the *Catechism of the Catholic Church*. Given the ambiguity

---

[1] St. Teresa of Jesus, *Interior Castle*, trans. and ed. E. Allison Peers (Garden City, N.Y.: Doubleday [Image Books], 1961): "Eventually they enter the first rooms on the lowest floor, but so many reptiles get in with them that they are unable to appreciate the beauty of the castle or to find any peace within it" (mansion 1, chap. 1, p. 33).

and confusion that surround this question, we should begin with a short summary of what that teaching is.

> Chastity means the successful integration of sexuality within the person and thus the inner unity of man in his bodily and spiritual being. Sexuality, in which man's belonging to the bodily and biological world is expressed, becomes personal and truly human when it is integrated into the relationship of one person to another, in the complete and lifelong mutual gift of a man and a woman.[2]

Chastity is first of all the integration of a biological fact into a human framework. This integration results in self-mastery, and this self-mastery is a training in human freedom. That is, either man governs the passions and finds peace, or he lets himself be dominated by them and becomes unhappy. Vatican II expresses this in the following way:

> Man's dignity therefore requires him to act out of conscious and free choice, as moved and drawn in a personal way from within, and not by blind impulses in himself or by mere external constraint. Man gains such dignity when, ridding himself of all slavery to the passions, he presses forward towards his goal by freely choosing what is good, and, by his diligence and skill, effectively secures for himself the means suited to this end.[3]

Since chastity involves self-mastery so that we can be free, we next have to ask what we do with this freedom. The *Catechism of the Catholic Church* answers that under the influence of charity, chastity is the way that allows us to be

---

[2] CCC 2337.

[3] Pastoral Constitution on the Church in the Modern World, *Gaudium et Spes*, (December 7, 1965), no. 17, in *Vatican Council II*, vol. 1: *The Conciliar and Postconciliar Documents*, ed. Austin Flannery, new rev. ed. (New York: Costello Pub. Co., 1996), p. 917.

able to give ourselves to others, particularly in friendship and in imitation of the Lord who has chosen us as friends.[4] In other words, the freedom that chastity brings with it is not a selfish virtue, but is to be used for others. Self-mastery is ordered to the gift of self.

We saw earlier that friendship was the key St. Thomas used to understand what charity or love really means. Now we see this same idea of friendship used to show how self-mastery in relation to sex leads to a capacity to love other people for the good that is in them and not merely because they are attractive or useful to us. To modern ears this teaching often seems thin and unconvincing, but it is the teaching of the saints. The alternative visions with which we have been presented have led not only to unhappiness but have taken the zest out of the Christian witness to the modern world. No doubt continence is sometimes the refuge of the cautious, the timid, and the censorious, but everyone who is serious about faith has to try to live chastely, as understood by the Church, generously and in a way that shows the compassion of Christ.

The *Catechism of the Catholic Church* lists offenses against chastity that find their source in *lust*. "Lust is disordered desire for or inordinate enjoyment of sexual pleasure." [5] Sexual pleasure is morally disordered when sought for itself, isolated from its procreative and unitive purposes. "Among the sins gravely contrary to chastity are masturbation, fornication, pornography, and homosexual practices." [6]

"The inordinate enjoyment of sexual pleasure" is a definition of lust, and definitions in themselves are of little use against the demands of our fallen human nature. But

[4] See CCC 2347.
[5] CCC 2351.
[6] CCC 2396.

definitions are necessary and useful for spiritual exercises, exercises that involve not only the will but also the intellect. Without some effort to live in the truth of Christ's revelation, we will never be able to live a chaste life. This means that the battle for chastity must take the teaching, as set out, for example, in the *Catechism of the Catholic Church*, as a given set of principles that guide the struggle to lead a chaste life. That is, once the guidelines themselves become matters for debate, the war is in fact lost. Unless we see this question within the clear rules of the Catholic faith, the practice of chastity becomes very problematic indeed. This is not to say there are not good arguments based on reason for living a temperate life, but the Christian teaching demands a sort of heroism from many people that no argument from reason alone can sustain when it comes actually to practicing the Christian way of life.

St. Augustine said: "Grant me chastity and continence, but not yet";[7] this is at least half the difficulty. Chastity seems not only unobtainable; it also seems undesirable. It may be that someone wants to follow Christ more seriously, but he believes, or has been taught to believe, that he cannot live without "exploring his sexuality". Yet once this exploring has begun, habits are quickly established that not only lead to repetition of the acts but, even more importantly, weaken any inclination there might be to live a chaste life. The struggle for chastity soon comes to be seen as unsophisticated or unrealistic or useless or unnatural and harmful. From this it is a short step to maintaining with the rest of society that chastity is an impossible virtue. We say "I cannot", when

---

[7] The passage continues: "I was afraid you might hear my prayer quickly, and that you might too rapidly heal me of the disease of lust which I preferred to satisfy rather than suppress" (*Confessions*, bk. 8, chap. 7, no. 17, trans. Henry Chadwick [Oxford and New York: Oxford Univ. Press, 1992], p. 145).

what we really mean is "I will not." St. Augustine was at least honest. He admitted the Christian imperative of chastity but was not prepared to risk everything on the promises of Christ. The modern approach seems to be, "I don't want to, and *therefore*, I cannot". From this it is a short step to saying that chastity is an impossible virtue and, because impossible, then something that should not be sought after. Newman is particularly trenchant about this *I cannot*:

> Say not, in excuse for others or for yourselves, that you cannot be other than Adam made you; you have never brought yourselves to will it,—you cannot bear to will it. You cannot bear to be other than you are. Life would seem a blank to you, were you other; yet what you are from not desiring a gift, this you make an excuse for not possessing it.[8]

It is, however, true that desiring the gift is also God's gift. It was not until St. Augustine threw himself unreservedly on the mercy of God that he both wanted and was given the grace to live a Christian life. For those already in the Church the gift is promised. If the practice of the virtue has become difficult, we have to clean up our mind in the light of Christ's truth. There must be an effort to work out the implications of our Christian faith and see that purity of heart is impossible without the virtue of chastity. We should meditate on the fact that a spiritual life without purity of heart makes no sense at all. Once this becomes clear to us, at least conceptually, we can pray for the grace to obtain a real desire for purity. And furthermore, no matter how we may sometimes feel about doing this, we must also begin to practice spiritual exercises to obtain this virtue.

---

[8] "The Power of the Will", sermon 24 in vol. 5 of *Parochial and Plain Sermons* (San Francisco: Ignatius Press, 1997), p. 1180.

The Spiritual Combat divides spiritual exercises designed to resist the sins of the flesh and undertaken within the above guidelines into three periods: (1) Before the temptation, (2) During the temptation, and (3) After the temptation.[9] By contemporary standards this is the outline of an extremely unsophisticated discussion of a sensitive subject. On the other hand, it does have the merit of intelligibility. Furthermore, it is not only intelligible, it is also an extremely useful analysis for actually dealing with difficulties about chastity. Spiritual exercises are supposed to be of practical use in the spiritual life and more than a theoretical discussion on the nature of virtue and vice. Scupoli's analysis is not packaged in a particularly attractive way, but, the subject matter itself, outside of sentimental literature and popular psychology, is often in reality not all that attractive. If Christian living has something to do with freedom, then one of the greatest obstacles to Christian living is, not the joy of sex, but the tyranny of lust. Lust has any number of different forms, but the shackles it gradually imposes on those who make no effort to fight result in the same loss of freedom.[10]

[9] SC 19, p. 44.

[10] The following example of a man under the tyranny of lust is taken from a rarified level of society; the symptoms, however, can be found everywhere. "Many people, particularly those who saw him only socially, found 'Don Juan' Palewski a figure of fun, with his rotund figure and slicked-back hair, to be seen at every party pursuing the pretty women like a Frenchman in a farce. To his English acquaintance, it was a ludicrous way for a man of his standing to behave. Regular guests at the British Embassy used to watch with amusement as Gaston [Palewski] selected his prey, pressing close to her on one of the huge sofas in the Salon Jaune, bouncing up and down on the cushions while urgently hissing in her ear, 'J'ai envie de toi! J'ai envie de toi!' To Gaston himself their opinions were a matter of indifference; he wanted to make love to as many women as he could persuade into bed, and what people thought or who these women were, was irrelevant. He tried them all: the wives of friends, the friends of friends, and Nancy knew that not even her own sisters would be left unattempted" (Selina Hastings, *Nancy Mitford* [London: Papermac, 1986], p. 191).

Before the Temptation

Scupoli says that there are five spiritual exercises for resisting the temptations of the flesh before they actually attack us, and these are: avoiding the occasions of sin, fighting sloth, practicing obedience, refusing to make false judgments, and being on the lookout for a false satisfaction with self that comes from a sense that our prayer is going well and that we are no longer susceptible to being tempted by the flesh.

1. We have to be on our guard against those places or people that, in our own particular case, are most liable to lead us into sin. St. Philip Neri said that in the battle for chastity it is the cowards who win, that is, it is those who run away from what causes the temptation who maintain their chastity.[11] Scupoli puts it this way:

> First, thou must combat the vice, but never confront it; on the contrary, avoid to the utmost of thy power every occasion and every person whence thou mayest incur the slightest danger.[12]

It is almost impossible to overestimate the importance of this remark. It is the key to the whole business. If we could avoid the occasions of this sin, that is, where it happens, what gives rise to it, and with whom it happens, chastity would become a much easier matter for us. It is extraordinary how devious people can be about this matter. They go into an occasion of sin in a state of double-think: they want to sin, but tell themselves they are going for another reason. Afterward they are overtaken by the sin and appear to suffer great remorse. Yet, with part of their being, they went into the

---

[11] "In the warfare of the flesh, only cowards gain the victory, that is to say, those who flee" (maxim for April 6, in *Maxims and Counsels*, arr. Fr. Faber [1890; reprint, Toronto: The Oratory, 1995]).

[12] SC 19, p. 44.

occasion knowing perfectly well they would sin just because they would be in a situation that in the past had led to bad conduct. For example, a man with a habit of reading pornography will convince himself he needs to buy razor blades at the corner drug store at which—he knows perfectly well— pornography is sold and which he will be unable to resist once he gets there.

"Once more I say to thee, Fly! for thou art as stubble."[13] Do not trust your good resolutions, not even in the well established habit of chastity, because you can lose the work of years in a moment.

> Neither be confident in thyself if thou art free, and during many years of such exercises hast continued free from temptations of the flesh; for this accursed vice makes its advances secretly, often doing in an hour what in many years it has failed to effect; and it hurts the more grievously, and wounds the more fatally, the more friendly the form it assumes, and the less ground of suspicion it seems to give.[14]

If we trust in our own strength and deliberately enter into an occasion of sin, sooner rather than later we will fall. It should also be spelled out that the word "occasion" does not mean only a place; it also means a person. Too great familiarity with anyone can lead to a fall, and if one is sexually tempted by someone, then the sensible thing is to stay away from his or her company. For, says Scupoli,

> inflamed by frequent stirring, the heat of the fire will gradually dry up the water of thy good resolve, and when thou are least on thy guard, it will so enkindle thee that thou wilt respect neither friends nor kindred, nor fear God, nor

---

[13] Ibid., p. 45.
[14] Ibid., p. 44.

regard life or honour, nor all the pains of hell. Therefore fly—fly unless thou wouldst be overtaken, captured, and slain.[15]

The real test of our seriousness in this matter is our willingness, or otherwise, to avoid the occasions of sin, and St. Philip Neri was especially strong on this point:

> It was a common warning with him, that when a man puts himself of his own choice into an occasion of sin, saying "I shall not fall, I shall not commit sin," it is an almost infallible sign that he will fall, and fall with especial damage to his soul. Hence he declared that he feared less for a man who had temptations of the flesh, and resisted them by avoiding the occasions, than for one who was not tempted at all, but did not avoid the occasions.[16]

2. Next, sloth or laziness is to be avoided. Sloth feeds unchastity, and unchastity feeds sloth. It is obvious that idleness leaves the way open for daydreaming, which can easily turn into sexual fantasizing and actions; and giving way to sexual temptation only reinforces our tendency to indolence and lack of self-determination.

The situation, however, is more complicated than at first appears because sloth, or what was traditionally called *accidie*, is a complex condition that is often hard to recognize and can be extremely harmful to our spiritual well-being. *Accidie*, that is, is not merely laziness; it also indicates a feeling of sadness and distaste that sweeps over us, and this experience leads Cassian to say that we may describe sloth as "weariness

---

[15] Ibid., p. 45.
[16] Pietro Bacci, *The Life of St. Philip Neri*, trans. F. A. Antrobus (London: Kegan Paul, Trench, Trübner, 1902), 1:286.

or distress of heart".[17] This weariness or distress of heart produces a laziness that is not only physical but spiritual as well. He uses the verse from the psalm that runs "My soul slept from weariness" to illustrate that the root of the trouble is in the soul, not in the body. "In truth", he says, "the soul which is wounded by the shaft of this passion does sleep, as regards all contemplation of the virtues and insight of the spiritual senses."[18] Nonetheless, although sloth is essentially a disease of the spirit, it finds expression in external activity as well. It has three principal observable effects. Sloth "produces dislike of the place, disgust with the cell, and contempt of the brethren who dwell with him. . . . It also makes the man lazy and sluggish about all manner of work."[19] Sloth, then, is characterized externally by three elements: an unwillingness to stay put, dislike of the people we must associate with, and laziness.

> And so the wretched soul, embarrassed by such contrivances of the enemy, is disturbed, until, worn out by the spirit of accidie, as by some strong battering ram, it either learns to sink into slumber, or, driven out from the confinement of its cell, accustoms itself to seek for consolation under these attacks in visiting some brother, only to be afterwards weakened the more by this remedy which it seeks for the present.[20]

The description should be recognizable. If we change the word "cell" to room or office or study, it could have been written yesterday. There is a kind of weariness or distress of

---

[17] John Cassian, *Institutes of the Coenobia*, bk. 10, chap. 1, in *Nicene and Post-Nicene Fathers*, ed. Philip Schaff and Henry Wace (Grand Rapids, Mich.: Eerdmans, 1978), 11:266.

[18] Ibid., bk. 10, chap. 1, pp. 267–68.

[19] Ibid., chap. 2, p. 267.

[20] Ibid., chap. 3, p. 267.

heart that sweeps over us. This weariness or distress produces three observable symptoms. First, our work seems boring and unprofitable, and we find we cannot stand our office or study, and so either we get onto our bed and go to sleep, or else we leave our room and look for someone to talk to. The people we find, however, seem to us to be covered with the same pall of boredom as is our room. Although they are necessary to us, we do not really like them, and we treat them with disdain. Finally, we can observe the evidence of sloth from the obvious fact that we are not working and our work does not get done. Of course, this only makes things worse. Everything gets more stale, and the work seems more boring when we get back to it. The whole thing is made worse by the fact that there is now even more work to do than there was when we first ran away from it.

It is clear that a person suffering from sloth is particularly prone to unchaste behavior. The inability to stay put, to get on with those around him, and the increasing unease about work not done leave him open to suggestions of lust because there is no steadying influence of work being done or of colleagues working toward a common goal. Furthermore, taking the easy way out and giving up on the task to be done weakens any ability a man might have to resist the passions.

These external manifestations of sloth, however, are only the signs of an interior disease of the spirit. The early writers on the spiritual life saw that laziness attacked not only the practical aspects of existence, but also our spiritual life and our relationship with God. Accidie is not fundamentally a distaste for doing our work in the world. Rather, it is a spirit of weariness or distress, which, if allowed to grow, can kill the joy and peace our faith brings to us. St. Thomas emphasizes this dimension of the matter and quotes St. John Damascene's definition that accidie is a "kind of oppressive sorrow";

and this sorrow, says Thomas, so depresses a man that he wants to do nothing; and some have said "it is a sluggishness of mind which neglects to begin good".[21] Thomas emphasizes that accidie is sorrow concerning spiritual things. That is, boredom, weariness, and indifference over work of any kind spread to spiritual goods and cast a gray pall over the enjoyment and zest that living in the friendship of Christ is supposed to bring to us. In its most concentrated form, or in its essence, accidie consists in being sad about God's goodness in relation to us personally. "To be sorrowful about the divine good, which charity rejoices in, now that does belong to a special vice. We call it spiritual apathy."[22]

Accidie can lead us to reject the friendship of God and the life of divine charity that God pours into our soul. Sloth, having thus struck at the root and the source of our spiritual life, kills the fruits of the Holy Spirit, which are love, joy, peace, patience, kindness, goodness, faithfulness, gentleness, and self-control (see Gal 5:22–23).

Sloth prepares the way for lust not merely because accidie ensures there will be plenty of time on our hands, but because it creates a state of mind, or a mood, that makes it certain that the battle for chastity is lost before it begins. If the world seems drab and gray, and if the promises of God seem irrelevant or even distasteful, then it is inevitable that sexual temptation will not be resisted.

It follows from this that every effort to fight against sloth will also help in the battle against lust. Cassian gives five ways to fight the spirit of accidie,[23] and each one of them

---

[21] ST 2a, 2ae, 35, 1.

[22] ST 2a, 2ae, 35, 2.

[23] Cassian, *Institutes*, bk. 10, chap. 7, p. 268. Here Cassian comments on a text from Thessalonians 4:9–10 to illustrate his remedies for sloth.

can also be viewed as a spiritual exercise for the development of chastity.

a. Live quietly. Cassian understood by this that we must learn to stay put and not go running around looking for distractions by visiting other people, listening to the radio, or watching TV. "Be not be disturbed by rumours," he says, "which generally spring from the wishes and gossip of idle persons, and so yourselves disturb others." [24]

If we examine ourselves, I think we will see that the minute we are supposed to be at work we suddenly convince ourselves that there is something we have to tell someone else, or there is some bit of news we have to find out about. "Shun all curiosity concerning worldly things and all attachment to them",[25] says Scupoli. That is the same point. It is not so much that interest in things of this world is wrong but that we let this interest interfere with the concentration required for the task at hand. We are driven away from our work, or allow ourselves to be driven away from it, all too often, by nothing more serious than the desire to gossip.

b. Mind your own business. If we do not attend to what we should be doing, we attend to what we should not be doing. In practice this means we start poking our nose into other people's affairs, "You should not want to inquire curiously of the world's actions, or, examining the lives of others, want to spend your strength, not on bettering yourselves and aiming at virtue, but on depreciating your brethren." [26] When we do not attend to our own work, we fill up our time by criticizing, speculating about other people's motives, and pretending we are doing something important

[24] Ibid.
[25] SC 20, p. 50.
[26] Cassian, *Institutes*, bk. 10, chap. 7, p. 269.

because we are talking big and judging the competence of others.

c. Work with your own hands. A person who is restless or anxious about other people's affairs is always one who is not satisfied to apply himself to the work of his own hands. This does not mean, necessarily, manual labor, although of course it could mean this. The point really is that we mind our own business by actually doing our own business. If we have an essay to write, the only way to avoid restlessness and involvement with other people's affairs is to get down to the job of actually writing the essay.

Scupoli has a practical point to make here:

> Never allow thyself one moment's delay; for that one little delay will soon be followed by another, and that by a third, and this again by others; and to the last the sense will yield and give way more easily than to the first, having been already fascinated and enslaved by the pleasure they have tasted therein. Hence the duty to be performed is either begun too late, or sometimes laid aside altogether, as too irksome to be endured.[27]

Putting off getting started is how we get enslaved by sloth:

> Thus by degrees, a habit of sloth is acquired, which, as we cannot disguise it from ourselves, we seek to excuse by vain purposes of future diligence and activity, while we are all the time held in bondage to it.[28]

We are all familiar with this: we tell ourselves we have wasted most of the morning so it is not worth writing for the three-quarters of an hour left before lunch. But, not to worry, I'll put in a really good morning's work tomorrow!

[27] SC 20, p. 50.
[28] Ibid.

d. Walk honestly with those who are without. If we do not stay put and do our own work, then we get involved with all sorts of people who will only encourage us in ways of talking and acting that reinforce our laziness.

> He cannot possibly walk honestly, even among those who are men of this world, who is not content to cling to the seclusion of his cell and the work of his own hands; but he is sure to be dishonest, while he seeks his needful food; and to take pains to flatter, to follow up news and gossip, to seek for opportunities for chattering and stories by means of which he may gain a footing and obtain an entrance into the houses of others.[29]

What Cassian is driving at here is that if we are not being honest with ourselves and our own work, then we will not be honest with other people either. The falseness that leads us to lie to ourselves about all the work we are going to do tomorrow spills over into our dealings with other people. The poison of sloth, says Scupoli:

> overspreads the whole man; not only infecting the will, by making exertion hateful to it, but also blinding the understanding, so that it is unable to see how vain and baseless are its intentions to do promptly and diligently at some future season what should be done at once, but is either wilfully neglected altogether or deferred to another time.[30]

If we could deal more fairly with others by not, among other things, wasting their time and leading them into sloth, this would help to combat the vice in ourselves.

e. Do not covet. Sloth is closely connected with envy. When we are wasting time, when we are not concentrating on what we should be doing, we have ample opportunity to think about others and to envy them for what they possess. Being unhappy ourselves we resent the goods and even the happiness of others. To cure sloth, we must stamp on envy. "If only I had X's opportunities, or Y's personality, or Z's money, I would be successful and happy." I torment myself with these thoughts, and I do nothing.

These five ways of resisting sloth, with its overpowering sense that nothing much matters, will make it easier to put into practice our resolutions about chastity. On the other hand, if we take no steps to fight sloth and we live in a state in which we are fed up with ourselves, and fed up with God, it is hardly surprising that we try to escape into living in the flesh.

3. We should not resist the will of our superiors, because in submitting to what may often displease us, we train our will not to be dominated by each passing feeling and emotion. The word "superior" is not much in vogue today, but even so it should not be difficult to see Scupoli's point. He is telling us that the necessity of doing what someone else wants, rather than what we would choose, can be used as a way of practicing our capacity to say no to our own immediate inclinations. Most people have jobs, and usually that involves doing what someone else wants, even if it is only serving a difficult customer in a store, and trying to please others often means not pleasing ourselves.

Instead of becoming resentful and unhappy like a child who is told to wash the dishes when he does not want to, we should use these times to build up a habit of distancing ourselves from what is immediately pleasing to us and so help to establish a capacity to reject the first promptings of lust.

4. We should also beware of forming rash judgments about other people in what concerns the sin. At first sight this may

not seem to have much to do with the matter in hand, but it does. One of the greatest obstacles to establishing the virtue of chastity is the failure of any given individual to identify and assess the gravity of his own sexual sin. To put the matter simply, the individual is usually easy on himself and rigorous about other people. This tendency arises from many different sources.

The first of these is the failure to recognize that lust is lust, and that while "one man's meat is another man's poison", nonetheless, from the perspective of establishing the virtue of chastity, pornography is as destructive as adultery. This is not to deny that objectively or in themselves some sexual sins are worse than others, but the point here is that a failure to recognize that the particular sin of the individual militates against chastity is often disguised from himself. And, it is disguised from himself because he focuses on other people's sexual sins, which he honestly finds distasteful and therefore of no danger, he thinks, to himself.

An even less attractive cause of harsh judgments is hypocrisy and fear. The sin of another is recognized as something the individual himself practices, and he tries to protect himself by an exaggerated condemnation of others. St. Philip Neri was a great saint whose chastity and perpetual virginity were officially recognized by the Church. Philip's general advice was that humility is the true guard of chastity; and therefore:

> that when we hear of anyone having fallen, we should be moved to pity and not to disdain, and that a want of compassion in such cases is a forerunner of a speedy fall in ourselves; and he used to add that in the matter of purity there is no danger so great as being without fear of danger.[31]

[31] Bacci, *Life*, 1:253.

If we have not imitated St. Philip in his purity, perhaps we could at least begin by taking his self-knowledge as our model; and whatever, exactly, the mechanism that connects harsh judgments and double-think to a fall in our own case may be, Scupoli's words express the reality of the causal connection:

> For if thou art forward to judge and despise others, God will correct thee to thy cost, and suffer thee to fall into the same fault in order to convince thee of thy weakness, that by such a humiliation both sins may be cured.[32]

5. Lastly, we should be careful that in times of spiritual consolation in prayer we do not gradually establish what Scupoli calls "a certain vain complacency" and begin to imagine ourselves as so spiritually advanced that we think we are secure from temptations against chastity:

> and that thine enemies are now no longer able to assault thee, because thou seemest to thy self to regard them with disgust, horror, and detestation. If thou art incautious in this matter thou wilt easily fall. [33]

St. Philip had as a penitent a young man who had broken off a sexual relationship with a woman.

> Some time after his conversion, thinking he had now gained sufficient stability in virtue, the desire came into his mind to convert her also; but instead of converting her he was perverted himself, and relapsed into sin.[34]

The young man broke with the woman again, and, because he was too ashamed to go to confession to Philip, went elsewhere. Finally, he did return to Philip, who immediately said:

[32] SC 19, p. 46.
[33] Ibid.
[34] Bacci, *Life*, 1:254.

There are some who, because they have gained a little spirituality, think they can do anything, and convert the world, and then they fall, and because they are ashamed to come to their own confessor, go and confess somewhere else.[35]

During the Temptation

Next we are told that during the time of temptation we should consider the causes of the temptation. This might seem to go against his advice that it is better to run from temptations against chastity than to confront them directly. But here Scupoli is talking about what might be called a predisposition to unchastity, or a long-standing condition of trouble in the area. His common sense is at work here, and he knew, long before the words were used in this way, that an effort to suppress the sexual instinct in the sense of pretending it is not there can be dangerous, while control of its manifestations is possible and necessary. That is to say, while we should not moon around and encourage sexual fantasies, nonetheless, we should have some understanding of the forces at work in our own case and of how best to deal with them. But, if we are going to do this, we have to see what are the persisting causes of sexual sin in ourselves.

The first thing to be done is to determine whether these causes are external or internal. By external causes he means such things as curiosity of the eyes or ears and conversations that excite to sin. The internal are "either the rebellion of the flesh, or thoughts of the mind proceeding from our own evil habits or from the suggestions of the devil".[36]

1. *The custody of the eyes and ears.* To take some sort of care over what we look at is essential if our imaginations are not going to be stored with an army of images that will come

[35] Ibid.
[36] SC 19, p. 47.

back to trouble us sooner or later. Too much television and, obviously, even so-called soft-porn are going to lead to trouble. When it comes to seeing things we cannot avoid, as when we are walking along the street in a city, there is still the discipline to be practiced of not letting our eyes slide back for a second look.

There are similar remarks to be made about what we listen to. We have to remember that one wrong speech provokes another, and it is easy to take part in a way of talking with others that in fact pulls us away from Christ:

> One wrong speech provokes another; and thus there grows up ... that miserable tone of conversation,—hinting and suggesting evil, jesting, bantering on the subject of sin, supplying fuel for the inflammable imagination,—which lasts through life, which is wherever the world is, which is the very breath of the world, which the world cannot do without, which the world "speaks out of the abundance of its heart", and which you may prophesy will prevail in every ordinary assemblage of men, as soon as they are at their ease and begin to talk freely,—a sort of vocal worship of the Evil One, to which the Evil One listens with special satisfaction, because he looks on it as the preparation for worse sin; for from bad thoughts and bad words proceed bad deeds.[37]

2. *The custody of the inner senses.* Sexual temptation is fueled by a biological drive that is not sufficiently integrated into the human person. It should be recognized that these temptations will never entirely disappear until, as Philip Neri says, we close

---

[37] J. H. Newman, "Intellect, the Instrument of Religious Training", in *Sermons Preached on Various Occasions* (New York and Bombay: Longmans, Green, & Co., 1904), pp. 9–10.

our eyes in death.[38] On the other hand, they can be controlled, and with time and practice they can also cease to be the focus of constant attention in the spiritual life.

Scupoli says the internal causes of temptation are either the rebellion of the flesh or thoughts of the mind proceeding from our own evil habits or the suggestion of the devil.[39]

a. A good deal of the temptations of the flesh are caused by the external senses and the imagination. There remains, however, the fact of the sexual appetite, which is itself a force and which Scupoli calls the rebellion of the flesh. This rebellion, because it is physical, has to be fought with physical instruments.

> The rebellion of the flesh must be mortified by fasts, disciplines, hair-shirts, vigils, and other similar austerities, as discretion and obedience may direct.[40]

The important thing about this list, whatever might be thought about the practices themselves, is Scupoli's insistence that what finds its source in the body has to be fought at the level of the body. It is true that he is teaching an asceticism of love, but we are not pure spirits or pure wills, and the body has to be trained, and sometimes in a negative fashion. The scriptural practice of fasting, at very least, should be practiced by those who are having a problem with the flesh.

b. Next Scupoli counsels prayer and meditation as another means for fighting lust. By prayer here he means what has been called "arrow prayer", or a prayer of aspirations. This sort of prayer is a short verse from a psalm or other part

---

[38] "We ought to fear and fly temptations of the flesh, even in sickness and in old age itself, aye, and so long as we can open and shut our eyelids, for the spirit of incontinence gives no truce either to place, time, or person" (maxim for March 24, in *Maxims and Counsels*).

[39] SC 19, p. 47.

[40] Ibid.

of Scripture, or a phrase from one of the saints, or even a sentence of one's own. The essential thing is that they should be few so that they be ready to hand when needed. Cassian writes of this sort of prayer in connection with lust:

> If carnal titillation suddenly pricks me while I am still struggling against the vices, and if it tries, with its caressing pleasurableness, to get me to consent as I lie sleeping, then, lest an alien fire blaze up and burn the sweetly scented blossoms of chastity, I should cry: "O God, incline unto my aid; O Lord, make haste to help me."[41]

The repetition of such a formula does at least two things. First of all, it deflects the mind away from the temptation, and, secondly, it strengthens the will to resist by reinforcing it with the strength of past victories that this prayer has helped to bring about. It is as though the force of a large express train had been redirected by throwing a railway switch, and the simplicity of this sort of prayer should not lead us to underestimate its importance.

The discussion of meditation here makes two points. In the first place, meditation on the temptation itself is to be avoided; and, secondly, we should meditate on the Passion and death of Christ. Meditation here means a sort of thinking that relates our present situation to the truths of our faith. We do this in a way that will result in a concrete resolution that will help to change the way we actually behave.[42] Meditation understood in this way as involving the connecting of ideas together has the disadvantage that it will all too easily link up with precisely the sort of thoughts we are trying to get rid of. Therefore at the time we are under pressure we

---

[41] John Cassian, *The Conferences*, bk. 10, chap. 9, no. 9, trans. and annotated by Boniface Ramsey, O.P. (New York: Paulist Press, 1997), p. 381.
[42] See below, chap. 8, the section on "Meditation".

should avoid any extended consideration of the nature of the vice itself. This is really an application of the principle that temptations against chastity are best met by running away from them. Scupoli says that meditations on the vileness of the vice, its insatiable craving and the ruin of estate, honor, and so on, that follow in its train are counterproductive if we try to use them while actually being tempted:

> For if the mind repels these thoughts on the one hand, on the other they afford an opportunity, and expose us to the danger of taking pleasure in, and consenting to, them. Therefore the true remedy in all these cases is flight, not from these thoughts alone, but from every thing, however contrary to them, which may bring them before us.[43]

Instead of trying to meditate directly on the temptation itself, we should meditate on the life and Passion of our crucified Redeemer. Even if we do take a lesson from our Lord's life that is unrelated to chastity, it will still require a serious effort to repel the suggestions of lust:

> And should the same thoughts again intrude themselves against thy will, and molest thee more than ever, as will very probably happen, be not discouraged on this account, nor leave off thy meditation, but continue it with all possible intensity.[44]

The effort to concentrate on, say, the patience of Christ is not going to remove entirely the thoughts of lust. The remedy is to pay no attention to them, and let them buzz around as though they were flies in the room. The flies can indeed distract us entirely from what we should be doing, but they do not absolutely have to. We should continue with our meditation:

[43] SC 19, p. 48.
[44] Ibid.

not even turning from it to repel such thoughts, but giving thyself no more concern about them than if they in no way belonged to thee. There is no better method than this of resisting them, how incessant so ever may be their attacks.[45]

This is an important piece of advice. Sometimes people give up praying altogether because the minute they begin they are troubled by obscene thoughts. The remedy is not to give up praying, but to fix the mind on the subject of the meditation and not be surprised or discouraged that this attention is difficult and appears to be divided. Indeed, I would say that it is just because the effort to continue meditating is difficult that we can be sure we are engaged in a real struggle, and we can be confident that if we persevere, our efforts will bring practical results. Nor, finally, should we reason with such temptations to find out whether we have consented to them or not:

> for this is a device of the devil, who seeks, under the semblance of good, to disquiet thee, and make thee distrustful and fainthearted, or hope, by entangling thee in such discussions, to draw thee into some sin.[46]

After the Temptation

When the temptation is over we should continue to keep away from everything that could begin another round of temptation, struggle, and perhaps even defeat. Often enough we let down our guard and begin discussions or frequent places that are not really necessary for us. With our unfathomable capacity for self-deception, we assure ourselves that

[45] Ibid.
[46] Ibid., p. 49.

we are doing these things from the highest motives, but, if we are not watchful, we will find ourselves with a hard and unnecessary struggle on our hands.

Father de Caussade has this to say about this necessary watchfulness, and while his rules may seem harsh, they will, if followed, help us to avoid a good deal of trouble.

1. We must, he says, cut back on all society that is not necessary with everyone of either sex to whom we are in danger of becoming too attached.

2. We have to learn to avoid any voluntary thought of these persons, to avoid occupying ourselves interiorly with them, to blot out their memory. To do this we have to turn gently, without strain, to God, who is the true object, the center of our rest, who alone can really content this heart of ours that is so vast in its desires.

3. If we have to do with these people, then we should return to God afterward and make sure that, as it were, we stick to business.

4. And if we find this a slow business, and if we fall, we must not be either surprised or impatient with ourselves or give ourselves over to vain regrets or become discouraged and think it was silly even to try. We must humble ourselves gently before God, confess our feebleness, thank him that things did not go farther, and affirm that we want to do better in the future. Finally we must realize that the fault itself teaches us about our own weakness and so makes us more humble to ask and receive the grace we need to do better.[47]

[47] Jean-Pierre de Caussade, *Lettres spirituelles*, ed. Michel Olphe-Galliard, S.J. (Paris: Desclée de Brouwer, 1962), 2:223–24.

CHAPTER SEVEN

PRAYER AS A WEAPON

As speech is the organ of human society, and the means of human civilization, so is prayer the instrument of divine fellowship and divine training.

> —J. H. Newman, "Moral Effects of Communion with God," *Parochial and Plain Sermons*

The fourth weapon of the spiritual combat is prayer, and Scupoli's treatment of prayer is focused on prayer as an instrument of the ascetical life. Asceticism in its most general sense, it will be remembered, has a twofold thrust. On the one hand, it involves an organized campaign against both the sinful aspects of the self and exterior temptation; and, at the same time, it requires a sustained effort to develop all those tendencies and habits in our nature that work for the perfection of our spiritual activities;[1] and so Scupoli writes about prayer as the most important element of this "organized campaign":

> If self-distrust, trust in God, and spiritual exercises, be so needful, as has already been shown, in this conflict, needful above all is prayer, (the fourth weapon above mentioned) by

[1] See above, p. 12, as well as prologue, n. 2.

146

means of which we may obtain from the Lord our God not these alone but all other good things.[2]

Prayer, within this context of the ascetical life, together with self-distrust, confidence in God, and spiritual exercises, is the most important means at our disposal and under our control through which we obtain purity of heart. It is through this struggle to obtain purity of heart that we gradually become united to God, which is the ultimate purpose of the spiritual life.

Ascetical Prayer and Mysticism

At the very beginning of the *Spiritual Combat* we were asked whether we wanted to attain in Christ the height of perfection and, by a nearer and nearer approach to God, to become one in spirit with him. We have to bear this final end of all our striving in mind when we deal with Scupoli's discussion on prayer. If we leave out of consideration that prayer is a means to union with God, what St. Robert Bellarmine called the treasure of our heart,[3] then the point of much of what Scupoli says will be lost. It will become easy to caricaturize his teaching as being dry and unhelpful; and, in fact, he has been criticized for having too narrow a view of prayer, not dealing with what are sometimes called more advanced states of prayer.

---

[2] SC 44, p. 113.

[3] "If you are wise, then, know that you have been created for the glory of God and your own eternal salvation. This is your goal; this is the center of your life; this is the treasure of your heart. If you reach this goal, you will find happiness. If you fail to reach it, you will find misery" (St. Robert Bellarmine, "On the Ascent of the Mind to God", quoted in *The Liturgy of the Hours* [New York: Catholic Book Publishing Co., 1975], 4:1412).

His teaching with regard to prayer reflects the teaching of his age and country in its most restrictive and unimaginative form. Out of nine chapters devoted to the subject, seven are wholly concerned with the practice of meditation, and there is no mention of the more contemplative forms of prayer except in one brief chapter entitled "mental prayer".[4]

This is hard on an age that included St. Philip Neri, St. Ignatius, St. Teresa of Avila, St. John of the Cross, and St. Francis de Sales. It is true that only St. Philip was an Italian, but it is difficult to see how the Spaniards or the Savoyard were noticeably different in their teaching about prayer as an instrument or weapon of the ascetical life. Still, it is easy enough to accept this criticism if we forget what Scupoli is trying to do, and at first sight his treatment on prayer does in fact seem restrictive and unimaginative. But the criticism can be pushed too hard. In the first place, he is talking about prayer within the context of what Newman called the moral effects of communion with God.[5] Christianity is a great deal more than morality, but Christianity does make serious demands on believers in the way of practice, and these demands are the focus of Scupoli's book. Again, secondly, it has to be remembered that these moral demands do not define Christianity or the entirety of the spiritual combat itself. Christianity is about loving God and neighbor. To love God and neighbor requires the practice of a serious ascetical life, and

[4] *Unseen Warfare: The Spiritual Combat and Path to Paradise of Lorenzo Scupoli*, ed. Nicodemus of the Holy Mountain and rev. by Theophan the Recluse; trans. E. Kadloubovsky and G. E. H. Palmer (London: Mowbrays, 1978), p. 40.

[5] J. H. Newman, "Moral Effects of Communion with God", sermon 15 in vol. 4 of *Parochial and Plain Sermons* (San Francisco: Ignatius Press, 1997), pp. 877–85.

asceticism is the way we attain to that purity of heart without which we will not see God. It is a serious mistake to say that asceticism is the final purpose of our existence, and Scupoli most definitely does not make this mistake.

The criticism of Scupoli is really based on the presupposition that prayer in connection with ordinary life and its problems is somehow of less interest and importance than mystical experience. Without wishing to set a value on the two sorts of praying, it can at least be said that the sort of prayer St. Teresa discusses in the *Interior Castle* is much less common than what Scupoli writes about. This does not mean that we should remain ignorant about the higher reaches of mystical experience, and some people find this knowledge a help and an inspiration in their daily life of a more ordinary sort of prayer. Von Balthasar has written that "although mysticism is a way taken by only a very few, it is nonetheless the model for every way of faith, precisely because it is the way of the one and only faith." [6] The tradition of Christian prayer sees mystical prayer as giving to ascetical prayer its ultimate meaning and justification. That is to say, the final purpose of prayer is about union with God, and whatever leads to that union, including ascetical prayer, receives its justification within this perspective. Nonetheless, to repeat the point at issue, ascetical prayer has value of its own, and it cannot be bypassed merely because of the reality of mysticism.

Ascetical prayer is not a sort of second-class prayer for those who cannot do any better. In *The Seven Storey Mountain* Thomas Merton characterizes the Spiritual Exercises of St. Ignatius in the following way:

[6] Hans Urs von Balthasar, *The Glory of the Lord*, vol. 3 (San Francisco: Ignatius Press, 1986), p. 106.

They are very pedestrian and practical—their chief purpose being to enable all the busy Jesuits to get their mind off their work and back to God with a minimum of wasted time.[7]

Thomas Merton wrote those words as a young man, but even so they are indefensible. The chief purpose of the Exercises was to assist in a total conversion of everything the exercitant was and had to Jesus Christ. Of course, this involved an integration of work, in an everyday sense, into the life of the one doing the Exercises, but to say that the Exercises have as their defining purpose the escape from this work seems to me ludicrous. However, it is the put down of ascetical prayer that is at issue here, not the interpretation of the Exercises.

St. Teresa was obviously perplexed by the question of why there were not more contemplatives,[8] but she saw two things very clearly. In the first place, contemplation is not required for perfection, and, secondly, many of those who are not so called do in fact lead saintly lives. She writes:

It does not follow that, because all of us in this house practise prayer, we are all *perforce* to be contemplatives. That is impossible; and those of us who are not would be greatly discouraged if we did not grasp the truth that contemplation is something given by God, and, as *it is not necessary for salvation and God does not ask it of us before He gives us our reward*, we must not suppose that anyone else will require it of us [my emphasis].[9]

[7] Thomas Merton, *The Seven Storey Mountain* (New York: Harcourt, Brace & Co., 1948), p. 268.

[8] See especially chap. 17 of the *Way of Perfection*.

[9] St. Teresa of Avila, *Way of Perfection*, chap. 17, trans. and ed. E. Allison Peers (Garden City, N.Y.: Doubleday [Image Books], 1964), p. 124.

Secondly, she is clear that a high degree of sanctity is possible through the ordinary practices of the ascetical life.

> I know a very old woman, leading a most excellent life—*I wish mine were like hers*—a penitent and a great servant of God, who for many years has been spending hours and hours in vocal prayer, but from mental prayer can get no help at all; the most she can do is to dwell upon each of her vocal prayers as she says them. There are a great many other people *just* like this; if they are humble, they will not, I think, be any the worse off in the end, but very much in the same state as those who enjoy numerous consolations.[10]

Abbot Chapman, who was abbot of Downside Abbey in the 1930s and had a great deal of experience of contemplative monasteries and convents, came to the same conclusions as St. Teresa and presents a much more balanced view than Merton's:

> It seems to me that people can get a very extraordinary sanctity, and wonderful love of God and familiarity with Him, by the loftier kinds of Meditation.[11]

This testimony is important because the abbot was a spiritual director who had great authority on the beginnings of contemplative prayer. These beginnings, which mark a new stage in our relationship with God, displace the usual practices of the ascetical life and entail a darker and more obscure life of prayer. The subject is complex and used to be much discussed, but what is important for our purposes here is to see that an authority on this darker and more obscure

[10] Ibid., p. 125.
[11] John Chapman, *Spiritual Letters* (London: Sheed & Ward, 1935), p. 113.

life of prayer insisted that the methods of the ascetical life are to be used for as long as they can be. For many, perhaps most, people, that means they will be the staple of spiritual exercises for a lifetime.

> The surest way towards the partial restoration of *integra natura* is by the practice of the virtues, assisted by the sacraments and by the prayer of petition. The science of Christian ascetics deals with this mortification for the taming of our lower nature and its subjection to reason enlightened by grace.[12]

Approaching God in the Right Way

In the *Spiritual Combat* Scupoli writes about prayer from the perspective of its being one of the ways in which we build up the virtues and fight the vices. Prayer, although it is undertaken because of the grace of God, is still a human activity that can be thought about, refined, and practiced more effectively. Scupoli lists six ways in which our prayer can be strengthened. These six means for strengthening prayer are not instructions on how to pray or descriptions of prayer but should be looked on as dispositions or attitudes that must be developed or cultivated if prayer is to become a more adequate conversation with God. These six points bring together many of the arguments that Scupoli has already discussed, and he now applies them to the life of prayer.

1. We must deepen our desire to serve God in an effective and real way. To do this we should try to stir up in ourselves a sense of the greatness, the majesty, and the beauty of God. This deeper sense of the reality of God will begin to create a real sense that we should serve God. Furthermore,

---

[12] Ibid., p. 315.

we should also remember that our Lord labored and suffered for thirty-three years to serve us:

> binding up and healing the putrefying sores envenomed by the poison of sin, not with oil, or wine or linen, but with the precious stream that flowed from his most sacred veins, and with his most pure flesh torn by scourges, thorns, and nails.[13]

We should also think quietly about the great value of serving God. Through the serious effort to serve God, we gradually gain the mastery over Satan and ourselves and are made the children of God himself.

2. We should pray with a lively faith and with deep confidence. Confidence in God, as we have seen[14] does not mean a vague sort of optimism. What it does mean is the well founded hope, which comes from our faith, that God will give us everything we need to enable us to do what he wants and everything we need for our own good.

> This holy confidence is the vessel which divine mercy fills with the treasures of his grace; and the larger and more capacious it is, the more richly laden will our prayer return into our bosom.[15]

If our prayer is pinched, dry, and shallow, then how will we be able to receive anything but the smallest particles of what God wants to give to us? The saints pray with great confidence, and they receive—in part, anyway, because they establish a real contact with God through a living and confident faith.

[13] SC 44, p. 114.
[14] See above, in chap. 3, "Hope in God".
[15] SC 44, p. 114.

3. We should learn to pray so that God's will, and not our own, will be fulfilled. In our prayer we should pray for what we need, things both spiritual and temporal. Yet we should always do this in the spirit of the Lord's Prayer—*thy* will be done. We should pray because God wishes us to pray, and we should desire to be heard insofar as and no farther than he wills. "Thy intention, in short, should be to unite thy will to the will of God, and not to draw his will to thine." [16]

4. We should make sure that our prayer is accompanied by good works. The exercise of prayer must continually be accompanied by self-discipline. Prayer involves the effort to lead a life conformable with our prayer, and our prayer is deepened and strengthened by this effort to lead a more serious Christian life.

> Be careful when thou goest to prayer to adorn thyself with works corresponding to thy petitions; and after thou hast prayed, labour more earnestly still to fit thyself for the grace and virtue thou desirest to obtain. [17]

5. Our prayer should contain an element of thanksgiving for past mercies. Thanksgiving should always be an element in our prayer; thanksgiving for past mercies, but also for difficulties that may arise in the present. If, for example, we are praying for patience, then we should try to thank God when a chance to exercise patience comes up:

> And if, while thou art praying for any particular virtue, some painful occasion for its exercise should present itself fail not to return thanks to God for the opportunity thus afforded thee, which is no small token of his loving kindness. [18]

[16] Ibid., p. 115.
[17] Ibid.
[18] Ibid., p. 116.

6. We should persevere in prayer with great confidence, "for humble perseverance vanquishes the invincible". God is merciful and desires our salvation. Therefore we must go on praying until we obtain what we need.

> Therefore, unless there be some fault on thy part, thou may-est rest assured either of obtaining all thy petition, or some-thing which will be more profitable for thee, or, it may be, both together; and the more he seems to repulse thee, the more do thou humble thyself in thine own sight, consider-ing thy own demerits, and fixing thine eyes steadfastly on the mercy of God.[19]

One of the purposes of apparently unanswered prayer is to teach us perseverance. To go on when things seem to be dark and unhopeful strengthens us not only in the particular difficulty we are experiencing, but it also makes us stronger when other difficulties present themselves. "Establish thus more and more thy confidence in God, which will be most acceptable to thy Lord, if thou maintain it the more lively and entire the more it is assailed."[20]

Language and Prayer

Ascetical prayer has it own intrinsic value and is the most important element in the spiritual combat. Next we have to see that language is an indispensable element in the practice of prayer.

Newman says that prayer is *conversing* with God:

> We converse with our fellow-men, and then we use familiar language, because they *are* our fellows. We converse with

God, and then we use the lowliest, awfullest, calmest, con-
cisest language we can, because He *is* God. Prayer, then, is
divine converse, differing from human as God differs from
man.[21]

Newman then develops this thought of prayer as language.
Our intercourse with our fellowmen, he says, is "not by sight,
but by sound, not by eyes, but by ears. Hearing is the social
sense, and language is the social bond." [22] If our relationship
to God is to be a human relationship, it must involve language, and so "prayers and praises" are the way a Christian
enters into a deeper awareness of the reality of God and the
reality of the unseen world.[23]

> Thus St. Paul says, "Our conversation is in heaven,"—not
> indeed thereby meaning converse of words only, but inter-
> course and manner of living generally; yet still in an especial
> way converse of words or prayer, because language is the
> special means of all intercourse.[24]

Without prayer we will not become familiar with God; we
will not know how to act and react when finally the reality
of God and of the unseen will no longer be matters of faith
but of sight. Without prayer we are like foreigners who do
not necessarily behave badly in a society not their own, but
who behave differently; they have no automatic responses,
and their training and their background have not provided
them with the means to deal adequately with quite ordinary
situations. If we do not want to be foreigners in the presence

---

[21] Newman, "Moral Effects", p. 878.

[22] Ibid.

[23] "He who does not pray, does not claim his citizenship with heaven, but
lives, though an heir of the kingdom, as if he were a child of earth" (ibid.).

[24] Ibid.

of God, we have to get to know him through the language of prayer. Ascetical prayer is a process of familiarizing ourselves with God through a loving conversation that uses language, even if the conversation "includes intercourse and manner of living generally".[25]

This "conversation with God" is vocal prayer and takes many forms, and we have already seen the role it should play in spiritual exercises. In times of temptation, for example, we noticed how a simple plea for God's help in the form of a prayer of aspirations, or "arrow prayer",[26] is often the only way we can pray. Scupoli says explicitly that we are to make use of our tongue when the superior will seems to be wholly stifled and overcome by the temptation:

> And if at any time the foes should so violently assail and press upon thee as almost to stifle thy will, so that it seems to have no breath to produce any opposing act of volition, yet do not lose courage, nor throw down thine arms, but make use of thy tongue in thy defence, saying "I yield not, I consent not".[27]

Again we have encountered the notion of meditation as a sort of thinking that relates our present situation to the truths of faith in a way that will result in a concrete resolution to fight a particular manifestation of the vice we are struggling against or help to establish the virtue we are striving to build up.[28] An example of this informal sort of meditation that emphasizes the verbal aspect of prayer is to be found in Scupoli's discussion of how to resist sudden impulses of the

[25] Ibid.
[26] Chap. 6, pp. 141–42, no. 2b.
[27] SC 14, p. 35.
[28] See p. 142.

passions.[29] If we are faced with an insult or trial, he says, we should rouse ourselves, lift up our heart to God, and then reflect on his goodness and love, which have chosen these means to help us fight our sins and establish Christlike virtues. This sort of "mini-meditation" needs to be driven home in a way that will affect the way we behave, and so he says:

> And, knowing how greatly he is pleased that thou shouldst suffer [the insult or trial], turn to thyself, and with a sharp rebuke say, "Oh, why wilt thou refuse to bear this cross, and embrace it with all possible patience and joy, saying, 'Oh cross, formed by divine Providence ... nail me now to thee, that so I may give myself to him who died on thee for my redemption'".[30]

Scupoli intends we should actually say the words, at least to ourselves. Language is at the heart of ascetical prayer, even if the language of individual prayer may gradually become very simple. St. Thomas says that vocal prayer is necessary for three reasons:[31]

1. It arouses interior devotion.

2. It gives homage to God with our body as well as with our soul.

3. It gives expression to spiritual sentiments that flood the soul in prayer.

The *Catechism of the Catholic Church* expresses the tradition concerning the necessity of vocal prayer:

> Vocal prayer, founded on the union of body and soul in human nature, associates the body with the interior prayer of

---

[29] SC 18, p. 42.
[30] Ibid., p. 43.
[31] ST 2a, 2ae, 83, 12.

the heart, following Christ's example of praying to his Father and teaching the Our Father to his disciples.[32]

There is something very contemporary about the importance Thomas and the tradition give to the importance of language, and this insistence on the importance of language ought to make what he says more accessible to us. George Steiner has said that the secret of human behavior is to be found in man as a "language animal",[33] and this is more immediately believable than the classical definition that "man is a rational animal." That definition is something our contemporaries find it hard to accept. The definition is obviously wrong if we understand it to mean that human beings always behave in a way that shows their actions are determined by reason. This impression is only reinforced when we remember that the definition has also carried with it the idea that reason and morality are closely connected: that is, man is a rational animal, and it is through his reason that he achieves happiness, good living, and a well-ordered society. We have only to look at the newspapers or the TV, or think about the cruelty and stupidity of so much of the twentieth century, to understand why so many people find the definition either unintelligible or completely wrong-headed.

There is, of course, much to be said in defense of the classical definition, but it is worth noting that "rational" in the phrase "rational animal" comes to us from the Latin, which is an effort to translate the word *logos*. Aristotle writes about *echein logon*,[34] that is, *having logos*. *Logos* is a word that, to use Charles Taylor's phrase, "straddles speech and thought"

[32] CCC 2722.

[33] Cited in Charles Taylor, *Human Agency and Language* (Cambridge and New York: Cambridge Univ. Press, 1985), p. 217.

[34] E.g., *Nichomachean Ethics*, 1, 13, 18 (1103 a).

and reminds us that language is not an irrelevance that can be treated with carelessness and even contempt.[35] The subject is a large one, but to ignore language, or to say that all the questions about its use have been solved, is to put oneself firmly in the eighteenth century, not in the vanguard of progress either in theology or prayer. Language matters, and it should not be disdained as though it were some kind of obstacle to real intimacy with God.

Petition and Prayer

The Catechism of the Catholic Church teaches that the "*forms of prayer* revealed in the apostolic and canonical Scriptures remain normative for Christian prayer",[36] and petition is one of these basic forms of prayer. Scupoli discusses vocal prayer from the perspective of petition, that is, of asking God for what we need, both spiritually and temporally. This makes perfect sense within the context of the ascetical life, which is concerned with fighting vice and establishing virtue. We should ask for God's help both in situations of sudden temptation and also in the more long-term efforts to train the intellect and the will to operate in a more Christian way. Christian prayer in the Bible and in the tradition of the Church is dominated by prayer understood as a humble request to God for what we need:

> The vocabulary of supplication in the New Testament is rich in shades of meaning: ask, beseech, plead, invoke, entreat,

---

[35] "It straddles speech and thought, because it means, inter alia, word, thought, reasoning, reasoned account, as well as being used for the words deployed in such an account. It incorporated in its range of meanings a sense of the relation of speech and thought" (Taylor, *Human Agency*, p. 218).

[36] CCC 2625.

cry out, even "struggle in prayer" (cf. *Rom* 15:30; *Col* 4:12). Its most usual form, because the most spontaneous, is petition: by prayer of petition we express awareness of our relationship with God. We are creatures who are not our own beginning, not the masters of adversity, not our own last end. We are sinners who as Christians know that we have turned away from our Father. Our petition is already a turning back to him.[37]

We have seen that Scupoli insists that the purpose of the prayer of petition is not to bend the will of God, but to pray for what we need in conformity with his will.[38] St. Thomas teaches that "Our Lord taught his disciples to ask definitely for those things which are contained in the petitions of the Lord's prayer."[39] It is God's will for us that we should ask for something definite when we pray in this way. In the prayer of petition, we grow gradually into a sense of the reality of our dependence on God and develop the confidence to ask him for what we need. The simple, familiar business of asking for what we require, if we are going even to begin to live the Christian life, is the foundation of our response to the call of God. It is through the prayer of petition that we begin to relate ourselves in a real way to the God who was before all things and is in all things.

The use of the prayer of petition is often neglected today for various reasons. Some people have a sense that it is an irrational activity that is hardly compatible with the mentality of sophisticated modern man. We have become accustomed to thinking that to put God at the center of our world view is to demean our human dignity. The use of the prayer

[37] CCC 2629.
[38] See p. 154, no. 3.
[39] ST 2a, 2ae, 86, 5.

of petition displays, so it is felt, a cowardice in the face of the difficulties of life and reveals a childish dependence on God that is unworthy of free men. This sense, of the autonomy of our humanity, is part of the cultural legacy of the Enlightenment.[40] It is important to be aware of this element in our contemporary climate of opinion, but at the same time it must be clearly recognized that it is incompatible with the Christian view of the providence of God and of our dependence on his will.[41]

There is, however, another difficulty about the prayer of petition that is more important, as it arises from a misunderstanding of the Christian world view itself. Serious Catholics sometimes worry as to whether the prayer of intercession is really compatible with a whole-hearted acceptance of God's providence. If, that is, God is all-powerful and all-loving, then surely, so it is argued, the prayer of petition is not only superfluous, but it also betrays a lack of faith in God and trust in his promises. There are, certainly, passages in the Bible that seem to teach that we should trust in God and not be concerned about the practical matters of life:

> Consider the lilies of the field, how they grow; they neither toil nor spin; yet I tell you, even Solomon in all his glory was not arrayed like one of these. But if God so clothes the grass of the field, which today is alive and tomorrow is thrown

---

[40] Jaroslav Pelikan, *The Christian Tradition*, vol. 5 (Chicago: Chicago Univ. Press, 1989), p. 60: "When applied to the Christian tradition and its doctrines, the Enlightenment represented what has been called the 'revolution of man's autonomous potentialities over against the heteronymous powers which were no longer convincing', namely, the heteronymous authority of the church and of its dogma and ultimately of the objective authority of Scripture and of transcendent revelation itself." The reference is to Paul Tillich's *Perspectives on 19th and 20th Century Protestant Theology*.

[41] See above, pp. 31–32.

into the oven, will he not much more clothe you, O men of
little faith? Therefore do not be anxious, saying "What shall
we eat?" or "What shall we drink?" or "What shall we wear?"
For the Gentiles seek all these things; and your heavenly Father knows that you need them all. (Mt 6:28–32)

Whatever exactly this passage is teaching, it does seem to be
creating at least an attitude of "God knows best, God loves
us, so trust in him and don't harass yourself about what you
think you might need." This attitude was sometimes in the
past pushed so far that even concern about our own salvation was held to display a want of perfect faith and trust in
God, because desiring anything for ourselves, even our hope
of heaven, supposedly showed a lack of a pure love of God.[42]
Or, to put the same point in a slightly different way, if I
desire anything for myself, even my own salvation, then I am
thinking about myself and not the will of God.

Love, as we have seen, is a desire for an object; we have,
that is, to love something if we are to love at all.[43] A pure
love of God that excluded wanting to be with him is nothing we could recognize as love. Hugh of St. Victor had the
matter right when he wrote:

Hear these wise men (these false mystics); they say: "We love
God; but we do not desire him." It is as if they said: "We
love him, but are not concerned with him." I am a man
and would not like to be loved by you at this price: if you
loved me without concerning yourself with me, I would give

[42] This favorite doctrine of the Quietists was discussed in a clear and accessible manner by Mgsr. Ronald Knox in chap. 12, "Quietism: The Doctrine", of *Enthusiasm* (Oxford: Clarendon Press, 1962). Father de Caussade's
On Prayer, bk. 1, dialogues 8 and 9, discusses the question of desiring our own
salvation in a precise manner.

[43] See above pp. 32–33.

nothing for your love. Judge then if a love that a man might reasonably reject with reason could be worthy of God! ...Those who speak in this way are ignorant of the very nature of charity; *for what is the love of God if it is not desire to possess him?*[44]

We cannot love God without desiring him for ourselves; and our desire for him is essential if our love is to be a human response to his call. Our desire for happiness is an ineradicable aspect of our nature, and it is because we desire happiness that we try to follow Christ's example and follow in his steps[45] and so reach our beatitude in the beatific vision.[46]

Someone might still say that while he accepts the fact that we cannot love God without also desiring him, that does not mean that he is supposed to pray for everything he happens to desire—for example, good health or a new job. Here we have to try to keep in mind both that God wants us to ask for what we need and that this prayer has to be in conformity with the will of God. If we need health or a new job to do what we are convinced is the will of God, then we are bound to ask for these goods. Yet because we do not always

---

[44] Cited in de Caussade, *On Prayer*, bk. 1, dialogue 9 (London: Burns & Oates, 1964), p. 87, n. 2 (emphasis mine). Hugh continues (in the same footnote): "Desiring him alone, and naught else, is loving him with a gratuitous love. If you desire other things besides him, your love is not disinterested, but [if] you desire nothing but him you love, you yet desire something, and what you desire is the object of your love. *For if you had no desire you would have no love*" (my emphasis).

[45] "For to this you have been called, because Christ also suffered for you, leaving you an example, that you should follow in his steps" (1 Pet 2:21).

[46] Jacques Bossuet wrote: "Nothing can remove from the heart the desire to be happy; and if we could master ourselves and cease to be concerned with ourselves, then we should no longer be subject to God, who could make us neither happy nor unhappy, could neither reward nor punish us, except perhaps by annihilating us; which again would be uncertain, supposing that we could be indifferent to that fate" (cited in de Caussade, *On Prayer*, bk. 1, dialogue 9, p. 93, n. 2 [iv]).

know what is really good for us, we should ask with the condition of our desire being in accordance with the will of God;[47] and we model our petition on the model of our Lord's prayer in the garden: "not as I will, but as thou wilt" (Mt 26:36–44).

There are other things, however, for which we should pray without condition, and these are goods that are bound up with our search for perfection. St. Thomas says, in the passage we have already noted concerning the petitions of the Lord's Prayer:

> There are certain goods which man cannot ill use, because they cannot have an evil result. Such are those which are the object of beatitude and whereby we merit it: and these the saints seek absolutely when they pray, as in Psalm 80, 3, Show us thy face Lord and we shall be saved, and again in Psalm 119, 35, Lead me into the path of thy commandments.[48]

It is these sort of goods that are treated in the ascetical life. Fighting the vices and working to establish the virtues are ways in which we increase in merit and make ourselves over, with God's grace, into the sort of people who will be able to enter into the joy of the Lord.

The practices of the ascetical life are an indispensable aspect of a serious Christian life, and if we are to persevere and to be successful in the ascetical life, then we must pray for self-distrust, for hope in God, and for the strength to go on fighting the vices and establishing the virtues.

> By prayer, well used, thou wilt put a sword into the hand of God wherewith to fight and conquer for thee.[49]

[47] See ST 2a, 2ae, 83, 6: "Whether man ought to ask God for temporal things when he prays".
[48] ST 2a, 2ae, 83, 5.
[49] SC 44, p. 113.

PART TWO

THE DEVELOPMENT OF PRAYER

Lift up thine heart unto God with a meek stirring of love;
and mean himself and none of his gifts.

— *The Cloud of Unknowing*

Spiritual combat is undertaken because we desire to know
Christ Jesus and him crucified; and the ascetical life must be
seen within this framework of preparing ourselves for sharing
in the divine nature. At every Mass the priest says, "may we
come to share in the divinity of Christ, who humbled himself
to share in our humanity",[1] and Scupoli's outline of prayer is
oriented toward this sharing in the divinity of Christ through
purity of heart. Yet knowledge of the final goal does not suddenly make the combat disappear or mean that prayer as a
weapon in the war against sin and in the campaign to acquire
the virtues is no longer necessary. Any effort to make a detour
around ascetical prayer usually ends in both failure in Christian living and frustration of the search for union with the divine.

Asceticism is an indispensable aspect of Christian living,
and prayer is an enduring element in this effort to fight sin
and draw closer to God. But just as asceticism does not constitute all there is to the spiritual life, so prayer cannot be
restricted to its role as a weapon in spiritual combat. Living
of any sort involves change, and spiritual combat is based
on the belief that change for the better is a real possibility. Inevitably development in the spiritual life will entail

---

[1] Prayer at the Offertory.

development in the life of prayer, even though this necessity often goes unrecognized by those who are satisfied with the particular form of ascetical prayer they have achieved.[2] Scupoli provides us with a practical guide to prayer as related to fighting sin and working at acquiring the virtues. Furthermore, his outline of prayer is oriented toward purity of heart and union with God and so escapes the criticism that his teaching is as narrow and unimaginative as has been suggested.[3] On the other hand, his treatment is so condensed that it is easy to lose sight of this final end of our prayer, and, to compound this difficulty, there are important discussions of some forms of vocal prayer in the section on spiritual exercises.

In order to make up in some way for this situation I have placed his discussion within a larger context, a context that shows both how Scupoli's outline of prayer is related to other types of prayer and how the serious practice of ascetical prayer points the way to a greater freedom in the spiritual life. St. John of the Cross says that "God leads each soul along a different road and there shall hardly be found a single spirit who can walk even half the way which is suitable for another."[4] This should not be understood to mean that St. John is recommending we ignore ascetical prayer, but he is saying that ascetical prayer leads to an intimacy with God that is not bound by rules.[5]

---

[2] St. Teresa in the third mansion of the *Interior Castle* has a characteristically incisive and unsentimental analysis of those who think they have the life of prayer safely organized and under their control and who tend to think they have no need of further progress.

[3] See above, chap. 7.

[4] St. John of the Cross, *Living Flame of Love*, first redaction, stanza 3, no. 51, in *Complete Works*, trans. and ed. by E. Allison Peers, new ed. (London: Burns & Oates, 1954), 3:81.

[5] "[Spiritual directors] . . . ought to give these souls freedom, for, when they would seek to better themselves, their directors have an obligation to put a good face upon it, since they know not by what means God desires such a soul to make progress" (ibid., no. 52, 3:81).

In seeking to provide the reader with a larger context, I have organized this section around a discussion found in the *Scala Claustralium*, sometimes known in English as the *Ladder of Monks*.[6] This twelfth-century work is clear, condensed, and while covering much of what Scupoli says, manages to put it in a more accessible framework and relate it to other forms of prayer.

It is important to see that these other forms of prayer are a development out of ascetical prayer and are not an alternative beginning to the life of the spirit. That is, I believe that any doctrine of what today is called *centering prayer*, which is indifferent to the demands of the ascetical life, is seriously in error. In dealing with this question I have made use of *The Cloud of Unknowing*, as this book has often been taken as justifying a method of prayer that is explicitly condemned by the unknown author of this famous treatise on contemplation.

[6] See below, p. 192.

CHAPTER EIGHT

PRAYER IN CONTEXT

There is not one who does not love something, but the
question is, what to love. The psalms do not tell us not to
love, but to choose the object of our love. But how can
we choose unless we were first chosen? We cannot love
unless someone has loved us first.

—St. Augustine, Sermon 34

There are many ways of praying, but all these different ways
affect one another and provide a background for the particular sort of prayer that is the focus of attention at any
given time. If we ignore this background, we will end up
with an impoverished view of prayer in general as well as
an inadequate understanding of the particular sort of prayer
that is dominant in our own life at any given time. Ascetical prayer is an essential and continuing component in our
efforts to draw nearer to God, but this prayer as a weapon
in spiritual combat has to be seen within a wider context,
and I have said that the *Scala Claustralium* of Guigo II can
be used to provide this context. In this book the author
says that the ladder by which we obtain union with God
has four rungs; these are: reading, meditation, prayer, and
contemplation.

Reading is the careful study of the Scriptures, concentrating all one's powers on it. Meditation is the busy application of the mind to seek with the help of one's own reason for knowledge of hidden truth. Prayer is the heart's devoted turning to God to drive away evil and obtain what is good. Contemplation is when the mind is in some sort lifted up to God and held above itself, so that it tastes the joys of everlasting sweetness.[1]

Reading

"Reading is the careful study of the Scriptures, concentrating all one's powers on it." Reading in the monastic tradition not only provided the indispensable basis for prayer but was itself prayer. In chapter 48 of his *Rule*, St. Benedict says that the brethren must be occupied at stated hours in *lectio divina*, that is, in reading the Bible.[2] For St. Benedict and the monastic tradition, this *lectio* was the sum total of nonliturgical prayer, and there has been a great deal of research and discussion about what this actually entailed within the tradition of monastic prayer,[3] but here I mean only the careful and attentive reading of either the Bible or some other book concerned with faith.

---

[1] Guigo II, *The Ladder of Monks*, no. 3, trans. with an introduction by Edmund College, O.S.A., and James Walsh, S.J. (New York: Doubleday [Image Books], 1978), p. 82.

[2] *Rule of St. Benedict*, chap. 48: "Idleness is the enemy of the soul. The brethren, therefore, must be occupied at stated hours in manual labour, and again at other hours in sacred reading" (*The Rule of St. Benedict*, ed. and trans. Abbot Justin McCann [London: Sheed & Ward, 1972]).

[3] The most accessible book that discusses the monastic tradition is Jean Leclercq, O.S.B., *The Love of Learning and the Desire for God* (New York: Fordham Univ. Press, 1961). Fr. Leclercq brings out just how much this tradition packed into the notion of *reading*.

St. Paul says that faith comes from what is heard—*ex auditu*.[4] Hearing and preaching involve the use of language to convey a message. Assuredly the message is more than merely words, but without the words there is no message. If we are to come into contact with the "preaching of Christ", then this preaching has to be accessible to us. One of the ways this preaching is in fact accessible in the modern world is through the reading of books. In spiritual reading we read to learn about Jesus Christ and about his Gospel, and even if this reading is not a hearing in the literal sense (as it was for the monks who actually read out loud and listened to themselves),[5] nonetheless, reading is the way our spirit is nourished by a truth that is greater than ourselves and that comes to us from outside ourselves. The first purpose of spiritual reading is to learn about this truth. A spiritual life that is not based on Christian truth may not inevitably be headed for shipwreck—at least in this world—but even if such a life survives, it will not be a Christian one. That ought to count for more than it often seems to today.

When it comes to the choice of what books should be read, there are two principles to be kept in mind. First of all, the reading must be related in a direct way to God's revelation in Christ. Obviously the Bible ought to be a major element at least some of the time. Closely related to the Bible there is the Liturgy of the Hours, and especially the Office of Readings, which contains three psalms, a passage of Scripture, and a passage usually from the Fathers. Then there is

[4] "So faith comes from what is heard, and what is heard comes by the preaching of Christ" (Rom 10:17).

[5] "They read usually, not as today, principally with the eyes, but with the lips, pronouncing what they saw, and with the ears, listening to the words pronounced, hearing what is called the 'voices of the pages.' It is a real acoustical reading" (Leclercq, *Love of Learning*, p. 19).

the Missal itself, with its ordered sequence of Scripture readings. In addition to these texts, there are well-known works, such as the *Imitation of Christ*, that focus directly on the person of Christ and on his demands on us. The second principle concerning the choice of what to read is that the reading should speak to the reader personally. This requires a certain amount of experimentation, and, while shopping around just to find something new is counterproductive, it remains true that the reading has to speak directly to the reader. Not everyone has the same needs, and it is a mistake to try to force everyone into the same pattern and feed him with the same sustenance.

The reading ought to be done regularly, and that means finding out what the reader can do even when he is tired or overworked or bored or tempted. The wise words of St. Philip Neri are to the point here:

> It is not a good thing to load ourselves with many spiritual exercises; it is better to undertake a little and go on with it, for if the devil can persuade us to omit an exercise once, he will easily get us to omit it the second time and the third, until at last all our pious practices will melt away.[6]

Once having determined the book to be read, and how much of it is to be read every day, the next thing to do is to read slowly and attentively with a serious intention of making the message it contains a part of oneself. If this entails reading so slowly that the reading is not finished, that does not matter. The important thing is that the truth should begin to assume a direct and compelling lesson for the reader. De Caussade puts it this way:

---

[6] Maxim for June 11, in *Maxims and Counsels*, arr. Fr. Faber (1890; reprint, Toronto: The Oratory, 1995).

When I read, it will not be to satisfy my curiosity or natural desire of the spirit to know things, nor for the purpose of remembering beautiful things, but only for tasting and savoring divine things, to nourish my soul with this taste, because these tastes of divine things are the marrow that nourishes and fattens the soul. The words and the thoughts are like the dregs and the lees which one rejects once one has experienced the marrow and the substance.[7]

In the Sermon on the Mount we read "Blessed are the pure in heart, for they shall see God" (Mt 5:8). Anyone can read those words and see that they are important, but they may also arrest the reader's attention as applying to himself. Guigo says we come across "a short text of Scripture, but it is of great sweetness, like a grape that is put into the mouth filled with many senses to feed the soul":

So, wishing to have a fuller understanding of this, the soul begins to bite and chew upon this grape, as though putting it in a wine press, while it stirs up its powers of reasoning to ask what this precious purity may be and how it may be had.[8]

The reader has learned a lesson, and then it strikes him personally. He wants to know more and to enter more deeply into what has struck him. Like Nicodemus, who heard that to see the kingdom of God he had to be born again, so we too must turn our hearts to God and ask what Christ's words can possibly mean for us.

[7] "Seulement pour goûter et savourer les choses divines, pour me remplir de ce goût, pour nourrir mon âme de ce goût, car ce goût divin, ces saintes impressions sont comme le suc et la substance dont notre âme se nourrie et s'engraisse" (Lettres spirituelles, ed. Michel Olphe-Galliard, S.J. [Paris: Desclée de Brouwer, 1962], 2:220).

[8] Ladder, no. 4, p. 83.

Meditation

"Meditation is the busy application of the mind to seek with the help of one's own reason for knowledge of hidden truth".[9]

Meditation has become a *bête noire* for those who want an approach to God that is, as they see it, free and unstructured. It may be that meditation was sometimes presented in the past in such a formal and precise way that it became a burden rather than a help in maintaining our conversation with God. But some sort of meditation is essential if we are going to stabilize our relationship with God by assimilating the truths of revelation in a way that will affect our conduct. We educate ourselves, with God's help, to know God, to rejoice in him, and to live for him. We have already seen how a meditation in the form of considerations can be of help in everyday life.[10]

Meditation is the way we make the life of Christ real enough to ourselves to ensure that it will affect the way we actually behave. This involves developing a deeper hold on the mysteries of Christ's life and a growing realization of our own sins and weaknesses. Christ, however, is no longer with us in a visible way, and we have to use our ordinary faculties, the intellect, the will, and the imagination, to bring that life before our consciousness. We have to try to see how the lessons of that life apply to the particular person who is making the meditation—to me myself. Finally, we resolve to put these two insights into practice so that in fact we will take a step forward in eliminating the sins that hold us back from union with Christ and will develop the virtues that will help us on our way to that union. All this is clearly stated by the *Catechism of the Catholic Church.*

[9] Ibid., no. 5, p. 83.
[10] See above, the section on "Language and Prayer", pp. 155–60.

Meditation engages thought, imagination, emotion, and desire. This mobilization of faculties is necessary in order to deepen our convictions of faith, prompt the conversion of our heart, and strengthen our will to follow Christ.[11]

If this is what is meant by Christian meditation, it should be clear why it is important. To act in a Christian way, we have to have a grasp of the truths of our faith that is real enough and personal enough to influence *our* conduct. Furthermore, unless we do have this real assent to the truths and commands of our faith, we will not have anything to counterbalance the more immediate and the more obvious attractions of the world, the flesh, and the devil.

A modern Carmelite, Sr. Ruth Burrows, has written very simply and to the point concerning the necessity for feeding the mind with good material if we are to pray seriously.

My mind has to supply strong motives for choosing God and his will in concrete instances. Here, I would say, lies our chief weakness, not sufficient importance is attached to the work the mind must do to set before the heart the motives for choosing what is not immediately and sensibly appealing. This deficiency implies a lack of seriousness and an unwillingness to take trouble. Anyone who really wants God will ceaselessly be thinking of what to do in order to go forward. They will have an eagerness to learn and willingly go to endless trouble. There is a tendency to think that good desires and strong motives will be infused; that if we remain quietly before the Lord in prayer, they will be borne in on us; that, when we are tempted and troubled we have only to go before the Lord and we will be changed.[12]

---

[11] CCC 2708.
[12] Ruth Burrows, *Interior Castle Explored* (London: Sheed & Ward, 1981), p. 23.

It is clear that meditation is not prayer in the way that petition, thanksgiving, or adoration may be called prayer. Meditation is using our head about what we have read and then applying it to ourselves. Using the example of "Blessed are the pure in heart, for they shall see God", Guigo shows how we might consider that it is the pure in heart, not in body, who will see God. So it is not enough to have hands clean from evil deeds unless our minds are cleansed from impure thoughts. He thinks about biblical figures, such as Job, and how he practiced purity of heart. Then he thinks about the rewards of seeing God face to face:

> After meditation has so pondered upon purity of heart it begins to think of the reward, of how glorious and joyful it would be to see the face of the Lord so greatly longed for, fairer than all the sons of men, no longer rejected and wretched, not with that earthly beauty with which His mother clothed Him, but wearing the robe of immortality and crowned with the diadem which His Father bestowed upon Him on the day of His resurrection and glory, the day which the Lord has made.[13]

The text thus passes through what Guigo calls "the anvil of meditation" and so acquires a new dimension. The text now holds out to the one meditating the promise of a joy possessed by the pure of heart, and he begins to sense "a first intimation of that sweetness" possessed by the pure in heart, but it is only a hint or a vague presentiment of this purity that his meditation has shown to be so full of joy:

> As long as it is meditating, so long is it suffering, because it does not feel that sweetness which, as meditation shows, belongs to purity of heart, but which it does not give.[14]

[13] *Ladder*, no. 5, p. 83.
[14] Ibid.

Meditation deepens and enriches our understanding and appreciation of the text, but it remains a kind of thinking *about* something. Christian meditation, based on God's revelation, begins with receiving some aspect of the Gospel and then working on this given truth; "meditation chews it and breaks it up" so that we may understand it better. The more we understand, the more we want to possess the object of our meditation, but meditation by itself will never unite us with the object of our desire.

The requirements for meditation are knowledge of the faith, which comes to us from reading, and knowledge of self, which comes from the examination of conscience. Meditation is made about ourselves, in the light of faith, in order to reform what needs reforming and to strengthen what should be strengthened. A person trying to develop the virtue of chastity has to know what the demands of Christianity are concerning this virtue. Then he has to see how he meets these demands and where he fails. From the habitual examination of conscience he will determine that he has a particular sort of failing in relation to chastity that leads, if unchecked, to actually sinning. From a particular examination of conscience in connection with this particular sin, he will conclude that he must resolve, say, to avoid a particular occasion of sin. From the general examination of conscience at the end of the day, he will see not only how this resolution has been kept, but also how it has fitted into a pattern of wrongdoing in other areas of his life. Perhaps things are developing for the better; perhaps there has been a serious fall; but in either case he will have to pray, and go on praying, for the virtue in a general way, but also for the strength to comply with one particular aspect of the virtue as it applies to him.

Prayer

> So the soul, seeing that it cannot attain by itself to that sweet-
> ness of knowing and feeling for which it longs, and that the
> more "the heart abases itself", the more "God is exalted",
> humbles itself and betakes itself to prayer, saying: Lord, you
> are not seen except by the pure of heart.[15]

Meditation has led to understanding of what we need and
then to wanting it. We also begin to see that we are going to
need help if we are ever to obtain what we want, and we
turn to prayer. For example, I have begun to understand in
a way that touches me personally that purity of heart is indispensable, because without it I will never see God. I then
begin to desire it, but I soon realize that without God's grace
I will never be able to achieve it. So, I turn to prayer. Scupoli says that mental prayer "is the lifting up of our heart to
God in actual or virtual supplication for anything we desire".[16] This prayer is actual when we put our petition into
words, for example, "O Lord, grant me this grace for thine
honour." [17] Or if we are tempted, we can send a cry for help
to God: "Be thou at hand, O God, to help me, that I yield
not to mine enemies." [18] We have already seen, how this
"arrow prayer" can be used.[19] By virtual supplication, he
means "the lifting up the heart to God to obtain some grace;
simply showing him our need, without further speech or
discourse".[20] There is also another sort of virtual prayer,
"which consists in a mere glance of the mind to God im-

[15] Ibid., no. 6, p. 86.
[16] SC 45, p. 117.
[17] Ibid.
[18] Ibid., p. 118.
[19] See above, pp. 141–42, no. 2b.
[20] SC 45, p. 118.

ploring his aid, which glance is a silent remembrancer and supplication for the grace which we have asked before".[21]

It seems to be an almost inevitable mistake to think that at this stage our prayer becomes nothing but an unformulated, nonverbal striving for what we need. This, however, is a serious mistake, and we have to ask in a human way for what it is we need. Asking in a human way involves the use of language, and prayer as Scupoli and the tradition understand it, is prayer that uses words, either, as he says, actually or virtually, for what we need.

Guigo puts it this way:

So give me, Lord, some pledge of what I hope to inherit, at least one drop of heavenly rain with which to refresh my thirst, for I am on fire with love. So the soul by such burning words inflames its own desire, makes known its state, and by such spells it seeks to call its spouse.[22]

Contemplation

But the Lord, whose eyes are upon the just and whose ears can catch not only the words, but the very meaning of their prayers, does not wait until the longing soul has said all its say, but breaks in upon the middle of its prayer, runs to meet it in all haste.[23]

Contemplation, as Catholic spiritual theology has understood it, means first of all a direct experience of God, and, secondly, an awareness that this experience is the gift of God. Contemplation understood in this way is not a form of

---

[21] Ibid., p. 119.
[22] *Ladder*, no. 6, p. 86.
[23] Ibid., no. 7, p. 87.

ascetical prayer. Ascetical prayer is prayer in which, assisted
by the grace of God, we use our ordinary faculties to read,
to meditate, and to ask for what we need. Contemplation
begins when the life of prayer begins to be dominated by the
Holy Spirit in ways that can be neither foreseen nor controlled. All we can do is to prepare ourselves to receive this
gift through reading, meditation, and prayer, but this preparation is not a guarantee that supernatural contemplation
will result. This is just the way things are, and St. Teresa
taught, as we saw above, that those who are not so called
would be greatly discouraged if they did not grasp the truth
that contemplation is something given by God and does not
depend on merit.

There is, however, a simplified form of meditation that
has sometimes been called *acquired contemplation* and that St.
John of the Cross calls a *prayer of loving attention*.[24] It seems to
be the case that meditation as "the busy application of the
mind to seek with the help of one's own reason for hidden
knowledge of the truth", that is, as a constant looking for
new considerations that will move the will to love and serve
God, often becomes more and more difficult. One reason
for this is a perfectly natural one. If, for example, we have
meditated for years on the agony in the garden, there are
probably relatively few new considerations that will be discovered. But considerations are a means to a greater love of
God and a deeper desire to serve him. They are not an end
in themselves. If we lose sight of this truth, then prayer will
become burdensome in an unhelpful way. Rather than forc-

---

[24] For example, "Since God, then, as giver, is communing with the soul by
means of loving and simple knowledge, the soul must likewise commune with
Him by receiving with a loving and simple knowledge or advertence, so that
knowledge may be united with knowledge and love with love" (St. John of
the Cross, *The Living Flame of Love*, stanza 3, no. 32, in *Complete Works*, trans.
and ed. by E. Allison Peers, new ed. [London: Burns & Oates, 1954], 3:69).

ing the mind to look for new considerations that will move the soul to love God, we should remain quietly in his presence. This prayer of loving attention is often called affective prayer. St. Jane Frances de Chantal says that this form of simplified meditation is:

> to keep ourselves simply in God's presence, by looking at Him with the eyes of faith in each mystery, conversing with Him by words full of confidence, heart to heart, but very secretly, as if we did not wish our good angel to know it.[25]

There is not anything necessarily mystical about this prayer, although as a means to our salvation it requires the grace of God. It represents the natural development of perhaps years in which gradually our mind and heart turn more readily to God and the things of God. Through a natural activity of habituating ourselves to making the divine presence real to ourselves, we begin to be able to content ourselves with that presence rather than trying to arrive at the position in which we are aware of its existence. The prayer is said to be simpler because it is one in which thinking plays a relatively small part. It is not simple in the sense that it is always easy to do, but because considerations, the "busy application of the mind", no longer play a large part in our prayer.

In the first half of the twentieth century there were endless debates as to whether or not contemplation was the best name for this sort of prayer and how exactly it was to be understood. Should it be looked on as a kind of halfway house between ascetical prayer and mystical prayer, or did it really mark a radical break with ascetical prayer and the beginning of mystical experience? These and similar questions were debated with a great deal of energy, and as a writer in

---

[25] St. Jane Frances de Chantal, *The Spiritual Life*, compiled by the Sisters of the Visitation (London: Sands, 1928), p. 180.

the *Dictionnaire de spiritualité* rather plaintively remarks, the arguments were abandoned more because of the death of the combatants than because any very clear results had been obtained.[26]

On the other hand, it does not seem to have been denied that a great many people who pray regularly experience this *simplifying* and *slowing down* of prayer, coupled, often enough, with an active distaste for meditation. Now assuming this is not the result of sin, carelessness, or bad health, then this means a simpler, less active prayer is called for. There should be no disquiet or worry about adopting this simpler form of prayer. We should not force it on ourselves, but if it develops, then it should be accepted and used.[27]

In her autobiography St. Teresa talks about how meditation often grows into a quieter, less active form of prayer, a form of prayer that is dominated by the will. We meditate by using our minds on, say, some scene of the Passion. We reflect for a time and think of the pains Christ bore for us, why he suffered them, who it was that bore them, and with what love he suffered them. She goes on, in a very characteristic way, to say:

> But we must not always tire ourselves by going in search of such ideas; we must sometimes remain by His side with our

---

[26] "La controverse finit moins par un accord de principe que par défaut de combattants. La mort avait éclairci leur rang" (*Dictionnaire de spiritualité*, ed. Marcel Viller, S.J. [Paris: G. Beauchesne et ses fils, 1932–], vol. 10, col. 1937). On the other hand, the author admits that the problems themselves have remained.

[27] In *The Living Flame of Love*, St. John of the Cross denounces the "Three Blind Guides of the Soul". The first of these are spiritual directors who try to force everyone into a form of prayer suitable only for beginners ("and please God they would even know this much"). But persons called to a prayer of loving attention must be allowed to develop through its use (stanza 3, nos. 29–54, 3:67–82).

minds hushed in silence. If we can, we should occupy ourselves in looking upon Him who is looking at us; keep Him
company; talk with Him; pray to Him; humble ourselves
before Him; have our delight in Him; and remember that
He never deserved to be there. Anyone who can do this,
though he may be but a beginner of prayer, will derive great
benefit from it, for this kind of prayer brings many benefits:
at least, so my soul has found.[28]

We tend to forget that the practice of prayer is itself an ascetical discipline. That is, prayer is one of the ways we train
ourselves toward leading a life that is pleasing to God. The
practice of any good habit strengthens other virtues, and prayer
does at least this. Of course there is more to it than merely
getting up regularly in the morning, but, nonetheless, it is
important to remember that the discipline of regular prayer
is one of the ways we strengthen the whole moral system.
But, because prayer involves the intellect and will, it is also
true that the training of these two faculties in prayer will
bring about changes in the way we think and desire. Meditation and discursive prayer will gradually become easier as
they become a habit, and the will, over the years, gradually
learns to respond to the suggestions and promptings of the
intellect in an immediate and peaceful way that gradually
leads to a closer union with God.[29]

---

[28] St. Teresa of Jesus, *Life*, chap. 13, in vol. 1 of *Complete Works*, trans. and
ed. E. Allison Peers (London and New York: Sheed & Ward, 1946), p. 83.

[29] Jordan Aumann, *Spiritual Theology* (London: Sheed & Ward, 1980). Fr.
Aumann puts it this way: "Because affective prayer is essentially an operation
of the will, it serves to deepen the union of the soul with God by acts of love.
And since all the infused virtues are increased with the increase of charity,
affective prayer is a powerful means for growth in virtue. It is likewise a great
stimulus for the practice of the Christian virtues because of the sweetness and
consolation it gives. It is, lastly, an excellent disposition and preparation for the
prayer of simplicity" (p. 325).

Yet the prayer of the will, or affective prayer, is ascetical; that is, it is a training in virtue in a much more serious way than a mere strengthening of our good habits. Affective prayer is a prayer that requires the development of a good deal of humility and simplicity for its practice; and these virtues, of humility and simplicity, are themselves developed through the practice of affective prayer. Humility is forced on us because we are made to realize that we do not pray very well, and we become more and more aware that we are dependent on God for the sort of prayer life we in fact have. Then, again, simplicity is strengthened because we gradually learn to trust in the providence of God as it shows itself in our prayer.

Many people whose prayer seems to be moving toward this more affective, or simpler, sort of prayer are at times troubled by the thought that they may be wasting their time and that the dryness and difficulties they experienced when they were trying to use a prayer of considerations were their own fault. Sometimes they try to force themselves back into using a prayer of considerations. At other times, perhaps, they even suspect that the whole enterprise of prayer has been a mistake and that the strength and delight they may have experienced in prayer at an earlier period of their lives were really an illusion.

Insofar as the prayer of simplicity is a quasi-natural development, then it is, at least in the abstract, easy enough to see whether this development toward a simpler sort of prayer is a good one. We have to ask two questions. These questions concern the success and the profit of the prayer. By success, I only mean a certain ease with this kind of prayer. Is it at least as easy to do as meditation based on considerations? If the prayer of simplicity is in any way forced, it will quickly prove more difficult than meditation. Affective prayer is supposed to be simpler and less tiring than a prayer of considerations. Well is it? That is the first test: Does this kind of prayer work for us? If we end up afterward limp and tired like a wet rag, and perhaps even with a headache, then it is clear we are forcing things and that we should once again try to use a prayer based more on the imagination or considerations.

The second test is the effect this prayer has on our lives. The test of good prayer, as Abbot Chapman says over and over again, is the effect it has on our lives, not how we feel during the prayer.[30] Affective prayer should stimulate us, in no *less* degree (at the very least), to a strengthening of the virtues and fighting the vices than does a prayer of considerations.

It should be noted that the standard of comparison is the prayer of the person actually doing the praying. Obviously an ordinary person's affective prayer is not going to be as effective as a prayer of considerations might have been for a saint. The point at issue is: Am *I* now being led to this kind of prayer, and, secondly, does it help *me* to strive after Christian holiness? If the answer is yes to both those questions, then it is time to engage in affective prayer.

Sometimes, this prayer is easy to do. One authority for the ease of this sort of prayer is St. Ignatius himself. In a letter he wrote:

> All meditation where the understanding works, fatigues the body. There are *other meditations*, equally in the order of God, which are restful, full of peace for the understanding, without labour for the interior faculties of the soul, and which are performed without either physical or interior effort.[31]

---

[30] "What matters is the result. *The after effects of good prayer are more definite than the prayer itself;* I mean a determination to follow God's Will, and to care for nothing else, without any reason to be given for the determination" (letter 17, "To a Literary Man", in John Chapman, *Spiritual Letters* [London: Sheed & Ward, 1935], p. 62).

[31] Cited in A. Poulain, S.J., *The Graces of Interior Prayer*, trans. Leonora L. Yorke Smith, pref. by D. Considine, S.J. (London: Paul, Trench, Trübner, 1910), p. 45.

On the other hand, sometimes this prayer is very difficult indeed. St. Jane Frances de Chantal, who was a great proponent of this sort of prayer, faced up frankly to this:

> You put me to confusion by asking me about my prayer. Alas! Daughter, it is usually nothing but distractions and a little suffering; for what can a poor pitiful mind filled with all sorts of business do? I tell you plainly in confidence, that for about twenty years God has taken away from me all power of any prayer of the understanding and reflection—that is meditation. And all I can do is to suffer and keep myself very simply before God, clinging with complete abandonment to His action within me, making no acts unless incited to them by Him, waiting there for whatever in His goodness he will give me.[32]

The difficulties in this sort of prayer do not come from having to meditate when in fact we cannot, but in trying to keep distractions at bay. We have to go slowly and be sure that we are drawn to the prayer of loving attention, that is, that we have not *forced* ourselves into a false state of quiet. If we can use our imagination, and even simple considerations, then we should do so. St. John of the Cross and St. Teresa both teach that there are periods when we swing back and forth from a prayer of considerations to that based largely on the will. The thing is to be quiet and to be attentive to the way God is leading us. We must try to conform ourselves to the will of God, even in our life of prayer, and not try to draw the will of God down to our level so that we try to make it conform to what we want.

One way of ensuring that we are not being lazy, and that we are not wasting our time, is to have a few verses of a psalm or the saying of a saint or a few lines of a hymn that

---

[32] Jane Frances de Chantal, *Spiritual Life*, p. 148.

we can gently use when we find ourselves distracted. For example, consider the following lines of St. Bernard of Clairvaux:

> Jesus, the very thought of Thee
> With sweetness fills my breast;
> But sweeter far Thy Face to see,
> And in Thy presence rest.[33]

If you are practicing a prayer of loving awareness of God but have begun to lose the sense of his presence, or if you seem to have completely given yourselves over to distractions, then try quietly saying those lines. Do not try to force all your attention onto the poem, because that will draw your will away from the love of God. On the other hand, if you say the lines quietly without concentrating on them, then the imagination has something other to work on than the distractions that are perhaps very nearly pulling you away from attending to God. The resulting state is that you are paying attention to something you know not what, but at the same time you are aware that you are saying the lines of the poem and that those lines have a meaning of which you are dimly aware. But, to repeat the point, it is not the meaning of the lines that is the focus of your attention. On the contrary, it is the love for God that dominates your consciousness in an obscure way.

---

[33] St. Bernard of Clairvaux, "Jesu dulcis memoria", trans. Edward Caswall, in the *St. Gregory Hymnal and Catholic Choir Book*, comp. Nicola A. Montani (Philadelphia: St. Gregory Guild, Inc., 1940), no. 17.

CHAPTER NINE

THE PRACTICE OF PRAYER

Remember, sweet Jesus, whom I seek to please, that it is
thee I desire to love above all. Make me joyfully fulfil thy
commands, so that I may see thy face for ever, and deal
with me so mercifully before I die that I may know that
I love nothing so much as God.

—The Monk of Farne, "Meditation Addressed to Christ
  Crucified," *The Meditations of a Certain Monk*

Reading, meditation, prayer, and contemplation are all activities of one process that, with the saints, ends in a union
of love with God, a union that begins in this life and ends
with the vision of the Blessed Trinity in eternity. So Guigo
writes:

These degrees are so linked together, each one working also
for the others, that the first degrees are of little or no use
without the last, while the last can never, or hardly ever, be
won without the first.[1]

---

[1] Guigo II, *The Ladder of Monks*, no. 13, trans. with an introduction by
Edmund College, O.S.A., and James Walsh, S.J. (New York: Doubleday [Im-
age Books], 1978), p. 93.

192

Analyzing an activity always risks detaching its various components into a series of disparate parts that have lost their interconnection. This is very true of the spiritual life. We have to remember that its various stages are all meant to apply to aspects of a lived experience, an experience in which at different times one theme will have the focus of attention and then another. At the beginning, the struggle with obvious sins will usually dominate, to be followed by periods in which strengthening of the virtues will take the center stage. Later on, it will be a desire for union with God that will cause other considerations to fall into the background.

There is an order to be observed, and so, although contemplation is the crown and glory of the spiritual life, that does not mean we should begin by trying to be contemplatives. Guigo says that contemplation can "hardly ever" be won without the other stages being in place. This "hardly ever" is his formulation of the truth that, because we are dealing with experiences in which God is the principal cause, we cannot deny the possibility and the reality of exceptions. The freedom of the individual must be respected, not only because freedom is a good in itself, but also because it may be that in any particular case, God is calling that individual in a special way.

People are very different, and the way God gradually awakens a person's heart and soul to turn to him varies from one soul to the next. For this reason there must be a real element of freedom in each one's approach to God. St. Teresa puts it this way:

> It is very important that no soul which practises prayer, whether little or much, should be subjected to undue constraint or limitation. Since God has given it such dignity, it must be allowed to roam through these mansions—through those above, those below and those on either side. It must not be compelled to

remain for a long time in one single room—not, at least, unless it is in the room of self-knowledge.[2]

On the other hand, St. Teresa herself insists time and time again that meditation, especially on the person of Jesus Christ, is the usual gateway to contemplation. In this she is at one with St. John of the Cross and the tradition of Catholic mysticism. Freedom must be preserved, but this is no blanket dispensation from the ordinary, run-of-the-mill progression that is the lot of most people. The exceptions are the consequence of God's activity, and because they are exceptions, it cannot be assumed ahead of time that they will happen. Certainly the spiritual life should not be based on the assumption that they will happen.

Guigo argues that ordinarily one stage not only precedes another but also causes the succeeding one. We cannot meditate unless we read. If we do not read and hear about Jesus Christ, then we will not be able to consider his life and see how it applies to us:

> Reading comes first, and is, as it were, the foundation; it provides the subject matter we must use for meditation.[3]

Reading is also a cause of meditation because it leads us to penetrate into the deeper meaning of what we read:

> Meditation considers more carefully what is to be sought after; it digs, as it were, for treasure which it finds and reveals, but since it is not in meditation's power to seize upon the treasure, it directs us to prayer.[4]

---

[2] St. Teresa of Avila, *Interior Castle*, mansion 1, chap. 2, trans. and ed. E. Allison Peers (Garden City, N.Y.: Doubleday [Image Books], 1962), p. 37.

[3] *Ladder*, no. 12, p. 92.

[4] Ibid.

The purpose of meditation is to put the way we live our lives into relation to the example of Christ, so that we can imitate him more perfectly. This involves wanting something for ourselves that we realize is only possible with God's help. We are seeking purity of heart, but this is not going to be achieved without the practices of the ascetical life. Prayer in connection with meditation may ask for something uncomplicated, such as avoiding an occasion of sin or for patience with a particular person. As progress is made, the prayer may become more and more an overwhelming desire for union with God.

> Prayer lifts itself up to God with all its strength, and begs for the treasure it longs for, which is the sweetness of contemplation. Contemplation when it comes rewards the labours of the other three; it inebriates the thirsting soul with the dew of heavenly sweetness.[5]

The degrees of the spiritual life are linked together, and in the ordinary way of things they follow one another "not only in the order of time but of causality".[6] This unity of time and causality is important for actually practicing the spiritual combat.

We have already seen enough of Guigo's teaching to understand that temporal priority does not mean that the preceding stage is left behind for good. He is teaching us that one stage is required before the next is undertaken. To pray we must know something about what the Gospel tells us about God and ourselves, and we must also know something about how God's promises and demands apply to ourselves and what we should do to bring our lives into harmony with these demands. This does not mean that once we have begun

[5] Ibid.
[6] Ibid.

to pray for the means to develop a particular virtue, we can give up reading and meditation for good. There is an order to be observed, and a certain causality is at work, but the order is constantly to be repeated, and the causality is reciprocal.

> From this we may gather that reading without meditation is sterile, meditation without reading is liable to error, prayer without meditation is lukewarm, meditation without prayer is unfruitful, prayer when it is fervent wins contemplation, but to obtain it without prayer would be rare, even miraculous.[7]

Reading and Meditation

St. Paul wrote that "what we preach is not ourselves, but Jesus Christ as Lord, with ourselves as your servants for Jesus' sake" (2 Cor 4:5). If this is to be accepted in any serious way, we have to understand what it means and apply it to ourselves. This point has already been discussed in several places.[8] Building on what has already been said, we can apply the principles directly to the practice of prayer.

Our reading will be sterile, that is, it will have no effect on our lives, unless we meditate on what we read. On the other hand, unless we read, our meditation, and the prayer based on it, will not be Christian. We have to "tie down" or apply what we read to our own lives, and we have to ensure that we see our own lives in the light of Christian truth. One of the great obstacles to this reciprocal relation is distractions.

---

[7] Ibid., no. 13, p. 93.

[8] For example, in chap. 5, in the section on "Spiritual Exercises concerning the Understanding".

Jesus said, "Peace I leave with you; my peace I give to you; not as the world gives do I give to you" (Jn 14:27); and he went on to tell us that because of this gift we are not to let our hearts be troubled or afraid. There are moments in the lives of most Christians when they have a vivid sense of this peace "which passes all understanding" (Phil 4:7). On the other hand, St. Paul in his Second Letter to the Corinthians says that when he came to Macedonia he was afflicted at every turn—"fighting without and fear within" (2 Cor 7:5); and without comparing ourselves to St. Paul, most of us know what he is talking about. We have been promised the gift of peace, but even the great Apostle appears to have had difficulties putting the gift into practice. Yet we have to pray as we are and where we are. We have gradually to detach ourselves from whatever interferes with our interior peace. Detachment does not mean we pretend our difficulties and our moods do not exist; but we have to resist the temptation to identify what we are with these difficulties and moods.

We are all familiar with the experience of being moved or inspired by something and then swinging to the other extreme and becoming lethargic and depressed either because we cannot attain what has inspired us or because it no longer seems to be inspiring. This is only a particular instance of the fact that our human nature is subject to moods and swings, which are often the result of factors that have little, apparently, to do directly with the spiritual life, such as health, the weather, or worry about practical things. Yet it is worth remembering that it is the same person who had a headache, is depressed by the rainy dark weather, or has to pay the mortgage who is trying to pray. We bring what we are, and what we are doing, to our prayer, and that is why we have to try to see our daily lives as a preparation for our prayer. It is inevitable that our prayer will seem unsatisfactory, even depressing, if we allow ourselves to be dominated by our external concerns and interior worries.

Cassian sometimes talks about our consciousness as an activity of the heart. This helps us remember that we are dealing with something that affects the whole man. He is not talking about thinking in abstraction from what he considers our fundamental task, the task, that is, of sanctifying ourselves with God's grace. This activity of the heart, this activity of the whole man, including thinking, he compares to a mill that is driven by water pressure.

> This activity of the heart is not inappropriately compared to millstones, which the swift rush of the waters turns with a violent revolving motion. As long as the water's force keeps them spinning they are utterly incapable of stopping their work.[9]

One way or another our minds seem to be working all the time. This activity may range anywhere from concentrated intellectual work to idle daydreaming. This has nothing to do with whether the ideas are good or bad but is merely to point out that the mind always seems to be working. Furthermore, we all know that we do not always seem to be entirely in control of what goes on in our minds. We may be trying to concentrate on writing an essay and find we are tempted to think about playing golf. We call this a distraction. What distracts us is not necessarily sinful, but it is something that gets in the way of what we are trying to do. In this case, what we are trying to do is to write the essay. Cassian

---

[9] Cassian, conference 1, "On the Goal of the Monk", chap. 18, no. 1, in John Cassian, *The Conferences*, trans. and annotated by Boniface Ramsey, O.P. (New York: Paulist Press, 1997), p. 57.

puts this in a very effective way by continuing his metaphor of the mill driven by water power:

> In the same way the mind cannot be free from agitating thoughts during the trials of the present life, since it is spinning around in the torrents of the trials that overwhelm it from all sides.[10]

The mind, then, is always in motion, and we sense that it is only by quieting the mind that we will find that peace necessary for a closer communion with God. How are we going to find this peace of heart that will enable us to become the temples of the Holy Spirit? There seem to be two sorts of answers. One, which is an old one but seems popular today, is to try to stop the mind from working. Try, so we are advised, to empty the mind of all thoughts and images, and wait peacefully for God. Leaving aside any theological considerations, it can at least be said this effort to empty the mind and to keep it still just does not work. The mind, as Cassian says, is like the mill driven by water power, and "it cannot cease operation at all so long as it is driven round by the pressure of the water." Trying to still the mind by our own efforts is to render ourselves less than human, not more than human. We have to use the water power for as long as we are driven by it.

We have then to use our minds and to try to feed its ceaseless activity with thoughts that will lead to peace of heart and so help in our sanctification. The mill is not going to cease operation, but it is possible for the person in charge of it to decide whether he prefers wheat or barley or weeds to be ground. "Indeed", he says, "only that will be ground which

[10] Ibid., no. 2, p. 57.

has been accepted by the person entrusted with the responsibility or the work." [11]

So, the lesson is clear. You cannot stop the mind from working, so feed it with good material rather than bad. The mind will gradually become fixed on what it thinks about. If we think about good things, we will gradually obtain a taste for them.

> For if, as we have said, we constantly return to meditating on Holy Scripture and raise our awareness to the recollection of spiritual realities and to the desire for perfection and the hope of future blessedness, it is inevitable that the spiritual thoughts which have arisen from this will cause the mind to dwell on the things that we have been meditating on. [12]

On the other hand, if we feed weeds into the mill, we must expect things to work out badly.

> But if we are overcome by laziness and negligence and let ourselves be taken up with wicked behaviour and silly conversations, or if we get involved in worldly concerns and unnecessary preoccupations, the result will be as if a kind of weed had sprung up, and this will impose harmful labour on our heart. And, according to the words of the Lord, the Saviour, wherever the treasure of our works and intentions is, there also will necessarily abide our heart. [13]

Meditation and Prayer

We have seen that prayer is one of the means we must use if we are to fulfill the moral demands of our Christian profes-

[11] Ibid., no. 1, p. 57.
[12] Ibid., no. 2, p. 57.
[13] Ibid., no. 3, p. 57.

sion,[14] and in this sense it follows on meditation. We have to look now at the other side of the matter and understand that without resolving to live as Christians, we will not be able to pray. In short, neglecting prayer is harmful to the practice of Christian morality, but neglecting meditation and morality is detrimental to prayer itself.

This teaching is an old one and was set out with force by Cassian, who emphasized the necessity of trying to practice the virtues if we are to pray well. At the same time, however, he insists that it is only by persevering in prayer that we will be able to live a virtuous life. In short, prayer requires the practice of the virtues, but the practice of the virtues requires constant prayer. If we are really serious about our prayer, we have, first of all, to struggle against our sins and then try to practice justice, temperance, fortitude, and the other Christian virtues. If we are going to build a spiritual and lofty tower, like the man in St. Luke's Gospel, we have first to "sit down and count the cost" (Lk 14:28). The cost is the willingness to struggle against our passions and to develop our potentiality for good. We can never have a stable and fruitful life of prayer unless:

> a complete purging of vice has been carried out first. And once the tottering and dead rubbish of the passions has been dug out, the firm foundations of simplicity and humility can be placed in what may be called the living and solid ground of our heart, on the gospel rock.[15]

This laying of the foundations of the spiritual life, by fighting the passions and beginning to practice the virtues, is, in Cassian's view, an integral part of the spiritual life. There can

---

[14] See above, chap. 7.
[15] Cassian, conference 9, "On Prayer", chap. 2, no. 3, p. 330.

be no life of prayer without these foundations, and the idea that we can reach the higher flights of mysticism by endeavoring to bypass the humdrum, daily effort to live in terms of the moral demands of the Gospel is a false one.

One clear argument in favor of the necessity of a moral foundation to prayer is a very practical one. Unless we try to live in the peace of Christ, by doing what he wants us to do, we will not be able to pray.

> For the mind in prayer is shaped by the state that it was previously in, and, when we sink into prayer, the image of the same deeds, words, and thoughts plays itself out before out eyes. This makes us angry or sad, depending on our previous condition, or it recalls past lusts or business, or it strikes us with foolish laughter—I am ashamed even to say it—at the suggestion of something ludicrous that was said or done, or it makes us fly back to previous conversations. [16]

And so, he concludes that "what we want to find ourselves like while we are praying, that we ought to prepare ourselves to be before the time for prayer." I do not think anyone has ever put this important truth more simply or more clearly. Without the effort to live a good life, we will not *in fact* be able to pray. Every time in our daily life that we deliberately sin, we are weakening our capacity to pray.

Cassian compares the nature of the soul to a very fine feather or very light wing, which, if it is not damaged or affected by moisture falling on it, is carried on high almost naturally to the heights of heaven by the lightness of its nature and the aid of the slightest breath of wind. On the other hand, if it is weighed down by moisture, it will not be carried aloft but borne down to the depths of earth by the weight

[16] Ibid., chap. 3, no. 3, p. 331.

of the moisture it has received. So our soul, if it is weighed down with faults that touch it and with the cares of this world or damaged by the moisture of injurious lusts, will sink to the earth and remain there. And so our Lord warns us: "But take heed to yourselves lest your hearts be weighed down with dissipation and drunkenness and cares of this life" (Lk 21:34).

Cassian is not teaching that we have to be perfect if we are going to pray. Nor is he telling us that a person in a state of mortal sin cannot offer up his prayer to God. He is, however, telling us, in no uncertain terms, that it is the same person sinning and praying and that we bring what we are, and what we have been, to our prayer.

> Therefore if we wish our prayers to penetrate not only the heavens, but even what is beyond the heavens, we should make an effort to draw our mind, purged of every earthly vice and cleansed of all the dregs of the passions, back to its natural lightness, so that thus its prayer might ascend to God, unburdened by the weight of any vice.[17]

If we are going to lead a Christian life, then, we must pray, because prayer, from the ascetical standpoint, is one of the ways we obtain the grace we need to lead a good life pleasing to God. On the other hand, without meditation and the resolution to lead a better life, our prayer will be lukewarm.

Prayer and Contemplation

We have seen that vocal prayer covers many sorts of activity; these include liturgical prayer, spiritual exercises such as the rosary, and nonliturgical devotions generally. It also includes

[17] Ibid., chap. 4, no. 3, p. 332.

the prayer of aspirations or ejaculatory prayer, and Scupoli pays a good deal of attention to this sort of prayer, although his extended treatment of it is to be found in the section on spiritual exercises. Aspirations are short phrases directed in an immediate or unreflective way to God and are usually described as coming from the heart. Because we desire to love God and to be united with him, so this prayer of aspirations comes from our love for God and expresses itself in a variety of ways and in the most diverse circumstances.[18]

It has been said that to pray is to desire—"Prier c'est désirer", said Fénelon;[19] and to desire something, in rather old-fashioned English, is to aspire after it. But when we pray, we are not only desiring to be united with God, we are also raising our mind and heart to him, and so St. John Chrysostom says that prayer is an elevation of the soul to God.[20] However, in the language of spirituality, the word "aspiration" is often used in a more specific way to designate prayer hurled, thrown, or flung from the heart or which springs forth from the will as sighs, lamentations, or bursts of joy and thanksgiving that are brief but fervent. St. Augustine, in a letter to Proba, talks about the prayers of the Fathers of the Desert that are "darted forth rapidly like arrows".[21] For this

[18] See "Aspirations", in *Dictionnaire de spiritualité*, ed. Marcel Viller, S.J. [Paris: G. Beauchesne et ses fils, 1932–], vol. 1, cols. 1017–25.

[19] Ibid., col. 1017.

[20] Ibid.

[21] "It is said the brothers of Egypt have certain prayers which they recite often, but they are very brief, and are, so to speak, darted forth rapidly like arrows, so that the alert attention, which is necessary in prayer, does not fade and grow heavy through long-drawn-out periods. By this practice they show quite well that, just as this attention is not to be whipped up if it cannot be sustained, so, if it can be sustained, it is not to be broken off too quickly" (*The Fathers of the Church* [New York: Fathers of the Church, 1953], 18:391).

reason this prayer has also been called ejaculatory prayer, from *jaculari*—to aim, to shoot at, and so to strive after, to seek.[22]

They are also called affections, because they have their source in the affective aspect of the soul and are at the basis of the will and sentiment. Galenius defines this prayer as "expeditus affectus erga Deum, ut summum bonum", that is, a prompt, or ready-to-hand affection or emotion directed toward God as our ultimate good.[23] This prayer has been given different names to highlight its different aspects:

> As touching the heart and will, it is an affection.
> As an élan (a rush, sally, bound, spurt), it is an anagogic movement.
> As a short and ardent prayer that raises the mind, it is ejaculatory prayer.
> As an expression of an intimate and profound desire, it is an aspiration.

This sort of prayer presupposes on the part of a believer the consciousness of his own powerlessness and his knowledge that there is a superior power capable of making up for this deficiency. It is a precise, specific appeal made by the soul in all humility and confidence to God, whom it knows is ready to hear it and is capable of helping it.

However, the mere knowledge of our helplessness and powerlessness is not in itself sufficient to give birth to the desire. There must be a movement from the thought to the desire, and this movement from the head to the heart will only happen if the soul is already penetrated by love. Fénelon said, "We pray only to the extent we desire, and we desire only to the extent we love." So aspirations find their deepest source

---

[22] *Dictionnaire de spiritualité*, vol. 1, col. 1018.
[23] Ibid.

in love, even though some exercise of the mind is required to formulate them and to remember them.

St. Francis de Sales writes about human love in which aspirations come almost spontaneously. He says:

> Those who love with a human and natural love have their thoughts incessantly engaged by the thing they love, their hearts filled with affection for it and their mouths ever employed in its praise. When absent, they lose no opportunity to testifying to their affection by letters. They do not come upon a tree without inscribing the name of their beloved on its bark. Thus, those who truly love God can never cease to think of Him, to sigh for Him, to aspire to Him, and to speak of Him.[24]

Often this love, without ceasing to exist, remains at it were latent, underneath the ideas at the forefront of consciousness and the daily occupation and duties of life. One can stimulate, wake up, or focus on this love by an act of the will; either by deliberately imagining the person loved or "by short but ardent movements of your heart to arouse yourself to a passionate and tender affect for this divine spouse".[25]

We know that the repetition of any act tends to strengthen the capacity to do the act another time. This psychological principle is at the basis of the establishment of both the virtues and the vices. So aspirations that are difficult to practice at the beginning become easier with practice. We are talking about the love of God; we know that this love is God's gift. On the other hand, supernatural love is practiced and devel-

---

[24] St. Francis de Sales, *Introduction to the Devout Life*, pt. 2, chap. 13, trans. and ed. John K. Ryan (New York: Harper & Brothers, 1950), p. 56.
[25] Ibid.

oped in the same way as natural acts. And so, in a way that may be difficult to untangle conceptually, but is quite clear in practice, the use of the prayer of aspirations both strengthens and deepens that love we have for God, and at the same time the acts themselves are facilitated by the activity of loving God through the prayer of aspirations.

Again, because love tends toward union, aspirations are a means for the heart to unite itself with the object of its love. They help us to distance ourselves from an over-intellectualist form of prayer, which can keep us from the deeper aspects of our being. And that is why St. Teresa of Avila said that the progress of the soul consists, not in much thinking, but in loving a great deal.

Aspirations are directed toward many different ends, but one of these is union with God. They move us toward the treasure of heart and prepare us to receive it:

> So give me, Lord, some pledge of what I hope to inherit, at least one drop of heavenly rain with which to refresh my thirst, for I am on fire with love.[26]

The practice of aspirations in made easier by the practice of recollection. St. Francis de Sales says that during the course of the day we should remember, or recollect, as often as we can that we are in the presence of God. In doing this, we do not create a new truth, but we train ourselves to recognize what is really the case. In the practice of recollection, we turn away from the distractions and worries of our daily life to the God who has his eyes fixed upon us "with an incomparable love".[27]

---

[26] *Ladder*, no. 6, p. 86.
[27] *Introduction to the Devout Life*, pt. 2, chap. 12, p. 54.

In the *Introduction to the Devout Life* he gives four different ways for putting ourselves into the presence of God.[28] These are based on the truths that God is everywhere, that God is within me, that Christ is watching me from heaven, and on the imaginative exercise that our Lord is sitting here with me in his humanity, helping me, consoling me, and strengthening me.[29]

First of all, we should consider the truth that God is in all things and in every place. We are like blind men who do not see the prince who is present among us but behave with respect when we are told of his presence. Although our faith assures us of his presence, we have to reflect on it if we are not to act as though he were far away.

Secondly, God is also present in a special way in the depth of our being. David calls him the God of my heart, and our Lord says, "I will love him and take up my abode with him." We have to balance the recognition of God's presence in the visible creation with his presence within us. He is nearer to us than our distractions, our thoughts, our desires, and our imaginings.

Then, says, St. Francis, we ought to try to think specifically of our Lord in his humanity watching us from heaven as we try to pray. It is as though he is looking at us through a chink in the wall, or looking over our shoulder. He is a watcher of whose presence we are aware but whom we cannot precisely identify.

Finally, we should imagine our Lord in his humanity, present with us, perhaps sitting beside us and helping us to

---

[28] Ibid., pt. 2, chap. 2, p. 42.

[29] These four ways of St. Francis should be compared to question 8 of the prima pars of the *Summa Theologiae* of St. Thomas. The question is on "The Existence of God in Things", and it provides the theological basis for St. Francis' teaching.

pray. If we are before the Blessed Sacrament, we ought to make a formal act of faith in his presence in the tabernacle.

> Remember . . . to retire occasionally into the solitude of your heart while you are outwardly engaged in business or association with others. This mental solitude cannot be prevented by the multitude of those who surround you. As they are not about your heart, but only about your body, your heart may remain in the presence of God alone.[30]

Recollecting that we are in the presence of God helps to establish the spiritual environment that makes the prayer of aspirations easier. At the same time, one way of establishing this awareness of the presence of God is through using the prayer of aspirations. Aspirations are usually described as coming from the heart, and using them helps us to return to the heart that desires to love God and to be united with him.

In the ordinary course of spiritual development, we begin with a determined effort to respond to the grace of God by fighting against those sins that would pull us back into a state of mortal sin. Later, if things go well, the effort to practice the virtues begins to be the center of our preoccupation. Finally, for a favored few, the desire to be united to Christ becomes the focus of attention. The life of prayer both follows this development and helps it to progress. Ascetical prayer is clearly connected with the first two stages and, also, in the form of the prayer of aspirations, is one of the means that prepare the way for contemplation.

Guigo makes it clear that to avoid this ordinary development would "be rare, even miraculous", and this is the teaching of the tradition of Catholic spirituality. One of the ornaments of this tradition is the unknown fourteenth-century mystic who wrote *The Cloud of Unknowing*. The work

---

[30] *Introduction to the Devout Life*, pt. 2, chap. 12, p. 54.

of this unknown author is of the highest intrinsic merit and has always enjoyed great authority in the Church. We turn to him for confirmation of the claim that there is no handy shortcut to the prayer of union. This can be simply demonstrated by taking four points from the text.

First of all, the author says that the contents of his book are only to be given to someone who is a serious Christian.

> I charge thee and I beseech thee ... [that] thou neither read it, write it, nor speak it, nor yet suffer it to be read, written, or spoken, by any other or to any other, unless it be by such a one or to such a one as hath (in thy supposing) in a true will and by a whole intent purposed him to be a perfect follower of Christ.[31]

Secondly, the Christian will have practiced reading, meditating, and praying as set out by Guigo.

> Nevertheless there be means in the which a contemplative prentice should be occupied, the which be these: Lesson, Meditation, and Orison. Or else, for thine understanding, they may be called: Reading, Thinking, and Praying. Of these three thou shalt find written in another book by another man much better than I can tell thee; and therefore it needeth not here to tell thee of the qualities of them.[32]

Thirdly, this thinking, or this meditation, is absolutely required to achieve genuine contemplation. He is very forceful that it is only by coming to know Jesus Christ that we will be able to enter into union with God. He uses the text from the tenth chapter of St. John, where Christ compares

---

[31] *The Cloud of Unknowing, Together with The Epistle of Privy Counsel*, prologue, ed. Abbot Justin McCann (London: Burns & Oates, 1952), p. 3.

[32] Ibid., chap. 35, p. 50.

himself to the door to the pasture, and says that those who try to get in by another way are thieves and robbers. The author of *The Cloud of Unknowing* says in his less well known *Epistle of Privy Counsel*:

> They enter by the door, that in beholding of the passion of Christ sorrow their wickedness, the which cause of that passion, with bitter reproving of themselves that have deserved and not suffered, and with pity and compassion of that worthy Lord that so vilely suffered and nothing deserved; and then lift up their hearts to the love and the goodness of his Godhead, in the which he vouchsafed to meek himself so low in our deadly manhood. All these enter by the door, and they shall be safe.[33]

It is only by reading, meditating, and praying on the life of Christ that we will enter into the pasture of contemplation. Nothing could be clearer, nor could be the author's view of those who teach anything else:

> And whoso entereth not by this door, but climbeth otherwise to perfection, by the subtle seeking and the curious fantastic working in his wild, wanton wits, leaving this common plain entry touched before and the true counsel of ghostly fathers: he, whatsoever he be, is not only a night thief, but a day skulker.[34]

He is a night thief because he leans "in his presumption to the singularity of his own wit and his will", rather than on any true counsel or sound tradition. He is a day skulker, that is, someone who lurks around avoiding work

[33] *The Epistle of Privy Counsel*, chap 9, in *Cloud*, p. 124.
[34] Ibid., p. 125.

and responsibility, because he steals the outward signs of contemplation "and hath not the fruit".[35]

Fourthly, the writer asks that anyone who reads the book
or talks about it should read the whole thing and try to present
the complete doctrine it teaches.

> And over this I charge thee and I beseech thee, by the au-
> thority of charity, if any such shall read it, write it, or speak
> it, or else hear it read or spoken, that thou charge them, as I
> do thee, for to take them time to read it, speak it, write it, or
> hear it, *all over*.[36]

If we do not follow the author's plea and read the whole
book, we are liable to take one part as stating his whole doctrine, without the necessary correctives and qualifications that
he in fact provides.

> Wherefore, if a man saw one matter and not another, per-
> adventure he might lightly be led into error. And therefore,
> for eschewing of this error both in thyself and in all other, I
> pray thee for charity do as I tell thee.[37]

Contemplation, as the tradition has understood it, develops
out of an ever closer identification with Jesus Christ, until
we can say with St. Paul, "it is no longer I who live, but
Christ who lives in me" (Gal 2:20). If we take the whole of
the *Cloud of Unknowing*, that is what it is teaching. The chapter on "How and why short prayer pierceth heaven"[38] has
to be read and understood in terms of our own Christian
principles.

[35] Ibid.
[36] *Cloud.*, prologue, p. 3 (my italics).
[37] Ibid., p. 4.
[38] Ibid., chap. 38, p. 54.

Simplicity in Prayer

If we are going to accept the teaching of Guigo, and of the *Cloud*, that prayer may lead to contemplation but also presupposes reading and meditation, we will have to learn to be less anxious about our spiritual lives. This simplicity is required whether the prayer is an ascetical prayer of loving attention or one of infused contemplation. Insofar as it is ascetical, it should not be confused with a deliberate effort either to empty the mind or to let God do everything without any acts of our own.[39] One of the greatest difficulties in persevering with any sort of ascetical prayer is the habit we quickly develop of watching ourselves praying and evaluating what we are doing. St. Jane Frances recognized this common failing and has some practical advice on how to deal with it. We have already seen the unflattering way she refers to her own prayer as "usually nothing but distractions and a little suffering",[40] and this arid, dry, and apparently ineffective prayer seems to have been the dominant note in her life.

> I speak about God, I give encouragement to others when opportunity arises, I write as if I feel and relish what I say, yet, all the while, it is with repugnance and against the grain: but it is impossible to explain this in the way I feel it.[41]

The saint is telling us that she cannot meditate; nonetheless, her dry and arid prayer must have been a very vital and valid form of prayer. We know from her life, altogether apart from what she has told us herself, that she was in fact an

[39] The same is true of infused contemplation, but that is not our subject here.
[40] See above, p. 190, quoting St. Jane Frances de Chantal, *The Spiritual Life*, compiled by the Sisters of the Visitation (London: Sands, 1928), p. 148.
[41] Ibid.

inspiration and support for a multitude of other people. Cardinal de Bérulle, the founder of the French Oratory, had written of her as a young widow:

> This heart is an altar where the fire of love never goes out; and it will burn so fiercely that not only the offerings of sacrifice but the altar itself will be consumed.[42]

Later in her life, at a time when she was suffering in a particularly painful way from interior trials, coming from conversation with her, the Cardinal said: "I have just been speaking with one of God's greatest lovers on earth."[43] St. Francis de Sales once wrote to her telling her to look after her health because she was needed by the Visitation order that he and she had founded together: "For", he says, "you know, my dear Mother, that you are in this enterprise the courage of my heart and the heart of my courage."[44] That is a very Salesian sort of sentence; not as clear, that is, as it might seem. Still, whatever it means exactly, it does indicate that St. Francis relied on St. Jane Frances, and that she had not failed him in the past.

And then, again, how accurate was the saint's description of her own prayer? Of course it was truthful in the sense that she described her habitual state, but she seemed to know a lot about other sorts of prayer as well. One of her compan-

---

[42] Elisabeth Stopp, *Madame de Chantal: Portrait of a Saint* (London: Faber and Faber, 1962), p. 192.

[43] Mother Françoise de Chaugy, *Life of S. Jane Frances de Chantal* (London: Richardson and Son, 1852), p. 19: "His Eminence the Cardinal de Bérulle, founder of the Fathers of the (French) Oratory, and who died in the odour of sanctity . . . went to visit her, and said on his return . . . that he had seen one of the greatest lovers of God on earth."

[44] Cited in "A Summary of the Instructions on the Virtues and on Prayer, Given by Saint Jane Frances Frémyot de Chantal" in *Spiritual Life*, p. 147.

ions, Madeleine de Chaugy, who had been secretary to the saint, and later on the superior of the monastery of Annecy, wrote the following:

> There was no way however secret, no road however isolated or unfamiliar, no path however narrow or obscure in the inward spiritual life with which this Blessed Mother was not thoroughly conversant. Upon whatever form of prayer of sublime union, or purified love or inward suffering she was consulted by the many souls who sought her guidance, her mind, illumined by God, satisfied the demand made upon it. . . . Those who consulted her felt an inward conviction that her teaching was not only the fruit of infused knowledge but likewise bought at the high cost of personal experience.[45]

From these precious insights into the prayer of the saint it seems clear that there is no correspondence between what she herself experienced in prayer and the value of her prayer. More goes on in prayer than we are aware of. Through, or by means of, the darkness and dryness of St. Jane's prayer, she was enabled to understand, to console, and to strengthen many other people. God, that is, worked through her prayer to accomplish what he wanted.

At the same time, however, it seems that, subjectively considered, the saint was being instructed about different sorts of prayer while she was praying in this dry and apparently pointless way. St. John of the Cross, who is, of course, a much greater theologian in the technical sense, confirms this assertion and says that some prayer involves a knowledge of God that is secret even to the understanding that receives it. The passage runs as follows:

[45] Ibid., p. 149.

And thus it is that contemplation, whereby the understanding has the loftiest knowledge of God, is called mystical theology, which signifies secret wisdom of God; for it is secret even to the understanding that receives it. For this reason Saint Dionysius calls it a ray of darkness. Of this the prophet Baruch says: "There is none that knoweth its way, nor any that can think of its paths." [46]

The point to grasp is that a lot more goes on in prayer than we are aware of, and for this reason it is pointless even to try to judge its value. So long as we are trying to pray as well as we can, there is no need for much reflection on what we are doing. We have to try to be simple about our prayer, that is, we have to try to fix our attention on our prayer without wasting time trying to see if we are praying well or praying as we think we ought to be. Abbot Chapman said, "Pray as you can, don't try to pray as you can't", [47] and that is the lesson of St. Jane Frances.

One of the constant themes in her teaching is the need for simplicity in prayer. The idea of simplicity is a very old one and goes back to the Old Testament, where it is found allied with such ideas as purity of heart, singleness of purpose, and upright living. A man who is simple in this sense is a man who is not two-faced or duplicitous but is honest through and through, or is, as we say, all of a piece and has his mind and heart fixed on God. St. Jane Frances understands simplicity in terms of an undivided intention fixed on God.

Perfect simplicity consists in having but one single aim in all our actions; that of pleasing God. The second practice which

---

[46] *Ascent of Mount Carmel*, bk. 2, chap. 8, no. 6, in *Complete Works*, trans. and ed. by E. Allison Peers, new ed. [London: Burns & Oates, 1954], 1:92.

[47] John Chapman, "Introductory Memoir", in *Spiritual Letters* (London: Sheed & Ward, 1935), p. 25.

follows upon this is, in everything good or ill that befalls us, to see only the will of God. Then whatsoever the event we shall always be tranquil because we shall have no love, no desire other than that of His adorable will. And this even though some happening may apparently delay our perfection at which nevertheless, we shall not cease to toil.[48]

This simplicity demands a real faith in providence. Providence, as we have seen, is God's activity in bringing about the perfection of his creatures, and it is, in the words of the *Catechism*, both "*concrete* and *immediate*".[49] A living faith in providence means that we are not distracted by worries about the future or regrets about the past, but that—in the here and now—we are free to keep our minds and hearts fixed on God.

> Truly we must be more generous, putting our satisfaction solely in God and abandoning ourselves absolutely to Him who is our only desire. How beautiful is simplicity! Believe me, daughters, a simple soul is a confident soul, she trusts in God and has nothing to fear. There are times when all seems lost, everything appears to go wrong; without confidence at such times where should we then be? Like Abraham, we must hope against hope and recommending everything to God abide in peace, never ceasing to trust in His sweet providence, for it will take care of us.[50]

Simplicity also has the sense of being an antidote to too much reliance on methods in prayer. The great Rhineland mystic Tauler complained against such excessive reliance and maintained that we do not find God through a technique or a

---

[48] Cited in *Spiritual Life*, p. 159.
[49] CCC 303.
[50] Cited in *Spiritual Life*, pp. 162–63.

method; we should look for him and allow ourselves to be found by him whose grace has drawn us to himself. It is so simple to love God, Tauler says. In St. Matthew we have our Lord's words: "I thank thee, Father, Lord of heaven and earth, that thou hast hidden these things from the wise and understanding and revealed them to infants; yea Father, for such was thy gracious will" (Mt 11:25).

St. Jane Frances says about this passage: "O lesson of innocence, of simplicity, of openness, of good faith, of artlessness, of perfect submission. What dost Thou say, Lord? Unless we become as little children; O terrible threat. We do not half weigh its import, its gravity."[51] Why does she say these well-known words of Christ are a terrible threat? It is because, although we have no difficulty in saying that the spiritual life is not reserved to theologians and intellectuals, we do have some trouble with admitting that something is required of the well-instructed. If it is to the simple and humble of heart that God has revealed himself, then simplicity is required of everyone.

Simplicity is also an antidote to thinking about the self in prayer or watching ourselves praying. Simplicity in prayer in this sense is to keep our mind and heart on God in a single-minded way, that is, not in a double way, which is to keep our mind and heart not only on God but on ourselves as well.

St. Francis de Sales has a passage in his *Treatise on the Love of God* that puts this point in a telling way:

He who in praying to God notices that he is praying, is not perfectly attentive to his prayer, for he diverts his attention from God to whom he prays, and turns it upon the prayer by

[51] *Spiritual Life*, p. 161.

which he prays. The very solicitude we have not to be distracted causes oftentimes a very great distraction; simplicity in spiritual actions is most to be commended. If you wish to contemplate God, contemplate him then, and that attentively: if you reflect and bring your eyes backwards upon yourself, to see how you look when you look upon him, it is not now he that you behold but your own behaviour—your self. He who prays fervently knows not whether he prays or not, for he is not thinking of the prayer which he makes but of God to whom he makes it.[52]

Ascetical prayer is not always a very exciting business, and reading some of the passages from St. Jane Frances we might conclude that she was a rather ineffective and depressed person. But that is anything but the truth. During her lifetime the foundress of the Visitation established eighty-six houses of her order, and she was the moving spirit of them all. Over two thousand of her letters remain, and it is estimated that she wrote eleven thousand. She kept three secretaries busily at work,[53] so it is clear that she lived in the turmoil of affairs and that her prayer, however difficult it may often have been for her, was the instrument that made a saint. If such sanctity requires the spiritual combat, and it does, then let us return to it.

---

[52] St. Francis de Sales, *Treatise on the Love of God*, bk. 9, chap. 10, trans. Henry Benedict Mackey (Westminster, Md.: Newman Press, 1953), p. 391.
[53] "The Saint's Prayer", in *Spiritual Life*, p. 147.

PART THREE

"WHAT IS VERY PLAIN ..."

What is very plain is sometimes taken for granted by those who know it, and hence is never heard by others at all.

—J. H. Newman, "The Incarnate Son, a Sufferer and Sacrifice", *Parochial and Plain Sermons*

The spiritual combat has little to do essentially with peace of mind or psychological wholeness, but it does have to do with how we are to follow Christ so that we may obtain our final destiny. The force and coherence of Scupoli's book derives in the first place from the fact that his teaching on the ascetical life is deeply rooted in the Christian view of existence. Self-distrust is based in the first instance, not on our own experience, but on the doctrine of original sin; hope in God is not the result of an easy optimism about the human condition, but on faith in the promises of God; spiritual exercises are not undertaken on the imperatives of human reason and calculation in order to develop useful virtues, but because they are the prescribed means for the following of Christ; finally, the practice of prayer is carefully meshed with the development of self-distrust, hope, and the development of the virtues.

The authority of Scupoli's statement of the Christian principles underlying the spiritual combat derives from his own painful experience of living those principles.[1] This experience enabled him to show how the use of these principles extends far beyond his own life and are, or should be, the

[1] See above, prologue.

foundation of the ordinary life of every Christian. Scupoli, however, was writing at the end of the sixteenth century, and some of the things he could take for granted are a great deal more problematic today even among Christians. In this part of *Spiritual Combat Revisited*, I want to spell out three key concepts of the Christian world view that in fact underlie much of what he says, even if he does not explicitly deal with them in any detail. To some these concepts may be so obvious as to be hardly worth mentioning, but to many others today they seem to be completely unknown. Yet unless there is some awareness of the following aspects of the Christian outlook on life, then much of what Scupoli says will seem either incomprehensible or ludicrous.

In the first place, we are people with a divided heart who do not know ourselves very well. We want God and the things of God with part of ourselves, but another part just as assuredly wants the world and the flesh and, if not so obviously, the devil. The call of Christ comes to ordinary people who either listen and try to follow or listen and refuse even to begin to follow or do begin and then fall away.

Secondly, there is a struggle ahead for those who do follow. The first joy and peace in believing that accompanies a generous response to follow Christ is sooner or later followed by the recognition that the acceptance did not go very deep, and we all too easily turn back to our former behavior and attitudes. To stay pointed in the right direction requires saying no to ourselves and trying to build up a network of Christlike responses to temptation, and this is "the hardest of all struggles",[2] as Scupoli puts it.

Yet, thirdly, what are we to understand by "being pointed in the right direction"? There seem to be so many directions

[2] SC 1, p. 5.

in which we can go. The right direction is the one that leads us to the happiness Christ has promised to those who are faithful, and this happiness consists in being united with God in an eternity of bliss. The spiritual combat is the way we perfect ourselves with God's grace so that we may inherit this beatitude. Yet it is clear from the human condition in general, and from our own experience in particular, that the fullness of perfection will never be obtained in this life. The cumulative effects of original sin in history and in our own lives as well as our own personal sins have resulted in a world full of social injustice and individual wrongdoing. It is not only the Psalmist who has seen the wicked "spreading himself like the green bay tree" (Ps 37:35 AV). Even if a perfect society were ever to be realized, a society in which the claims of all were to be recognized and acted on, this would do nothing for all those who had suffered in the past. If God's justice and mercy are to be operative for all, and if Christianity is to be anything more than a heroic, but ultimately futile, struggle in a hostile and meaningless world, then the Christian teaching of the resurrection of every individual into a life ordered totally by love and justice must be preached. It must be preached in the spirit of St. Paul who said: "For I am not ashamed of the Gospel" (Rom 1:16).

CHAPTER TEN

CHRIST'S CALL AND
THE DIVIDED HEART

There is nothing miraculous or extraordinary in His dealings with us. He works through our natural faculties and circumstances of life. Still what happens to us in providence is
in all essential respects what His voice was to those whom
He addressed when on earth: whether He commands by a
visible presence, or by a voice, or by our consciences, it matters not, so that we feel it to be a command. If it is a command, it may be obeyed or disobeyed; it may be accepted
as Samuel or St. Paul accepted it, or put aside after the manner of the young man who had great possessions.

—J. H. Newman, "Divine Calls,"
Parochial and Plain Sermons

We are divided creatures who do not know ourselves very
well. St. Paul wrote, "What person knows a man's thoughts
except the spirit of the man which is in him" (1 Cor 2:11),
and we have seen that St. Augustine went on to add that
"there is something of the human person which is unknown
even to the spirit of man which is within him".[1] Modern

---

[1] St. Augustine, *Confessions*, bk. 10, chap. 5, no. 7, trans. Henry Chadwick
(Oxford and New York: Oxford Univ. Press, 1992), p. 182; see above, pp. 55–56.

philosophy has been preoccupied with the nature of mental existence and the self.[2] Scupoli is not writing either theology or philosophy, but that does not mean his approach to human nature is simple-minded or naive. It is not simple-minded or naive because it is thoroughly biblical. He knows that the "imagination of man's heart is evil from his youth" (Gen 8:21), but he also realizes that one great difficulty, although certainly not the only one, in writing about the spiritual life is that of leading people to recognize the particular faults that in fact afflict them. The prayer of the Psalmist, "Give me understanding, that I may keep thy law and observe it with my whole heart" (Ps 119:34), is a plea for a self-knowledge that will enable him to keep the law of God.

The difficulty of recognizing and then speaking about individual experiences that are intensely personal and that are never exactly the same extends far beyond spiritual theology. The problem of how we are to describe what is particular and happens only once in terms of words that are used to describe what is general and repeated over and over again is an old one. Yet if there is going to be any writing about the spiritual life at all, we have to describe and categorize the various conditions of the spiritual life and then go on to trace their development. These descriptions, though, are at best accounts of what generally happens. The textbook case of the individual who is in fact suffering from sloth or pride or who is afflicted with scruples in a culpable way and who exhibits a set of well-defined characteristics that indicate his

---

[2] See, for example, Charles Taylor, *Sources of the Self: The Making of the Modern Identity* (Cambridge, Mass.: Harvard Univ. Press, 1989); and Roger Scruton, *Sexual Desire* (London: Phoenix, 1994), appendix 1, "The First Person", and appendix 2, "Intentionality".

condition is extremely rare. The reality is much more complex, and the recognition and identification of the spiritual movement in the individual case are harder to grasp than might at first appear.

The need for individuals who could discern, or diagnose, has been clear since the time of Cassian,[3] and the discernment of spirits plays an important role, to cite the best-known example, in the *Spiritual Exercises of St. Ignatius of Loyola*.[4] These Exercises are written from the point of view of providing a confessor or spiritual guide with the means to help a third party, and the "one giving the Exercises" is provided with questions to ask of the person being given the retreat. In the "Rules for the Discernment of Spirits", the retreat master is provided with matter for formulating the questions.

Unlike the work of St. Ignatius, Scupoli's *The Spiritual Combat* is a "do-it-yourself" book and is addressed to a "beloved daughter in Christ".[5] That is, it was intended for the reader trying to improve his spiritual condition, and not for a spiritual director or a preacher giving a retreat. Inevitably this results in a book that is less structured in approach but more personal and direct. Scupoli addresses his reader directly with the truths of Christianity and advice about the best way of putting these truths into practice; after that, he leaves it up to the reader to get on with it.

---

[3] John Cassian, second conference, "On Discretion", in *The Conferences*.

[4] *The Spiritual Exercises of St. Ignatius of Loyola*, sections 1–21, passim, ed. Louis J. Puhl, S.J. (Chicago: Loyola Univ. Press, 1951), pp. 1–10.

[5] "Figliuola in Christo amatissima". St. Francis de Sales used the same device in the *Introduction to the Devout life*, which is addressed to "dearest Philothea". Both books were designed for home consumption.

This approach has its drawbacks, because it is not always easy in the concrete to identify our spiritual condition or to see what we should do. Life does not present us, most of the time, with a series of choices that come, as it were, clearly marked as being of greater or lesser importance. Discernment involves seeing what is important in a situation for our spiritual welfare and then doing something about it. Often enough, it has to be said, the chance to do something slips away before we have even recognized the crucial character of the circumstances to which we have failed to respond. Human life is messy and confused, and the call of God is only one voice in a noisy world of competing claims. The response has to be the response of a particular human being who, especially at the beginning of a serious spiritual life, is hard put to recognize a true description of the situation in which he finds himself, much less to do very much about it. It is one thing to be vaguely dissatisfied with a sinful way of life and quite another to recognize this way of life for what it is and to seek and apply the needed remedies. Furthermore, it is unhappily the case that we may arrive at a situation in which we see clearly enough that we should be doing a good deal better, but for any number of reasons we are unwilling to put our house in order. Our hearts are divided, as Hosea said to the Jews,[6] and the life we lead not only obscures our vision, but it also weakens our will.

Sometimes, however, with clearer vision or a change of circumstances, a man is moved to do better. How this happens is as varied as there are conversions. Suddenly he may be drawn up short by a passage from Scripture; he may hear

---

[6] "Their heart is false; now they must bear their guilt" (Hos 10:2).

a word spoken at the right time and place that pierces him to the heart; it may be someone's act of charity that shows up his own shoddiness and moves him to tears, but, for whatever reason, he cries with St. Catherine of Genoa, "no more world, no more sin".[7] Something, somehow, stings his conscience, and he turns to Christ.

We have then the person who hears a call to do better but fails to respond; and we have the case of the man who hears, who listens, and who tries to follow. To illustrate these two cases, let us go to the New Testament and examine first of all how King Herod responded to the teaching of John the Baptist, and then how Nicodemus received our Lord and his teaching.

King Herod had a divided heart. He had married his brother's wife, and John the Baptist had told him this was breaking the law of God.[8] Herodias, his new wife, was inflamed with hatred for John and wanted him dead. For love of his new wife and to please her, Herod put John into prison. But, although John's message could not have been any more welcome to Herod than it was to Herodias, he refused, at first, to have him killed. He was, as St. Mark puts it, "much perplexed" (Mk 6:20).

The reason for Herod's hesitation is instructive. Herod, St. Mark tells us, was afraid of John because he recognized that the Baptist was a "righteous and holy man" (Mk 6:20). Somewhere in that confused, vicious, ambitious, and unprincipled nature that was Herod's, there was also a capacity to sense the austere beauty of a way of life he half recognized

---

[7] F. von Hügel. *The Mystical Element in Religion* (London: J. M. Dent & Sons, 1961), p. 105.

[8] Mt 14; Mk 6; and Lk 3. The most detailed account is in Mark.

as a rebuke to his own sordid existence. Herod heard what John had to say. He did not entirely shut out his message, but "he was much perplexed."

The cause of the perplexity was not that Herod failed to understand what John was saying; after all, that was all too clear. John kept telling him that it was not lawful for him to take his brother's wife. The perplexity arose because Herod did not know what to do about what he was being told. The Baptist's words were a condemnation of everything Herod was and did, and yet he heard John gladly (cf Mk 6:20). Part of Herod's nature was drawn to a better way of life than he was in fact living; but another part was firmly fixed in the status quo of ambition, lust, and power.

It was clear that something would have to give. The situation demanded some sort of resolution, as its elements were too volatile to admit of more than temporary equilibrium. Either the pressure from Herodias and his own desires would have to make way for the message of the Baptist, or else the call of the Baptist would, somehow or other, have to be suppressed. In the event, as we know, it was the message of John that was silenced. Herod was tricked, or allowed himself to be tricked, into having the Baptist beheaded. The daughter of Herodias danced for the king and his guests, and as a reward he promised her whatever she wanted, even half his kingdom. Urged on by her mother, the girl asked for the head of John the Baptist on a platter; and Herod, with every show of reluctance, had John executed. He murdered John not only to please the girl, but because he had made his promise in front of his courtiers, his officers, and the leading men of Galilee. So, lust and political expediency led him to silence the unwelcome voice.

There is no doubt that Herod heard the voice of John, and heard it gladly. There was something in his nature that responded to both the voice and the message; yet there were, as well, a great many other elements that fought against his acceptance of that voice and that message. In the end he chose Herodias and all she stood for and rejected John and what he represented. But the decision to get rid of the Baptist was Herod's own and no one else's. He put an end to the warfare in his own heart by choosing "the lust of the flesh and the lust of the eyes and the pride of life", which is "not of the Father but is of the world" (1 Jn 2:16).

We all have something of Herod in us. We are all like Herod, not perhaps because we commit incest, adultery, and murder, but because we are all divided creatures. Herod shows us a picture, painted in primary colors that cannot be mistaken, of the human situation in which we find ourselves. We are pulled toward God, toward love and righteousness, but we are also pulled toward the world, the flesh, and the devil. Our conscience and our reason are constantly trying to find a way of life that will lead us between the different calls and pressures of our existence. Like Herod, we want to listen to John, but we also do not want to give up Herodias. And, like Herod, we often turn away from the good that we obscurely sense is being offered to us.

But the divided heart sometimes turns toward the acceptance of the healing truth. In the case of Nicodemus, we see an original, tentative acceptance of the claims of the divine teacher grow into a whole-hearted and loving acceptance of Christ. It was, however, a slow and awkward process. At first Nicodemus was too confused and too frightened to profess openly that Jesus was the Messiah.

Now there was a man of the Pharisees, named Nicodemus, a ruler of the Jews. This man came to Jesus by night and said to him, "Rabbi, we know that you are a teacher come from

God; for no one can do these signs that you do, unless God is with him." [9]

Jesus said to his visitor that unless he was born anew, he would not see the kingdom of God. In spite of his professional knowledge of the Old Testament, which should have prepared him to understand what Christ was saying, Nicodemus did not seem to grasp much of what he was being told, and what he did understand he rejected. "Nicodemus said to him, 'How can a man be born when he is old? Can he enter a second time into his mother's womb and be born?'" (Jn 3:4).

Our Lord then made it plain to Nicodemus that if he could not understand what he had been told so far, he certainly was not going to be able to grasp anything more complicated and of greater significance. "If I have told you earthly things and you do not believe, how can you believe if I tell you heavenly things?" (Jn 3:12).

Nicodemus failed to grasp the message, but he did not reject it. Like Herod, he sensed that there was something important in what he was being told, but he was not at all sure what it was. Probably he went home and thought about what he had heard and kept an eye on the career of the teacher whom he was too frightened to acknowledge or to follow openly. And echoing in his heart, there must have been the

---

[9] Jn 3:1–2. Who Nicodemus was exactly, and what his position in the Jewish community was, is a matter of debate among scholars. He is mentioned only in St. John's Gospel, but the fact that he is mentioned is enough for our purposes. See C. K. Barrett, *The Gospel according to St. John* (London: S.P.C.K., 1962), p. 170. Raymond Brown, *The Death of the Messiah* (New York: Doubleday, 1993), says "I recognize that one should not jump to the conclusion that exclusively Johannine characters are not historical because their role suits the theology of the Gospel"; in the end Fr. Brown seems prepared to give Nicodemus some sort of existence; he sees "no reason for denying Nicodemus a possible historicity" (p. 1279).

Lord's words: "And this is the judgment, that the light has come into the world, and men loved darkness rather than light" (Jn 3:19).

The next time we hear of Nicodemus is in the last week of Jesus' life. The Pharisees had sent the temple guards to arrest Christ, and they returned empty-handed. It seems there were enough people in the crowds who believed in Jesus to have made it difficult to take him into custody. Perhaps, as well, the soldiers themselves were impressed. When they got back to the authorities, all they could say was that no one ever spoke like this man. They were then rebuked by the leaders of the Jews, who asked if they too had been led astray. None of the authorities, none of the Pharisees, the soldiers were told, had believed the claims of Christ, so why should the soldiers? It was only the unlettered crowd "who do not know the law" and were "accursed" who had any time for his claims (Jn 7:47–49).

It was at this point that Nicodemus made his intervention. He did not defend Jesus directly, and he certainly did not confess that he believed in Christ, but he did now have the courage to say to the Jews that they were breaking their own law: "Nicodemus, who had gone to him before, and who was one of them, said to them, 'Does our law judge a man without first giving him a hearing and learning what he does?'" [10]

This appeal to justice only landed Nicodemus in hot water and did nothing to help Jesus. Finally, after the crucifixion, Nicodemus had the courage to acknowledge Christ and in the daytime to help Joseph of Arimathea bury the dead body of Christ as well as to provide the spices required to

---

[10] Jn 7:50–51. By "who was one of them", St. John probably means that Nicodemus was still a Jew in good standing and not a follower of Christ.

anoint the body.[11] Unlike Herod, Nicodemus had finally come round to accepting the truth that he must be born anew in order to see the kingdom of God. Nicodemus conquered his own timidity and his concern to maintain an honored and useful place in his society, and he did this so that he could follow the light that is Christ. In the end he listened to the call of God and followed the demands that call made on him. "But he who does what is true comes to the light, that it may be clearly seen that his deeds have been wrought in God" (Jn 3:21).

All through the public ministry of Christ we come up against this double response. People are pulled toward him, and yet almost at the same time they are repelled by what they see and hear. We are here face to face with the fallen human heart, a heart divided and confused, yet which finally either revolts, like Herod, against the holiness of God or accepts, like Nicodemus, the claims of Christ.

If we are going to be serious in our response to Christ's call to follow him, if we want to avoid the turning away of Herod, and if we want to end up on the side of Christ like Nicodemus, then we are in for a struggle. We are in for a struggle because, like Herod and Nicodemus, we are people who want it both ways. If our hearts are to be changed, and if we are to learn to love the things of God, then we have to unlearn the love of this world. But this is going to mean

---

[11] There seems to be a difficulty in reconciling the account of the burial as recorded in John with the account given by the Synoptics. Raymond Brown writes of Nicodemus: "This additional character in the burial is found only in John, where he has appeared in two previous scenes (3:1 ff.; 7:50–52). To explain his presence here (where he is totally absent from the Synoptic burial account) an astounding number of suggestions have been made by scholars" (*Death of the Messiah*, p. 1277). However, Nicodemus does in fact appear in the Gospel, and his sayings and character are there for our instruction.

saying no to what our fallen nature craves. If we are going to live with Christ in the daylight, then we will have to wage war against whatever stands in the way of the claims he has on us. Newman wrote:

> To be righteous and obedient implies self-command; but to possess power we must have gained it; nor can we gain it without a vigorous struggle, a persevering warfare against ourselves. The very notion of being religious implies self-denial, because by nature we do not love religion. [12]

"A vigorous struggle, a persevering warfare against ourselves" is how Newman describes the Christian's existence. We are all familiar with this struggle, or at least we ought to be. Like Herod and the Jews, we hear Christ's voice and want to follow him, but all too often, like Herod and the Jews, we do not see clearly, and we give up trying when the going gets tough. But there is also the example of Nicodemus, and like him we must aim at moving from the shadows of life, from timidity and a desire for security, into an existence led courageously for Christ in the full light of day.

[12] J. H. Newman, "The Duty of Self-Denial", sermon 7 in bk. 7 of *Parochial and Plain Sermons* (San Francisco: Ignatius Press, 1997), p. 1470.

CHAPTER ELEVEN

THE HARDEST OF ALL STRUGGLES

A hard life is, alas! no certain method of becoming spiritually minded, but it is one out of the means by which
Almighty God makes us so. We must, at least at seasons,
defraud ourselves of nature, if we would not be defrauded
of grace.

—J. H. Newman, "Love, the One Thing Needful,"
Parochial and Plain Sermons

Both Herod and Nicodemus were touched by the call of
God, but afterward they traveled by different roads. Herod
ended not only by killing John the Baptist, but also by turning his back on the light by cooperating with Pilate at the
time of the Passion (Lk 23:8–12). Nicodemus, on the other
hand, was faithful to the voice beating on his heart and moved
from darkness into the light.

There is no reason to think that Nicodemus found the
struggle anything but a struggle. He was rich; he had a powerful position in society; and these were clearly at odds with
the demands of Jesus. It must have seemed to him at times
that he was being asked to risk his wealth and his power for
a will-o'-the-wisp. His struggle was not between something
external and evil, that is, his wealth and social position, and
something internal, that is, his spiritual call. No matter how

inward and how satisfying the thought of following Christ might have been, what was being asked of him was a new way of life, not just a new way of thinking. Inevitably this involved a struggle with himself, and it is this struggle with self that defines the spiritual combat.

> This is indeed the hardest of all struggles; for while we struggle against self, self is striving against us, and therefore is the victory here most glorious and precious in the sight of God.[1]

The truth of Christianity lies first in its teaching. But that same truth has also to be found in the witness of a life that testifies to the fruitfulness of this teaching. One of the reasons our minds are so blinded and our wills so unready to acknowledge and follow the law of Christ is because, as Newman put it, we are "busied in the pleasures and pursuits of this life"[2] and have lost any sense that Christianity makes serious demands on the way we should behave. It is true that people have always been "busied in the pleasures and pursuits of this life", but our time seems to have forgotten the need for a serious moral reformation in the light of the Gospel. Our faith is dim because our virtue is weak, and our hearts are divided. We are hesitant and anxious because we are always in fact saying no to God in the way we behave. Yet we constantly seek what we know will not satisfy us and turn away from the truth that will make us free. We are forever refusing the mercy and the forgiveness of God and turning back to what we know in our heart of hearts will not satisfy us. We want a new life, but that new life demands an

[1] SC I, p. 5.
[2] J. H. Newman, "The Immortality of the Soul", sermon 2 in vol. I of *Parochial and Plain Sermons* (San Francisco: Ignatius Press, 1997), p. 14.

effort on our part, and it is an effort in which we are reluctant to engage. St. Paulinus of Nola put it this way:

> To what purpose, pray, do you sadly and continually seek falsehoods with burdened hearts, and vainly love slippery pursuits? Amend your ways, burst asunder the chains of death, and offer your necks freely to the sweetest of yokes.[3]

"Amend your ways, burst asunder the chains of death, and offer your necks freely to the sweetest of yokes", says the saint, but it is easier said than done. First of all, we have to understand what is being asked of us in the light of our Christian faith, and secondly we must have some idea of how to overcome our built-in resistance to doing what our faith requires of us.

The ascetical dimension of Christianity is deeply rooted in the Bible,[4] even though some of its practices antedate Christianity itself. It is St. Paul who tells us that the Christian life is to be compared to an athletic contest and that we have to go into training if we are to be successful.[5] But the contest we are concerned with is not a game; it is a real battle against everything that will pull the Christian soldier

---

[3] St. Paulinus of Nola, *Poems*, Ancient Christian Writers, no. 40 (New York: Newman Press, 1975), p. 217.

[4] M. Villier et M. Olphe-Galliard, "L'Ascèse chrétienne—Les Origines scriptuaires", in *Dictionnaire de spiritualité*, ed. Marcel Viller, S.J. [Paris: G. Beauchesne et ses fils, 1932–], vol. 1, cols. 960–64.

[5] "Do you not know that in a race all the runners compete, but only one receives the prize? So run that you may obtain it. Every athlete exercises self-control in all things. They do it to receive a perishable wreath, but we an imperishable. Well, I do not run aimlessly, I do not box as one beating the air; but I pommel my body and subdue it, lest after preaching to others I myself should be disqualified" (1 Cor 9:24–26).

away from God, who is our true and only real happiness.[6]
Newman put the matter clearly enough in one of his Anglican sermons:

> St. Paul also, in addition to his "weariness and painfulness,"
> "hunger and thirst," "cold and nakedness," was "in watch-
> ings often," "in fasting often." Such were holy men of old
> time. How far are we below them! Alas for our easy sensual
> life, our cowardice, our sloth! is this the way by which the
> kingdom of heaven is won? is this the way that St. Paul fought
> a good fight, and finished his course? or was it by putting
> behind his back all things on earth, and looking stedfastly
> towards Him who is invisible?[7]

Newman was preaching to upper-class young men in the
thirties and forties of the nineteenth century who gave at
least a formal adhesion to the religion of the Anglican prayer
book, and this gave him a vocabulary his hearers would recognize and themes with which they would be familiar. But
even that beginning is denied to us. For nearly a generation
now the emphasis in Catholic spirituality has been to reject
what was seen as an overemphasis on the development of the
virtues and fighting the vices in an organized struggle. The
causes of this turning away from both the theory and the
practice of asceticism are complex. Some of these are aspects
of the general history of the development of the Church

---

[6] "For we are not contending against flesh and blood, but against the prin-
cipalities, against the powers, against the world rulers of this present darkness,
against the spiritual hosts of wickedness in the heavenly places. Therefore take
the whole armor of God, that you may be able to withstand in the evil day,
and having done all, to stand" (Eph 6:12–13).

[7] J. H. Newman, "Apostolic Abstinence a Pattern for Christians", sermon 3
in vol. 6 of *Parochial and Plain Sermons*, pp. 1204–5.

after Vatican II and are beyond the scope of this book. There are, however, two elements in the situation that concern us. The first of these has to do with asceticism and our approach to God, and the second with the theological underpinnings of the ascetical life.

It has often been maintained during the last thirty years that the freedom to enter into union with God was stifled by an overemphasis on the methods and techniques of the ascetical life. A life organized around developing the virtues and fighting the vices has been viewed as interfering with the Christian's freedom to seek God in his own way. For example, in his introduction to the mystical works of the unknown author of *The Cloud of Unknowing*, a modern authority on the spiritual life, Fr. George A. Maloney, S.J., has maintained that "spiritual seekers" have been deflected in their search for Divine Love by the "heavy rationalistic structure" of Western Christendom. What is needed, he claims, is a "complementary vision" that will revitalize the religious search of ordinary people.

> Such a "new" vision is not really so new. The God of the Old and New Testament is a God of mystery, met in wonder. Knowledge of him is grounded in intuition rather than in rational ideas. The Judeo-Christian God takes man's eyes away from himself as the exploiting center of the universe and demands a humble response to God's invitation to share his divine life.[8]

This line of reasoning has been enormously successful, and today we hear very little about either the theory or the prac-

---

[8] *The Pursuit of Wisdom*, trans., ed., and annotated by James A. Walsh, S.J. and George A. Maloney, S.J. (New York: Paulist Press, 1988), p. 6.

tice of asceticism. This, I think, is another example of throwing away the baby with the bathwater. It is true that the ascetical life, as discussed by Scupoli, St. Ignatius of Loyola, or St. Francis de Sales, does represent a spirituality that, in Fr. Maloney's words, focuses man's eyes on himself. Scupoli and other ascetical writers do in fact emphasize the human aspect of our encounter with God, although it is not very clear why this should be termed exploitive. What Scupoli and the others would, presumably, want to add to Fr. Maloney's account is that the mind is focused on the self so as to fit men to give the "humble response to God's invitation to share his divine life", which the modern seeker is said to be so desirous of obtaining.

The dangers of exaggeration and overemphasis in a spirituality that concentrates on asceticism are real, and too many people have identified asceticism as the enemy of Christian liberty to deny the perception. The perception itself, though, is a mistaken one, and the Christian imperative to "amend your ways" and to "burst asunder the chains of death" should still be an element in the practice of Catholicism. There are always dangers connected with a serious living of Christianity, but the evils associated with these dangers ought to be seen as evils arising from the corruption of what is both good and necessary. The dangers themselves have been recognized since the time of Cassian, who wrote about these matters in the fifth century.[9] In the 1930s Fr. De Guibert, the

[9] See, for example, the eighteenth conference, where Cassian shows that true patience is rooted in the heart and not in external practices: "True patience and tranquillity are not acquired or held onto without profound humility of heart. If they proceed from this source they will stand in need of neither the benefit of a cell nor the refuge of solitude" (John Cassian, conference 18, chap. 13, no. 1, in *The Conferences*, trans. and annotated by Boniface Ramsey, O.P. [New York: Paulist Press, 1997], pp. 644–45).

authoritative Jesuit theologian of the spiritual life, summa-
rized the practical dangers of asceticism under five headings:[10]

1. The danger of *naturalism*, that is, of a concentration on
the moral dimension of Christianity to such an extent that
the supernatural and infused elements of Christianity are
ignored;

2. The danger of *an exaggerated reliance on oneself*, and a
narrow interest in our own doings, so that the realities of the
supernatural life are forgotten and the overall aims of the
glory of God and the salvation of souls are ignored;

3. The danger of *self-love* and of taking pride in the practices of the ascetical life themselves;

4. The danger of *inflexibility* coupled with an inability to
adapt to the realities of the human situation;

5. The danger of *wasting time* in battles that are not really
central to our own spiritual needs.

The five headings represent real dangers, and it may be
that in the past the demands of the ascetical life were pressed
by those who did not possess Fr. De Guibert's wisdom and
experience. Nonetheless, the pendulum has swung too far
away from the ascetical life, and the perennial value of its
central tenets should once again be made clear. This is recognized in the *Catechism*, which reaffirms the importance of
the ascetical dimension of Christianity in the following
passage:

The way of perfection passes by way of the Cross. There is
no holiness without renunciation and spiritual battle (cf. 2
Tim 4). Spiritual progress entails the ascesis and mortifica-

---

[10] *Dictionnaire de spiritualité*, vol. 1, cols. 998–99. These headings are concerned with the application of the ascetical life, not so much with the theological objections to asceticism that are found in other parts of the article.

tion that gradually lead to living in the peace and joy of the Beatitudes.[11]

For Scupoli, the necessity of the ascetical life was seen as our response to Christ's warning to his disciples that they must deny themselves, take up their cross, and follow him (Mt 16:24). If the disciples are faithful unto death, they will be given the crown of life (Rev 2:10). Being faithful involves trying to live a Christian life. It is Christ who calls, but we must respond. Our response involves our own activity, and asceticism deals with this activity on our part. We are responsible for what we do and how we live, and our response to the grace given us will determine our future in eternity.[12]

The ascetical point of view depends on theological positions that have not been emphasized in the years since Vatican II. Often enough, these positions have not been actively denied, but the focus of interest has shifted. Because, for example, it was thought that social justice had not been sufficiently emphasized in the pre-Vatican II Church, there developed a much more horizontal or this-world presentation of Christianity. However we are to judge the merits of this new stance, it cannot be denied that it has resulted in turning men's hearts and minds away from any awareness of such truths as the particular judgment and the importance of personal striving after holiness. Often enough the witness to the reality of sin and of its terrible consequences has been

[11] CCC 2015.
[12] J. H. Newman, "That we are accountable for what we do and what we are,—that, in spite of all aids or hindrances from without, each soul is the cause of its own happiness or misery,—is a truth certified to us both by Nature and Revelation" ("Human Responsibility as Independent of Circumstances", sermon 8, sec. 3, in *Fifteen Sermons Preached before the University of Oxford between A.D. 1826 and 1843* [London: Longmans, Green, 1900], p. 137).

strangely muted. And yet the existence of the awesome struggle remains, as recognized by this passage from the Second Vatican Council:

> The whole of man's history has been the story of dour combat with the powers of evil, stretching, so our Lord tells us, from the very dawn of history until the last day. Finding himself in the midst of the battlefield man has to struggle to do what is right, and it is at great cost to himself, and aided by God's grace, that he succeeds in achieving his own inner integrity.[13]

Scupoli's book has to do with this "dour combat with the powers of evil", and his work can only be understood and valued when viewed against the background of the theological stance from which he wrote. Once this theological perspective is understood, what he says about Christian living can be seen to follow naturally, even if what he says may at first sight seem hard to accept. [14]

These theological underpinnings are important because what we are concerned with here is asceticism undertaken as a response to the grace of Christ, and not as an exercise in self-realization. Asceticism as a discipline is not exclusive to Christianity, and the Stoics, the Epicureans, and Socrates taught sophisticated and coherent methods in what Epictetus called "the art of living". All these methods involved self-

[13] Vatican Council II, Pastoral Constitution on the Church in the Modern World, *Gaudium et Spes*, December 7, 1965, no. 37, in *Vatican Council II*, vol. 1: *The Conciliar and Postconciliar Documents*, ed. Austin Flannery, new rev. ed. (New York: Costello Pub. Co., 1996), p. 936.

[14] It is not hard to show that the underpinnings of *The Spiritual Combat* are the same dogmatic formulations we find reaffirmed in the *Catechism of the Catholic Church*. In my presentation of Scupoli, I have taken the *Catechism* as normative, and I have not tried to argue for the theological positions it teaches.

denial and the reordering of our value systems in order to achieve inner peace and a serene acceptance of what could not be changed.[15] The asceticism of the Christian, like that of the Greek and Roman philosophers, is a way of life, but, unlike theirs, it is a way of life adopted for the love of the Crucified and with a desire to follow and imitate him. On the Christian view, God must call before we can respond. The ascetical life is thus a two-way street. If we forget about the grace of God or try to discuss asceticism in isolation from God's gifts, we do in fact lay ourselves open to the criticism that asceticism has no necessary connection with Christianity. If, in the past, there has been a tendency to think of asceticism as involving only our efforts, then it has to be said quite simply that this was wrong and was a deformed picture of the Christian life.

It is not hard to see how the temptation to view asceticism as a sort of technique for overcoming sin and establishing virtue arose. We are so conscious of our own confusion and ignorance that we are always in danger of imagining that our relationship to God consists only in our struggle to reach him. But that is not the case. The first and basic movement of the spiritual life is from God to us—not from ourselves to God.

Herod and Nicodemus were first confronted with a divine initiative that held out to both of them something that, in an obscure way, they both wanted; and their response was just that, an answer to something other than themselves. Neither was clear about what was being offered to them, but they grasped enough to realize that it satisfied something their natures craved. There are some lovely words of comfort

---

[15] Pierre Hadot, "Spiritual Exercises", in *Philosophy as a Way of Life: Spiritual Exercises from Socrates to Foucault*, ed. Arnold Davidson, trans. Michael Chase (Oxford: Blackwell, 1999). See above, p. 77.

addressed to the Christian soul in *The Living Flame of Love* by St. John of the Cross which express this truth: "First of all it must know that, if the soul is seeking God, its beloved is seeking it much more." [16] God loves us, and he wants our love in return. Yet while God wants our love, we do not return it to him with an undivided heart. Our desire may be perfectly genuine, but there are other things we want in an equally serious way. Answering the call of God involves the effort to make sure that our love of God gradually dominates and reorders our other loves. Loving God is not an abstract or ethereal activity apart from or other than our everyday self. The love of God is a desire that gradually takes over our unstable nature and enables us to love God with an undivided, stable, and pure heart—if, that is, we will cooperate and work with the grace given to us. It is from this perspective that St. Augustine was able to write that "the entire life of a good Christian is in fact an exercise in holy desire." [17]

But what are we to understand at a more down-to-earth level about the response on our part to God's calling? Surely it must be at least to try to get ourselves into shape to follow Christ in a somewhat adequate way. Newman wrote that "while Christianity reveals the pardon of sin and the promise of eternal life through the mediation of Christ, it also professes to point out means for the present improvement of

[16] St. John of the Cross, *Living Flame of Love*, stanza 3, no. 27, in *Complete Works*, trans. and ed. by E. Allison Peers, new ed. (London: Burns & Oates, 1954), 3:60.

[17] St. Augustine, *Tractates on the First Letter of John*, reprinted in *The Liturgy of the Hours*, Office of Readings, Friday, sixth week of ordinary time (New York: Catholic Book Publishing Co., 1975): "The entire life of a good Christian in fact is an exercise of holy desire. You do not yet see what you long for, but the very act of desiring prepares you, so that when he comes you may see and be utterly satisfied" (3:220).

our moral nature itself." [18] Newman thought that our contribution to our own development in the life of grace, if we could put it simply, was to try to live better lives. Expressed this way, it may seem a somewhat pedestrian concern measured against the excitement of a free-wheeling, unstructured spiritual life. But Newman was right, and a genuine response to the call of Christ is in part an effort at moral reformation. If the reaction to overplaying the role of the ascetical has led to a denial of the importance of a personal struggle for holiness, the distrust of asceticism has gone too far.

Scupoli's book was intended to provide a practical outline for at least the foundations of Christian living, and these foundations are ascetical in nature. If we are to take up Scupoli's book is a serious way, we will have to take to heart the ascetical ideals upon which it is based. What is required is not just to revisit a book but, as the *Catechism* reminds us, to engage in the battle with which it deals.

[18] J. H. Newman, "Evangelical Sanctity and the Completion of Natural Virtue", *Fifteen Sermons*, no. 3, sec. 1, p. 37.

CHAPTER TWELVE

PERFECTION, BEATITUDE, AND IMMORTALITY

God, infinitely perfect and blessed in himself, in a plan of sheer goodness freely created man to make him share in his own blessed life.

— Catechism of the Catholic Church

God works for a purpose, and the meaning of our lives is to be found in trying to be holy and blameless in his sight so that we may share in his beatitude. Behind everything Scupoli says about the necessity of the struggle to work for perfection by fighting sin and becoming more Christlike in our behavior, there is the clear presence of the principle that all this is undertaken so that we can be united with God through love in this world and finally see him face to face in the next. This union is the ultimate purpose of our lives. The *Catechism* puts this truth in the following way: "The Beatitudes [of the Sermon on the Mount] reveal the goal of human existence, the ultimate end of human acts: God calls us to his own beatitude." [1]

---

[1] CCC 1719.

The realities denoted by words and phrases such as working for perfection, purpose, and beatitude are principles of the Christian faith, but in the present climate of opinion they are either ignored or contested. This means that if we consider them merely as philosophical ideas, about which it is possible to debate, then they do not seem to be the best place from which to start a discussion on the practice of the moral and sacrificial aspects of Christian living.[2] Scupoli's approach would be that we work for perfection and hope for beatitude, not because this seems to be a sensible conclusion to a metaphysical argument, but because acting in this way is one aspect of what it means to be a Christian.

Newman said that the philosopher "aspires towards a divine *principle*; the Christian towards a *Divine Agent*"[3], and it is the "Divine Agent" who has told us how we are to understand and live our lives:

Such ... is the Revealed system compared with the Natural—teaching religious truths historically, not by investigation; revealing the divine Nature, not in words, but in

[2] The following is a good example of what I take to be the generally accepted position about human life held today by most non-Christians: "That human life has no external point or τέλος; is a view as difficult to argue as its opposite.... I can see no evidence to suggest that human life is not something self-contained. There are properly many patterns and purposes within life, but there is no general and as it were externally guaranteed pattern or purpose of the kind for which philosophers and theologians used to search. We are what we seem to be, transient mortal creatures subject to necessity and chance. That is to say that there is, in my view, no God in the traditional sense of that term; and the traditional sense is perhaps the only sense" (Iris Murdoch, "The Sovereignty of Good over Other Concepts", in *Existentialists and Mystics* [London: Chatto and Windus, 1997], pp. 363–85; here, pp. 364–65).

[3] "The Influence of Natural and Revealed Religion Respectively", sermon 2, sec. 20, in *Fifteen Sermons Preached before the University of Oxford between A.D. 1826 and 1843* (London: Longmans, Green, 1900), p. 28.

action; not in His moral laws, but in His spoken commands; training us to be subjects of a kingdom, not citizens
of a Stoic republic; and enforcing obedience, not on Reason so much as on Faith.[4]

The will of God comes to us in the form of imperatives. We
are told to love God, not recommended to put him first;
we are told to be honest, chaste, and kind, not advised that
we will probably be happier if in fact we try to be moral.
The same consideration obtains concerning our existence as
a whole; that is, when we are told that our destiny is to be
united with the eternal beatitude of God through incorpo-
ration in Jesus Christ, we are not being presented with one
option among many others, but with the truth about the
way things are. The "glorious liberty of the children of God"
(Rom 8:21) of which St. Paul speaks, is only going to be
obtained by freely living out in our own lives the plan of
God, not by trying to frustrate it, nor by trying to invent a
new purpose to life. "This is your goal, this is the center of
your life; this is the treasure of your heart", as St. Robert
Bellarmine so finely and so concisely put it.[5]

We have come across all these ideas in the course of this
book. Now we should look at them more carefully. First of
all, we have to examine in more detail how striving for
perfection is related both to charity and to everyday life;
then we must go on to consider how perfection is related
to beatitude; and finally we need to outline the argument
that beatitude requires immortality.

---

[4] Ibid., sec. 23, p. 30.
[5] St. Robert Bellarmine, "On the Ascent of the Mind to God", quoted in
The Liturgy of the Hours (New York: Catholic Book Publishing Co., 1975),
4:1412; see above, chap. 7, n. 3.

Perfection

Scupoli does not present us with a theology of perfection, but, assuming the Catholic doctrine of grace, he teaches how this perfection is in practice to be worked for.[6] Sanctifying or deifying grace is given by God to us in such a way that it brings about a real change in our nature and is the source of our sanctification. This initiative of God, however, demands man's free response in the here and now of everyday existence. It is this free response and the obstacles to it, which constitute the subject matter of ascetical theology.

There are two objections that can be leveled against this concentration on the virtues and vices of ordinary life. The first of these maintains that Scupoli's perspective substitutes a moral ideal for the truly Christian goal of perfection, which is charity or love; while the second insists that any sort of concern with conduct misses the real point of religion.

Perfection and Charity

It is true that Christian perfection must be understood as a perfection in the growth of charity or love, but this perfection of love necessitates the other virtues. This is "very plain", but it is often misunderstood or ignored and has to be repeated and enlarged upon.

Perfection was understood by St. Paul and the Fathers, not merely as the following of certain rules or external precepts, but as trying to become like Christ. "Have this mind among yourselves, which was in Christ Jesus" (Phil 2:5); try, in other words, to have the same mentality as the Lord. And, in other places, St. Paul tells his disciples to imitate him (Paul),

[6] See CCC 1996–2005.

as he has imitated Christ Jesus.[7] Seeking perfection means following Christ and trying to imitate his virtues. St. Augustine summed up the Catholic tradition when he wrote: "For, what is it to follow him except to imitate him?"[8]

Once we begin to pay attention to the words we are liable to be overwhelmed with this ideal of imitating Christ. There seems to be "a great chasm" fixed (Lk 16:26) between the holiness of the Lord and what even the best of human beings can achieve. Given this impression, it is not surprising that many have thought, and still think, that we must try to follow Christ and not worry too much about our own pathetic efforts to practice virtue and fight vice. Or, to put the same issue in a different way, ascetical practices based on the mortification of the intellect and will do not seem to have much to do with Christian perfection. The important thing is to love God and to try to follow him and not to worry too much about everyday existence.

It is very true that we should be deeply aware of our own darkness in contrast to the holiness of God, and we have already seen that distrust of self and hope in God are indispensable for living a Christian life. Yet it does not follow from this that spiritual combat has suddenly been rendered obsolete by a deeper sense that Christian asceticism is based on the love of God and on the need to imitate Christ. We

---

[7] For example, "Be imitators of me, as I am of Christ" (1 Cor 11:1).

[8] *De Sancta Virginitate*, 28: "Quid est enim sequi, nisi imitari?", in *Collectio SS Ecclesiae Patrum* (Paris: Parent Debarres, 1839), 26:27. "You deservedly follow him wherever He goes because of your virginity of heart and of body. For, what is it to follow Him except to imitate Him? 'For Christ has suffered' for us, 'leaving' us 'an example', as the Apostle Peter says, 'that' we 'may follow in His steps'. Each one follows Him in that in which he imitates Him'" ("Holy Virginity", *The Fathers of the Church*, reprinted as a pamphlet [Boston: Daughters of St. Paul, 1961]).

can see this from St. Paul, who is quite clear about both the centrality of charity and the truth that it does not stand alone. In his famous hymn in praise of love he says:

> If I speak in the tongues of men and of angels, but have not love, I am a noisy gong or a clanging cymbal. And if I have prophetic powers, and understand all mysteries and all knowledge, and if I have all faith, so as to remove mountains, but have not love, I am nothing. If I give away all I have, and if I deliver my body to be burned, but have not love, I gain nothing. (1 Cor 13:1–3)

This teaching from St. Paul can be found all through the New Testament. Christ himself tells us that upon the love of God and of neighbor depend the whole law and the prophets (Mt 22:35–40). "Over all these virtues", says St. Paul, "put on love, which binds the rest together and makes them perfect" (Col 3:14, NAB). Charity establishes the mutual love of friendship between God and ourselves. We were created to live in communion with God, united to God, as St. Augustine says, and it is by charity that we enter into this union. Indeed, the union itself is a union of love.

Charity is the essence or center of Christian existence, but it does not follow from this great truth that it is the only virtue. Because nothing without charity is of any use, it does not follow that there is nothing else to strive after. This is a point about which a lot of people go wrong today. They seem to think that because of the central importance of charity, it follows that the other virtues do not really matter. But faith and hope, as well as the moral virtues, have their own intrinsic importance and are of essential importance in living the Christian life. This is what St. Paul has to say:

> Love is patient and kind; love is not jealous or boastful; it is not arrogant or rude. Love does not insist on its own way; it

is not irritable or resentful; it does not rejoice at wrong, but rejoices in the right. Love bears all things, believes all things, hopes all things, endures all things. (1 Cor 13:4–7)

St. Paul is teaching us here that charity requires other virtues, like patience, kindness, and endurance, and that vices such as jealousy, boastfulness, irritation, and resentment have a reality that can destroy charity. These virtues and these vices are something different from charity, and although closely connected to charity, they must be practiced—or fought, in the case of the vices—in order to develop real charity. We have to live our lives in a way pleasing to God, and we do this, not merely to obey a law, but so that the deepest needs and desires of our heart will one day be satisfied in the vision of the Blessed Trinity. In the meantime we have to learn to practice the virtues and fight the vices so that, as Scupoli puts it, we will "attain in Christ the height of perfection".

The end we are seeking is beatitude, or the kingdom of God, but we will only achieve this if we are willing to sacrifice in order to achieve purity of heart. Cassian laid down the fundamental principle of this asceticism of love in the early years of the fifth century, and he sums up this teaching in his own way by saying:

For the sake of [purity of heart] everything is to be done and desired. For its sake solitude is to be pursued; for its sake we know that we must undertake fasts, vigils, labours, bodily deprivation, reading, and other virtuous things, so that by them we may be able to acquire and keep a heart untouched by any harmful passion, and so that by taking these steps we may be able to ascend to the perfection of love.[9]

---

[9] John Cassian, conference 1, chap. 7, no. 1, in *The Conferences*, trans. and annotated by Boniface Ramsey, O.P. (New York: Paulist Press, 1997), p. 45.

The road we must travel to obtain this purity of heart is the way of Christ's new commandment of love, but this has to be properly understood in a way that includes "fasts, labours, bodily deprivation, reading and other virtuous things". In other words, Christian living involves asceticism, and asceticism must include the moral dimension of Christianity. Furthermore, to live a Christian moral life requires that we adopt the means necessary to ensure we do in fact lead such lives.

Everyday Life and Religion

Christian perfection requires that we concentrate on our ordinary experience and try to correct what is sinful and imperfect in our daily lives as well as work to develop the virtues that we actually need. Scupoli says that one of the ways the devil deflects us from an effective spiritual combat is, first of all, "to turn away our attention from the enemies who are close at hand to injure and assail us" and then, secondly, "to fill us with resolutions and desires after higher degrees of perfection".[10]

> And while we cannot endure the least thing or the slightest word which crosses our will, we waste our time in long meditations and resolutions to endure the acutest sufferings on earth or in purgatory for the love of God. And because our inferior part feels no repugnance at these things in the distance, we flatter ourselves, miserable creatures as we are, into the conceit that we belong to the class of patient and heroic sufferers.[11]

[10] SC 30, p. 77.
[11] Ibid., pp. 77–78.

It is clear, then, that the struggle for perfection, as understood by Scupoli, is focused on ordinary moral experience, and Newman reinforces this perspective:

> It is the saying of holy men that, if we wish to be perfect, we have nothing more to do than to perform the ordinary duties of the day well. A short road to perfection—short, not because easy, but because pertinent and intelligible. There are no short ways to perfection, but there are sure ones.[12]

Newman, as we saw in the first chapter, said that we all know what it is to give God *im*perfect service, and from this poor performance we can grasp the idea of perfection. Furthermore, in pointing out that we are going to understand perfection by examining our own imperfect religious actions, Newman reminds us that the perfection demanded of us is to be understood as Christian perfection. That is, spiritual combat is not concerned with the perfection of a soldier or an athlete or a lawyer, as such, but with the perfection of human beings, as human beings, in their relation to God. As it is the perfection of human beings, as human beings, that is at issue, then perfection must be open to all. If "the poor and maimed and blind and lame" (Lk 14:21), are not excluded, then Christian perfection cannot be based on natural talents or good fortune or in itself require anything out of the ordinary: "[Perfection] does not mean any extraordinary service, anything out of the way, or especially heroic—not

---

[12] Placid Murray, O.S.B., quoting Newman's chapter address of September 27, 1856, in "Newman's Oratory Papers", in *Newman the Oratorian* (Dublin: Gill and Macmillan, 1969). Also reprinted, with omissions and alterations, as "A Short Road to Perfection", in *Meditations and Devotions*, in *Prayers, Verses, and Devotions: The Devotions of Bishop Andrewes, Meditations and Devotions, Verses on Various Occasions* (San Francisco: Ignatius Press, 2000), pp. 328–29, here, p. 328.

all have the opportunity of heroic acts, of sufferings." [13] It might be said that Newman's emphasis on conduct in everyday life is misplaced because Christianity is concerned with the development of the spiritual dimension in man, or an appreciation of "higher values", and neither this spiritual dimension nor this appreciation of higher values has much to do with the tedious round of everyday existence. This is a large and complex subject, but we ought to keep in mind the following points:

1. Christianity is not only a doctrine, but a way of life. Jesus said, "I am the way, and the truth, and the life" (Jn 14:6). The Church brings us the revelation of God in Jesus Christ. But this revelation is a *saving* knowledge. That is, God gave us his truth so that we could make "the glory of God and our own eternal salvation" the treasure of our heart by living in a certain way. The way we live has to be based on truth, but the truth was not given to us merely to satisfy our intellectual needs, but so that we might use it to live as God wants us to live. It was with good reason that the early Christians sometimes referred to Christianity as *the Way*, [14] for the religion of Christ is not solely truth; it is also life and the road over which we must travel if we are to achieve our destiny and final happiness.

2. A way of life has to be related to ordinary existence as we find it. The whole idea of an interior life unrelated to everyday existence with its ordinariness, its complexities, and confusion is a mistaken one. Whatever Christian living is going to entail, it is going to require at least living in the world as it is, even if that world is a monastic one. Indeed, I would want to argue that without this reference to existence

---

[13] Newman, "Short Road", p. 328.
[14] "If he found any belonging to the Way": Acts 9:2.

as it really is, then whatever remains of the self is of little importance. In the *Phenomenology of Spirit*, Hegel describes what he acidly calls "the beautiful soul" that

> lives in dread of besmirching the splendour of its inner being by action and an existence; and, in order to preserve the purity of its heart, it flees from contact with the actual world, and persists in its self-willed impotence to renounce its self which is reduced to the extreme of ultimate abstraction.[15]

The beautiful soul disappears into nothingness, and what it leaves behind is unregenerate human nature. But our unregenerate human nature is what we have to begin with; it should not be what we end up with at the end of all our efforts.

There is no shortcut to an enduring relationship with Christ that bypasses the moral demands of faith, because the call of Christ is a summons to a better moral life. There is, however, a second reason for trying to follow the law of Christ in our daily lives, and this, as we have already seen, is that without at least trying to develop the Christian virtues, we are very quickly going to lose our grasp on the treasure of our hearts. It is in our daily experience that the will is trained and strengthened, and without this training and this strengthening we will waver and lose sight of our goal. It is only a will toughened up by trying to do the right thing in practice that can keep our minds focused on the truths of faith. Without a serious effort to live a moral life, we will weaken into the sort of people incapable of sustaining our end of the relationship with Christ.

The earliest monastic tradition was quite clear on this point. In the *Institutes*, Cassian teaches that it is only those who

---

[15] G. Hegel, *Phenomenology of Spirit*, trans. A. V. Miller (Oxford: Clarendon Press, 1979), p. 400.

have developed the virtues by living in community who should go on to live a more solitary life.[16] Solitude does not, by itself, cure our faults. This is the teaching both of experience and of the tradition. Solitude, Cassian remarks, "generally not only preserves but intensifies the faults of those who have undergone no correction".[17] These words are found in Cassian's discussion of patience, but the example is an admirable example of the general point that solitude is no way to perfect the virtues required for the foundation of the spiritual life:

> For a man appears to himself to be patient and humble, just as long as he comes across nobody in intercourse; but he will presently revert to his former nature, whenever the chance of any sort of passion occurs.... For when the opportunity for practising [the virtues] among men is removed, our faults will more and more increase in us, unless we have been purified from them.[18]

The desire for solitude, and an interest in the contemplative life, may, therefore, be based on an unwillingness to come to terms with ourselves and to undertake the difficult job of trying to become more Christian in our behavior toward other people and toward ourselves. And, without this effort at developing the virtues and fighting the vices, we will neither be equipped for the necessary warfare against everything that

[16] John Cassian, *Institutes of the Coenobia*, bk. 8, chap. 18, in *Nicene and Post-Nicene Fathers*, ed. Philip Schaff and Henry Wace (Grand Rapids, Mich.: Eerdmans, 1978), 11:262: "It is those who are perfect and purified from all faults who ought to seek the desert, and when they have thoroughly exterminated all their faults amid the assembly of the brethren, they should enter it not by way of cowardly flight, but for the purpose of divine contemplation, and with the desire of deeper insight into heavenly things, which can only be gained in solitude by those who are perfect."

[17] Ibid.

[18] Ibid.

pulls us away from Christ nor possess the strength and perseverance to remain close to him in the dark days. If we do
not want to be like Herod, who heard the Baptist gladly but
turned away when things got rough, then we must respond
to the call in the ordinary circumstances of our everyday
lives. We do this so that we may begin to strengthen our
hold on Christ, and even if the progress is slow and halting,
like that of Nicodemus, we will be turning ourselves into
the sort of people who will not only make of God the treasure of their hearts but also keep him there. It is an understandable mistake to think that we can deepen a living and
personal relationship with our Lord in isolation from other
people and the moral demands this living with others makes
upon us. But, understandable or not, it is a mistake to believe we can respond in an immediate way to the call of Christ
without any reference to the world we live in.

3. We cannot live in the truth of faith without a concern
for ordinary existence. A. N. Whitehead wrote that "conduct is a by-product of religion—an inevitable by-product,
but not the main point." [19] Well, perhaps not, but unless a
reasonable attention is paid to the moral dimension of our
faith the *main point*, whatever it is exactly, is going to be
missed. "The insistence upon rules of conduct", he continues, "marks the ebb of religious fervour." [20] This goes to
show that philosophers are in some ways ahead of their time.
One of the reasons for Catholicism's lack of cutting edge, in
North America at least, is contemporary efforts to present
the "main point" without any moral demands. I suppose it is
true that if morality is presented as merely restricting, and in

[19] A. N. Whitehead, *Science and the Modern World* (Cambridge: University
Press, 1932), p. 237.
[20] Ibid., p. 238.

some sense anti-life, then a case could be made out for White-head's judgment. But Christianity does have a moral dimension, and to leave it out is to present something that is not Catholic Christianity. The ascetical doctrine of life is very much concerned to teach us how to improve our practice of this moral aspect of our faith. We are called to love God above all things and to follow the demands of that love in our daily lives. Nicodemus had finally to change his way of life, and following Christ involves trying to do what he wants us to do. "He who has my commandments and keeps them, he it is who loves me", says our Lord in St. John's Gospel (Jn 14:21). It is quite true that Catholicism is more than morality, but that does not mean that morality is not one of its most important aspects.

Newman's "Short Road to Perfection" is very much of Scupoli's way of thinking. It was written as a chapter address to his fellow Oratorians in Birmingham, and so the details of the rule of life it prescribes may not be appropriate for everyone in all circumstances. What is universal in Newman's plan is the focus on everyday life as each person's school of sanctity. He writes that, "he, then, is perfect who does the work of the day perfectly", and continues:

> If you ask me what you are to do in order to be perfect, I say, first—Do not lie in bed beyond the due time of rising; give your first thoughts to God; make a good visit to the Blessed Sacrament; say the Angelus devoutly; eat and drink to God's glory; say the Rosary well; be recollected; keep out bad thoughts; make your evening meditation well; examine yourself daily; go to bed in good time, and you are already perfect.[21]

---

[21] "Short Road", pp. 328–29.

This has been called a "somewhat governess-like conception" of perfection.[22] But if perfection really is open to all and has to be worked at through ordinary life, then Newman's account is a clear and condensed version of the perfection required of a Christian. Furthermore, it makes no concessions to weakness and is much more difficult to live by than might at first appear.

Perfection and Beatitude

Working for perfection is an essential part of Christian living, but unless we remind ourselves that spiritual combat is undertaken because we desire to be united with Christ, then things will go wrong with us in at least two ways. In the first place, forgetting about beatitude leads to a focus on spiritual combat that distorts asceticism itself. Secondly, if we ignore the purpose of asceticism, we will not persevere.

When the spiritual combat becomes an end in itself, it degenerates into a refined sort of selfishness with all the emphasis on the fact that it is my own perfection that is being worked for with little concern either for other people or often, so it would seem, even for God. The safeguard against this danger is to remember that we seek perfection because Christ has told us to, and he has told us to so that, with his grace, we may become united with him. This has already been discussed in various places, but we must always remember the words of Cassian that "it is for the sake of purity of heart that everything is to be done and desired so that we may be able to ascend to the perfection of love."[23]

---

[22] By John Passmore, in *The Perfectibility of Man* (New York: Charles Scribner's Sons, 1970), p. 123.

[23] See above, pp. 241–42.

Secondly, if we forget the purpose of spiritual combat, we will not persevere in a struggle that is often painful, in which there is a large element of failure, and which at times seems pointless. Catholic morality knows nothing of Kant's "duty for duty's sake", but it does require the effort to be faithful to principles that at times make harsh demands on us. The obvious examples are those involved with the Christian imperatives about chastity, but these are by no means the only ones. Forgiveness in the face of real wrong, fidelity to serious commitments when they are no longer to our obvious advantage, courage to hold on and not give way to despair in the face of a fatal disease or the death of those we love, all these sorts of experience require something more than a concern for our own perfection if we are going to go on trying to live a Christian life. None of this means that the spiritual combat has suddenly become impossible or irrelevant, but perseverance requires a deep-rooted conviction of the reality of the promises of God held out to us in Jesus Christ.

But, how is this deep-rooted conviction to be acquired? There is a real difficulty here, because we are not asking about an intense experience of conversion. Rather, we want to know how an effective belief in the providence of God, and his promise of beatitude for each one of us personally, is to be acquired. Philip Neri said to the young John Leonard:[24] "You are a saint, but try to remain what you are."[25] It is one thing

---

[24] St. John Leonard was a pharmacist's helper who grew up during the Council of Trent, began priestly studies at twenty-five, and founded at Lucca the Clerks Regular of the Mother of God to carry out the ideals of priestly ministry projected by the Council of Trent. He wrote a catechism of Christian doctrine that remained in use for three centuries. St. Philip Neri persuaded him to have the new foundation keep to Italy as its mission field.

[25] Louis Ponnelle and Louis Bordet, *St. Philip Neri and the Roman Society of His Time*, trans. Ralph Francis Kerr (London: Sheed & Ward, 1932), p. 578.

to be overwhelmed, as was St. Peter, with the certainty that "You are the Christ, the Son of the living God" (Mt 16:16) and to be convinced that our happiness depends on really accepting and responding to this truth; but it is another thing to make this conviction a living and enduring reality in our lives. The catch is not so much to put Christ at the center of our lives from time to time as to keep him there. In other words, perseverance is also required. Doubt, temptation, and confusion all too easily blunt and obscure the perception of the goal of our existence. The treasure seems least like a treasure when we need it most.

This just seems to be the way things are, and it is often the effort to live in a Christian way that keeps our awareness of the goal alive. That is, in doing what God commands, we are brought back to a realization that there is a purpose to our lives and a goal to our existence. This is the case even though logically it is true that the value of our actions depends ultimately on whether or not they lead us to beatitude.

What is involved in trying to make and to keep Christ as the goal and treasure of our hearts? How are we, that is, going to be able to persevere in spiritual combat? First of all, we have to remember that no one else can fight the fight for us, and, secondly, the struggle must be based on a serious acceptance of the Christian faith.

The hope that it will be enough to conform to external rules is a mistaken one. Herod and Nicodemus responded each in his own way to "the drawing of this love and the voice of this calling";[26] one rejected the call, while the other accepted it. This reminds us that there is a personal element in answering divine calls that is crucial for the future of the

---

[26] *The Cloud of Unknowing, Together with The Epistle of Privy Counsel*, ed. Abbot Justin McCann (London: Burns & Oates, 1952), chap. 2, p. 6.

one responding or refusing to respond. No one else can say yes or no for us, and this personal responsibility cannot be shrugged off with talk about the influence of historical background or society or psychological conditioning.

> That we are accountable for what we do and what we are, that, in spite of all aids or hindrances from without, each soul is the cause of its own happiness or misery, is a truth certified to us both by Nature and Revelation.[27]

Pope John Paul II has argued for this unfashionable position by showing that a refusal to accept this fundamental responsibility is also to deny human freedom. It is, the Pope says, "a truth of faith, as well as confirmed by our experience and reason, that the human person is free".[28] This truth cannot be disregarded in order to place the blame for individuals' sins on external factors such as structures, systems, or other peoples.

> Above all, this would be to deny the person's dignity and freedom, which are manifested—even though in a negative and disastrous way—also in this responsibility for sin committed. Hence there is nothing so personal and untransferable in each individual as merit for virtue or responsibility for sin.[29]

The freedom being discussed here is not the imaginary capacity to become anything we want, or even the power to fulfill ourselves by realizing our talents. Rather, it means that at the core of each person's existence there is the real possibility of saying yes to what is good and no to what is evil.

---

[27] J. H. Newman, "Human Responsibility, as Independent of Circumstances", sermon 8, in *Fifteen Sermons*, p. 137.

[28] John Paul II, apostolic exhortation *Reconciliation and Penance* (*Reconciliatio et paenitentia*, December 2, 1984), sec. 16.

[29] Ibid.

Spiritual combat appears differently in different lives, but no matter what form it takes, it presupposes this freedom.

This free and personal adhesion to the call of Christ, however, has to be correctly understood. It is sometimes said that the call of Christ itself is so unlike any other experience that there is no need of further evidence or argument. This is true, but it is not the whole truth.

In a letter of 1874, Newman wrote:

> I should myself consider that his personal hold upon Him is the immediate evidence of divine truth to every consistent Christian; who has no need of having his answer in hand to every one of the multiform, manyheaded objections which from day to day he may hear urged against his faith. [30]

In other words, that the personal encounter with Christ, in whatever form it may take place, needs no further justification is true so far as it goes. The trouble is that it does not go far enough, because even religious experiences change, and if we base our relationship with God on what happens to be of interest to us at the moment, or on how we feel, then we will never establish anything solid. We will be like the man in the Gospel who built his house on sand and could not survive the rain and wind. [31]

Newman, after stating clearly that there must be a personal "hold" by the believer on Christ, then goes on to say

[30] Many Protestants, Newman says, would hold: "that *our Lord Himself* is all in all, evidence and proof as well as Object, of our faith; that we desire no better assurance that He is God Incarnate, than is conveyed in His own voice, 'It is I'" (*The Letters and Diaries of John Henry Newman* [Edinburgh: Thomas Nelson, and Oxford: Clarendon Press, 1978–], 27:109).

[31] "And every one who hears these words of mine and does not do them will be like a foolish man who built his house upon the sand; and the rain fell, and the floods came, and the winds blew and beat against that house, and it fell; and great was the fall of it" (Mt 7:26–27).

that there must also be a further safeguard if "our poor human nature" is to be protected against deception and change. "Religious experiences", he says, "and convictions, when right, come from God; but Satan can counterfeit them; and those may feel assurances who have no claim to them." [32] It is just because Newman's emphasis on the personal and immediate is so consistent through all his work that this insistence on a complement, or supplement, to the personal and immediate is so telling:

> And in matter of fact, men who have professed the most beautiful things, and with the utmost earnestness and sincerity believed in their union with our Lord, have often slipped away into some form of error on the ground of new experiences and assurances, nay into scepticism and infidelity. Looking over the letters of early friends, who are now unbelievers, I have before now come upon the expression of their faith and hope in Christ so simple and fervent, and of their experimental certitude so vivid, as to fill me with awe and tearful pity at the vision of such a change.[33]

The personal encounter with Christ can be real but still be lost; and if Christ is to remain the treasure of our heart, our relation to him will have to be based on something more than experience, no matter how genuine that experience may be. To experience must be added the objectivity of faith, and faith must be nourished by a Christian style of life.

The fact of change and emotional inconsistency is one of the reasons the masters of the spiritual life of the Church have always emphasized that a fruitful quest for God consists

---

[32] *Letters and Diaries*, 27:109. "But I consider too, that the Lover of souls, and Searcher of hearts has not thought it enough for us, has not felt it safe for our poor nature, to have no other safeguard for our faith than this."

[33] Ibid.

in the *knowledge* of the goodness and the greatness of God as well as knowledge about the human condition in general and knowledge about ourselves in particular. Faith, St. Thomas teaches, is more like knowledge than it is like willing or feeling;[34] and St. John says: "This is eternal life, that they *know* thee the only true God, and Jesus Christ whom thou hast sent" (Jn 17:3, emphasis added). Now knowledge is something stable and fixed and not so susceptible to change as anything based on emotions, moods, real suffering, or even a change in the weather. That is obvious, but what it is easy to forget is that intense and even genuine experiences of turning to God and away from sin are not fixed, and if they are to have an enduring effect in our lives, they will have to be worked into the structure of Christian belief.

This structure of Christian belief, this knowledge about who we are and about our destiny, comes from God. God reveals his loving plan for our salvation, and we receive this revelation in faith. In the Letter to the Hebrews, we read that whoever would draw near to God must believe that he exists and that he rewards those who seek him (Heb 11:6). In this sense faith is the foundation of the whole spiritual life, and so St. Thomas says that faith by its very nature precedes all other virtues.[35] Without God's gift of faith, we would not know that God has destined us for a life of bliss in the vision of God, nor would we be able to hope for this fulfillment of our longings. Without faith we would not know with any clarity how God wants us to live or what our nature is really like. The hidden mysteries of our destiny, of our nature, and of how we are to live are made known to us through Jesus Christ. The *Catechism* reminds us that it is Christ

[34] ST 2a, 2ae, 2, 2 and 3; 2a, 2ae, 4, 1.
[35] ST 2a, 2ae, 4, 7.

who reveals man fully to himself, making his exalted vocation manifest. It goes on to add: "Endowed with a spiritual soul, with intellect and with free will, the human person is from his very conception ordered to God and destined for eternal beatitude." [36] It is knowledge we need when subjective certainties seem to fade, and it is faith that brings this knowledge.

Really to possess Christ as the treasure of our heart requires a personal response to "the drawing of this love and the voice of this calling"; it also requires that this experience be nourished and guided by faith.

The spiritual combat is itself one of the ways we begin to experience the truths of the realities of our faith. The framework of the spiritual life is based on God's revelation in Christ, but this framework and this revelation have to be appropriated by the individual in his approach to God. From this perspective spirituality is intensely personal, but it is not, to repeat the point in a different way, an idiosyncratic or a free-wheeling approach to life. Christian asceticism, as Scupoli understands it, is an asceticism of love. Any sacrifice we make, any suffering we endure, should be seen as helping to make us over into the image of the Son of God who redeemed us and who makes himself and the truth of his Gospel known to us in the struggle to fight against the poverty and failures of our moral life.

In his little treatise *On Inward Peace* Scupoli says:

Thy heart was created by God for this end alone—to be loved and possessed by him. And by means of this love thou mayest do what thou wilt with it; and all things, however difficult, will thus become most easy to thee. The first thing, then, which thou hast to do, is so to fix and establish the

[36] CCC 1711.

intention of thy heart, that the exterior may flow from the interior.[37]

Scupoli, like Cassian, has moved the center of the spiritual life away from actions to purity of motive and intention. His move does not appear as a particularly surprising one today, but we should be clear that he has not substituted an ethics of authenticity, or self-legislation, for Catholic morality, and his book outlines one set of practices for responding to God's call in a more serious way and how to go about avoiding the double response of acceptance and rejection that so often seems to characterize the human heart when left to itself. To follow Christ with a less divided heart, and to seek to be united with him, means undertaking a journey in faith, a journey that will have its ups and down, its successes and its failures. But the most important thing is gradually to learn that it is a journey in which we will be accompanied by the stranger on the road to Emmaus (Lk 24:13–35), whom we will learn to recognize, and believe in, as we try to follow in his footsteps. Like the disciples, we will be able to say "Did not our hearts burn within us while he talked to us on the road, while he opened to us the scriptures?" (Lk 24:32).

Beatitude and Immortality

The morality associated with the ascetical life seems to have little relevance and even less authority in the modern world. One of the reasons for this is that spiritual combat is based on principles and judged by standards that are given to us by our Christian faith. Without these principles and standards, the ascetical life becomes an exercise in self-realization or,

---

[37] *On Inward Peace*, chap. 1, in Lorenzo Scupoli, *Spiritual Combat, Together with The Treatise of Inward Peace* (London: Burns & Oates, 1963).

even worse, a sort of spiritual athletics undertaken in the interests of self-discipline. One set of principles and standards that has a direct bearing on Christian living is based on belief in the resurrection and the hope of beatitude.

It is said that people today have ceased to believe in heaven and are not afraid of hell. This attitude just seems to be part of the present-day climate of opinion and so is taken for granted. Iris Murdoch, according to her biographer, thought "the Christian 'lie' about the conquest of death by Jesus deeply vulgar",[38] and in saying this she gave voice to what many people think today (or feel, as they would probably say). But, for the believer the promise of Christ, "deeply vulgar" or not, that "where I am, there shall my servant be also" (Jn 12:26) is an assurance that the spiritual combat makes us into the servants of the incarnate Son of God, who will take us finally to where he is now.

I have said that *Spiritual Combat Revisited* is not concerned to argue for the truth of Christianity but to show how the ascetical life is one of its essential aspects. I have accepted the *Catechism of the Catholic Church* as normative and argued within the context of this authoritative exposition of the Catholic faith. Bad taste, or not being socially or academically respectable, is not the point at issue. Newman thought a belief in immortality was the doctrine "which broke the power and the fascination of paganism".[39] He believed the doctrine to

[38] Peter Conradi, *Iris Murdoch: A Life* (New York, London: W. W. Norton & Co., 2001), p. 354.

[39] J. H. Newman, "The Immortality of the Soul", sermon 2 in vol. 1 of *Parochial and Plain Sermons* (San Francisco: Ignatius Press, 1997), p. 14. "Every one will say, and say truly, that this was the great and solemn doctrine which gave the Gospel a claim to be heard when first preached, which arrested the thoughtless multitudes, who were busied in the pleasure and pursuits of this life, awed them with the vision of the life to come, and sobered them till they turned to God with a true heart" (ibid.).

be true. Iris Murdoch thought it was a lie and, probably equally importantly for her, that it was also deeply vulgar. But Catholics are committed to a belief in the resurrection of the dead. The *Catechism* is quite clear and says that "Belief in the resurrection of the dead has been an essential element of the Christian faith from its beginnings." [40]

Iris Murdoch's views, of course, did not begin with her. The belief in immortality may have helped to establish Christianity in the ancient world, but by Newman's time the same belief was used as a prime example of what was wrong with religion. Beatitude as the vision of God in a future life began to be viewed as "pie in the sky" designed to distract the poor and the persecuted from the injustices and frustrations of this life. The ninetenth century saw endless variations on Ludwig Feuerbach's theme that God and heaven are nothing but human constructs that rob mankind of its best qualities: "The more empty life is, the fuller, the more concrete is God. The impoverishing of the real world and the enriching of God is one act. Only the poor man has a rich God." [41]

Belief in God and immortality are symptoms, for Feuerbach, of a deep-seated inner division or alienation in the psyche. Religion is not just a mechanical projection of these qualities into an empty beyond; it represents what we want to be the case. We seek in heaven what we cannot find on earth. The worse, that is, our experience of the human condition, the more we strain and strive to find perfection in a heaven of our own construction. The only cure for this, Feuerbach believed, is to realize that the perfections we ascribe to God are really our own. From this he argues that salvation does not lie in another world but depends on our

[40] CCC 991.
[41] Ludwig Feuerbach, *The Essence of Christianity* (New York: Harper & Row, 1957), p. 73.

taking back for ourselves those qualities that are really ours in the first place. Forget about heaven; do not become distracted with vague promises of a future life; and concentrate on enriching this world with the qualities religion has stolen from mankind.

The logic of Feuerbach's arguments may be shaky, but the force of their rhetoric is undeniable. George Eliot (Marian Evans), who translated Feuerbach into English in 1854, is an obvious but by no means untypical example.[42] Walking in the gardens of Trinity, Cambridge, she is reported to have said "with terrible earnestness" about the words God, immortality, and duty: "How inconceivable was the *first*, how unbelievable the *second*, and yet how peremptory and absolute the *third*".[43] George Eliot was a fair-minded woman who understood Newman's position at the time of the controversy with Kingsley that resulted in the *Apologia*,[44] but her words sound the quintessential note of Victorian scepticism.

We are not quite so high-minded today, and duty would probably not fare much better than either God or immortality. Since George Eliot and Feuerbach there have been Marx and Freud, liberation theology, as well as various forms of deconstructing any and all sorts of objectivity, which have helped to create a climate of opinion in which the Christian certainties about immortality, of which Newman spoke, now often seem insubstantial and deeply suspect from a moral point of view. Is it not morally wrong, we seem constantly to be

---

[42] She had also translated Strauss' *Life of Jesus* in 1846, which brought biblical criticism to the consciousness of the educated public.

[43] Cited in Kathryn Hughes, *George Eliot, The Last Victorian* (London: Fourth Estate, 1998), p. 400.

[44] She thought Kingsley's pamphlet against Newman was "thoroughly vicious", "a mixture of arrogance, coarse impertinence and unscrupulousness with real intellectual incompetence" (cited in Martin Svaglic's edition of the *Apologia* [Oxford: Clarendon Press, 1967], p. xxv).

asked, to think about the next world when this one is such a mess? Is it not the case that a repressive orthodoxy has yoked the Church with the established social order and used the Christian promise of immortality to discourage the development of a just society?[45]

If we are going even to begin to understand the spiritual combat inherent in Christianity, we will have to see it within the framework of a seeking for a beatitude that will never be completed in this life. This does not mean abandoning the high moral ground that the followers of Feuerbach seem to have occupied without protest, because there are powerful arguments for the necessity of immortality based on moral considerations. It must be fully and frankly admitted that this world is in fact full of injustice. The fact that the wicked prosper is, after all, one of the main themes in the Psalms, and Job's complaint is based on a realistic, if unsentimental, perception:

> Why do the wicked live,
>   reach old age, and grow mighty in power?
> Their children are established in their presence,
>   and their offspring before their eyes.
> Their houses are safe from fear,
>   and no rod of God is upon them. . . .
> They spend their days in prosperity,
>   and in peace they go down to Sheol.[46]

---

[45] George Eliot herself was much given to this sort of argument. "There was something about the aura of moral seriousness combined with the pedagogic tradition which always brought out the prig in Marian. Browning recalled how during dinner at Trinity (in 1868) 'she talked to me solemnly about the duties of life, about the shallow immorality of believing that all things would turn out for the best, and the danger of fixing our attention too much on the life to come, as likely to distract us from doing our duty in this world'" (Hughes, *George Eliot*, p. 400).

[46] Job 21: 7–9, 13. Also see Psalms 10, 14, 37, 73, 94:3, etc.

If Job's perception is correct, and it is, then immortality is required if justice is to be given to those who have suffered and, more generally, if the wrongs of this existence are to be rectified. This is not, as Kant saw, an unanswerable argument for the reality of immortality.[47] It is, however, a powerful suasion for the appropriateness of the Christian faith. It is not morally obtuse to accept the teaching of our faith that there is a recognizable identity between our personality after death and what it is now; and that, furthermore, we will take with us what we have made of ourselves for both good and evil. That is, it is a great stimulus to moral effort and a strong support to the human spirit if we can believe that the moral life is something more than a noble but desperate and ultimately unsuccessful enterprise undertaken against the background of a blind and indifferent universe.[48] Perhaps people have sometimes concentrated on the afterlife in a way that has in fact interfered with their Christian obligations in this world. It does not require an intelligence of surpassing power to suspect this may at times have been the case. Nonetheless, that is no reason to rewrite Christianity.

[47] Kant, *Critique*, p. 219.
[48] Kant says that "This principle of the moral destination of our nature, namely that it is only in an endless progress that we can attain perfect accordance with the moral law, is of the greatest use" both for moral philosophy and for religion (ibid.).

"AND THAT IS MEANT FOR ME"

—St. Frances de Chantal on her death-bed, quoted by
Elisabeth Stopp, *Madame de Chantal: Portrait of a Saint*

On the night before she died, Jane Frances de Chantal asked
to have read to her the tremendous passage in the *Confessions*
of St. Augustine, describing the mystical experience he and
his mother shared just before Monica died at Ostia on her
way home to Africa.

> We entered into our own minds. We moved up beyond them
> so as to attain to the region of inexhaustible abundance where
> you feed Israel eternally with truth for food. There life is the
> wisdom by which all creatures come into being, both things
> that were and which will be.... And while we talked and
> panted after it, we touched it in some small degree by a mo-
> ment of total concentration of the heart. And we sighed and
> left behind us "the firstfruits of the Spirit" (Rom. 8:23).[1]

"And that is meant for me", whispered Jane Frances, as she
too prepared to leave her body in a land that was no longer
her own and the reading from St. Augustine came to an end.
But her words also apply to the mystical experience itself

---

[1] St. Augustine, *Confessions*, bk. 9, chap. 10, in *Basic Writings of St. Augustine*
(New York: Random House, 1948), p. 24.

that St. Augustine describes. "The end of love", St. Francis had written in the *Treatise on the Love of God*, "is no other thing than union of the lover and the thing loved",[2] and as Jane Frances heard again St. Augustine's words, she also heard the echo of her own experience both as a mystic and as one who loved her daughters in religion, her own natural family, and, preeminently, Francis de Sales.[3]

Jane Frances knew firsthand about what Monica and Augustine shared. Most of the time her mysticism was what Sr. Ruth Burrows has called "lights off mysticism".[4] That is, she herself was not aware in any direct way of the working of God in her soul. Sometimes, though, God broke through into her experience. She did have visions; she was wrapped in ecstasy; and she did hear locutions, but most of the time, especially toward the end of her life, there was more darkness than illumination. Her own account of her spiritual condition, written under obedience, is a stern warning that the contemplative life is not a vocation for the faint-hearted.

> Sometimes, indeed often, my whole mind is just a confused turmoil of darkness and helplessness, casting up feelings of rebellion, doubts and every other sort of horror. When things are at their worst, this process is almost continual and gives me inconceivable anguish. I don't know what I would not do and suffer to be rid of this torture. On the one hand the

---

[2] St. Francis de Sales, *Treatise on the Love of God*, bk. 1, chap. 9, trans. Henry Benedict Mackey (Westminster, Md.: Newman Press, 1953), p. 39.

[3] One of the most concise and authoritative treatments of the experience at Ostia is to be found in A. Solignac, S.J., introduction to the *Confessions*, Bibliothèque augustinienne, vol. 13 (Paris: Desclée de Brouwer, 1962), p. 191. There is also a valuable bibliography on mysticism in the *Confessions* on p. 186.

[4] Ruth Burrows, "A Look at 'Experiences'", chap. 4 of *Guidelines for Mystical Prayer* (London: Sheed & Ward, 1976), pp. 45–55.

torment besets me and on the other I so much love my holy faith that I long to die for the least article of it.[5]

She herself described the life of St. Francis de Sales, and implicitly her own, as a martyrdom of love. The day-to-day abnegation of her own will, the generous, ever-increasing, gift of herself to God and to others, were the means God chose to unite her to himself; and these means were the proof and fruit of love.

Secondly, Jane Frances understood St. Augustine's strange compelling account of a shared mystical experience in a special way. Her own spiritual progress was inextricably bound up with that of St. Francis de Sales. Brémond wrote that the mystical development of the two saints was really only one and the same development.[6] The *Treatise on the Love of God* was written *for* Jane Frances, but more importantly, it was she, and the first members of her order, who were being written *about*.[7] The shared experience at Ostia has been described as an example of the "Society of Soul with Soul",[8] and Jane Francis knew all about that.

[5] Cited in Elisabeth Stopp, *Madame de Chantal: Portrait of a Saint* (London: Faber and Faber, 1962), p. 233.

[6] "Notre méthode ... toute historique et analytique nous impose donc de suivre d'un même regard l'ascension parallèle de ces deux âmes, leur épanouissement mystique, le rayonnement de l'une sur l'autre" (*Histoire littéraire du sentiment réligieux en France* [Paris: Librairie Blond et Gay, 1923], 2:538).

[7] Henri Brémond, "Sainte Chantal tient une grande place dans l'histoire intime du *Traité de l'Amour de Dieu*. C'est pour elle et près d'elle que ce livre a été écrit: mieux encore, c'est elle qu'il nous raconte et les premières visitandines" (ibid.).

[8] Robert J O'Connell, S.J., *St. Augustine's Confessions, the Odyssey of Soul* (Cambridge, Mass.: Harvard Univ. Press, 1969), p. 115.

It is sometimes said that the contemplative life is not sufficiently ordered toward the Church. Hans Urs von Balthasar, in discussing St. John of the Cross, says that there is a "remarkable lacuna in St John's thought, the yawning gap where the Church should be".[9]

> Where, in the whole of John's work, is the neighbour? Where is the communion of saints? Where is the Johannine criterion for love of God: love of the brother?[10]

Whether or not this criticism can be sustained in the case of St. John of the Cross, it certainly does give expression to the suspicion that the spiritual life is essentially a selfish one. It is thought to be selfish, that is, both in the sense that it is an isolated and introverted cultivation of the self as well as in the sense of its having no interest in, or concern for, other people. Neither of these understandings of selfishness can be taken as applying to either St. Jane Frances or St. Francis. At the center of the most fundamental relationship of all, that is, between the soul and God, there is (for both of them) the presence of the beloved other; a beloved loved indeed, in God, and not in the place of God, but loved and served as what God has created and God loves.

But, there is no Christian love, and no mystical experience, without spiritual combat, and this combat remains until the end. It may not always be the focus of attention, but the continual imitation of the Crucified is a necessary mark of any genuine Christian spirituality. Scupoli taught this to

[9] Hans Urs von Balthasar, *The Glory of the Lord*, vol. 3 (San Francisco: Ignatius Press, 1986), p. 166.

[10] Ibid., p. 167. Von Balthasar goes on to suggest that St. John did not take seriously enough the *reality* of the images of the New Testament, "the reality of the God who *descends*, who comes down into flesh and pain and death" (ibid.). This judgment is in my view, as the Scots would say, "not proven".

Francis de Sales, and he to Jane Frances. Newman learned it from the Fathers, and it was reenforced by his reading of Scupoli and Francis. If we today, with some right, demand a more open and less constricted way to divine intimacy, then we must also relearn the Gospel lesson, repeated by the saints and prophets of the spiritual life, that the pearl of great price does not come cheap. We will have to learn to make the words of the dying saint our own: "And that is meant for me."

Abbreviations

CCC   *Catechism of the Catholic Church*, 2d ed. Vatican City: Libreria Editrice Vaticana, 1997.

SC   Lorenzo Scupoli, *Spiritual Combat, Together with The Treatise of Inward Peace*. London: Burns & Oates, 1963.

ST   St. Thomas Aquinas, *Summa Theologiae*

Bibliography

Anonymous. *The Cloud of Unknowing and Other Treatises*. Edited by Abbot Justin McCann. London: Burns & Oates, 1952.

Anonymous. *The Pursuit of Wisdom*. Translated, edited, and annotated by James A. Walsh, S.J., and George A. Maloney, S.J. New York: Paulist Press, 1988.

Anscombe, G. E. M. *Intention*. Oxford: Basil Blackwell, 1957.

Aristotle. *Nichomachean Ethics*. In *The Basic Works of Aristotle*. New York: Random House, 1941.

Augustine, St. *Confessions*. Translated with notes by Henry Chadwick. Oxford and New York: Oxford Univ. Press, 1992.

———. *Confessions*. Bibliothèque augustinienne, vol. 13. Paris: Desclée de Brouwer, 1962.

———. "Holy Virginity". In *The Fathers of the Church*. Reprinted as a pamphlet. Boston: Daughters of St. Paul, 1961.

Aumann, Jordan. *Spiritual Theology*. London: Sheed & Ward, 1980.

Bacci, Pietro. *The Life of St. Philip Neri*. Translated by F. A. Antrobus. London: Kegan Paul, Trench, Trübner, 1902.

Balthasar, Hans Urs von. *The Glory of the Lord*. Vol. 3. San Francisco: Ignatius Press, 1982.

Barrett, C. K. *The Gospel according to St. John*. London: S.P.C.K., 1962.

Baur, Benedict, O.S.B. *Frequent Confession, Its Place in the Spiritual Life*. Translated by Patrick C. Barry, S.J. Dublin: Four Courts Press, 1984.

Benedict, St. *The Rule of St. Benedict*. Edited and translated by Abbot Justin McCann. London: Sheed & Ward, 1972.

Bernard of Clairvaux, St. "Jesu dulcis memoria". Translated by Edward Caswall. In *Lyra catholica*. London, 1849.

Brémond, Henri. *Histoire littéraire du sentiment réligieux en France*. Vol. 2. Paris: Librairie Blond et Gay, 1923.

Brock, Stephen L. *Action and Conduct*. Edinburgh: T&T Clark, 1998.

Brown, Raymond. *The Death of the Messiah*. New York: Doubleday, 1993.

Burrows, Ruth. *Guidelines for Mystical Prayer*. London: Sheed & Ward, 1976.

————. *Interior Castle Explored*. London: Sheed & Ward, 1981.

Camus, Jean Pierre. *The Spirit of St. François de Sales*. New York: Harper, 1952.

Cassian, John. *The Conferences*. Translated and annotated by Boniface Ramsey, O.P. New York: Paulist Press, 1997.

————. *Institutes of the Coenobia*. In vol. 11 of *Nicene and Post-Nicene Fathers*, edited by Philip Schaff and Henry Wace. Grand Rapids, Mich.: Eerdmans, 1978.

Caussade, Jean-Pierre de. *Abandonment to Divine Providence*. Translated by John Beevers. Garden City, N.Y.: Doubleday, 1975.

————. *Lettres spirituelles*. Edited by Michel Olphe-Galliard, S.J. Paris: Desclée de Brouwer, 1962.

————. *On Prayer*. 2d rev. ed. London: Burns & Oates, 1949.

————. *Traité sur l'oraison du coeur*. Edited by Michel Olphe-Galliard, S.J. Paris: Desclée de Brouwer, 1979.

Chadwick, Owen. *John Cassian: A Study in Primitive Monasticism*. 2d ed. London: Cambridge Univ. Press, 1968.

Chapman, John. *Spiritual Letters*. London: Sheed & Ward, 1935.

Chaugy, Mother Francoise de. *Life of S. Jane Frances de Chantal.* London: Richardson and Son, 1852.

Collectio SS Ecclesiae Patrum. Vol 26. Paris: Parent Debarres, 1839.

Conradi, Peter. *Iris Murdoch: A Life.* New York and London: W. W Norton and Co., 2001.

Dictionnaire de spiritualité. Edited by Marcel Viller, S.J. Paris: Gabriel Beauchesne et ses Fils, 1937–1996. 16 vols.

The Fathers of the Church. Vol. 18. New York: Fathers of the Church, 1953.

Feuerbach, Ludwig. *The Essence of Christianity.* Translated by George Eliot. New York: Harper & Row. 1957.

Francis de Sales, St. *Introduction to the Devout Life.* Translated and edited by John K. Ryan. New York: Harper & Brothers, 1950.

———. *Treatise on the Love of God.* Westminster, Md.: Newman Press, 1953.

Gilson, Étienne. *The Christian Philosophy of St. Thomas Aquinas.* New York: Random House, 1956.

Guigo II. *The Ladder of Monks.* Translated with an introduction by Edmund College, O.S.A., and James Walsh, S.J. New York: Doubleday (Image Books), 1978.

Hadot, Pierre. *Philosophy as a Way of Life: Spiritual Exercises from Socrates to Foucault.* Edited by Arnold Davidson. Translated by Michael Chase. Oxford: Blackwell, 1999.

Hamon, André J.-M. *Vie de St. François de Sales.* Paris: Gabalda, 1920.

Handbook of Prayers. Princeton, N.J.: Scepter Publishers, 1995.

Hastings, Selina. *Nancy Mitford.* London: Papermac, 1986.

Hegel, G. *Phenomenology of Spirit.* Translated by A. V. Miller. Oxford: Clarendon Press, 1979.

Hügel, F. von. *The Mystical Element in Religion.* London: J. M. Dent and Sons, 1961.

Hughes, Kathryn. *George Eliot: The Last Victorian*. London: Fourth Estate, 1998.

Ignatius of Loyola, St. *The Spiritual Exercises of St. Ignatius of Loyola*. Edited by Louis J. Puhl, S.J. Chicago: Loyola Univ. Press, 1951.

Jane Frances de Chantal, St. *The Spiritual Life: A Summary of the Instructions on the Virtues and on Prayer Given by Saint Jane Frances Frémyot de Chantal*. Compiled by the Sisters of the Visitation. London: Sands, 1928.

John of the Cross, St. *Complete Works*. Translated and edited by E. Allison Peers. New ed. London: Burns & Oates, 1954.

Kant, Immanuel. *The Critique of Practical Reason*. Translated by Thomas Kingsmill. 6th ed. London: Longmans, Green and Co., 1909.

Knox, Ronald. *Enthusiasm*. Oxford: Clarendon Press, 1962.

Leclercq, Jean, O.S.B. *The Love of Learning and the Desire for God*. New York: Fordham Univ. Press, 1961.

Liturgy of the Hours, The. New York: Catholic Book Publishing Co., 1975.

McCabe, Herbert, O.P. *God Matters*. 1987; reprint, London and New York: Mowbray, 2000.

Merton, Thomas. *The Seven Storey Mountain*. New York: Harcourt, Brace and Co., 1948.

Monk of Farne, The. Edited and introduced by Dom Hugh Farmer, O.S.B. London: Darton, Longman and Todd, 1961.

Murdoch, Iris. *Existentialists and Mystics*. London: Chatto and Windus, 1997.

Murray, Placid, O.S.B. *Newman the Oratorian*. Dublin: Gill and Macmillan, 1969.

Newman, J. H. *Apologia*, New York: Doubleday (Image Books), 1956.

_____. *The Apologia*. Edited by Martin J. Svaglic. Oxford: Clarendon Press, 1967.

_____. *Fifteen Sermons Preached before the University of Oxford between A.D. 1826 and 1843*. London: Longmans, Green, 1900.

_____. *The Idea of a University*. New York: Doubleday and Company (Image Books), 1959.

_____. *The Letters and Diaries of John Henry Newman*. Edinburgh: Nelson; Oxford: Clarendon Press, 1978—. Thirty volumes are planned, but the edition is as yet incomplete.

_____. *Parochial and Plain Sermons*. San Francisco: Ignatius Press, 1997.

_____. *Prayers, Verses, and Devotions: The Devotions of Bishop Andrewes, Meditations and Devotions, Verses on Various Occasions*. San Francisco: Ignatius Press, 2000.

_____. *Sermon Notes of John Henry Cardinal Newman 1849–1878*. Edited by Fathers of the Birmingham Oratory. London: Longmans, Green, 1913–1914.

_____. *Sermons Preached on Various Occasions*. London: Longmans, Green, 1904.

O'Connell, Robert J., S.J. *St. Augustine's Confessions; the Odyssey of Soul*. Cambridge, Mass.: Harvard Univ. Press, 1969.

Passmore, John. *The Perfectibility of Man*. New York: Charles Scribner's Sons, 1970.

Paulinus of Nola, St. *Poems*. Ancient Christian Writers, no. 40. New York: Newman Press, 1975.

Peers, E. Allison. *Spirit of Flame*. London: S.C.M. Press, 1943.

Pelikan, Jaroslav. *The Christian Tradition*. Vol. 5. Chicago: University of Chicago Press, 1989.

Philip Neri, St. *Maxims and Counsels*. Arranged by Fr. Wilfrid Faber. Dublin: M. H. Gill, 1890. Revised by two priests of the Toronto Oratory. Toronto: privately printed, 1995.

Ponnelle, Louis, and Louis Bordet. *St. Philip Neri and the Roman Society of His Time*. Translated by Ralph Francis Kerr. London: Sheed & Ward, 1932.

Poulain, A., S.J. *The Graces of Interior Prayer.* Translated by Leonora L. Yorke Smith. Preface by D. Considine, S.J. London: Paul, Trench, Trübner, 1910.

Rist, John M. *Augustine: Ancient Thought Baptized.* Cambridge and New York: Cambridge Univ. Press, 1994.

Ryle, Gilbert. *The Concept of Mind.* Watford, Herts.: William Brendon and Son, 1949.

Scruton, Roger. *Sexual Desire.* London: Phoenix, 1994.

Scupoli, Lorenzo. *Combattimento Spirituale.* Milan: Edizione Paoline, 1992.

_____. *The Spiritual Combat and Path to Paradise of Lorenzo Scupoli.* Edited by Nicodemus of the Holy Mountain and revised by Theophan the Recluse. Translated by E. Kadloubovsky and G. E. H. Palmer. Introduction by H. A. Hodges. London: Mowbrays, 1978.

_____. *The Spiritual Combat and The Path of Paradise.* Translated with an introduction by E. B. Pusey. London: n. p., 1849.

_____. *Spiritual Combat, Together with The Treatise of Inward Peace.* Printed in Belgium by N. V. Splichal-Turhout. London: Burns & Oates, 1963.

Stewart, Columba, O.S.B. *Cassian the Monk.* New York: Oxford Univ. Press, 1998.

Stopp, Elisabeth. *Madame de Chantal: Portrait of a Saint.* London: Faber and Faber, 1962.

Taylor, Charles. *Human Agency and Language.* Cambridge and New York: Cambridge Univ. Press, 1985.

_____. *Sources of the Self: The Making of the Modern Identity.* Cambridge, Mass.: Harvard Univ. Press, 1989.

Teresa of Jesus, St. *Complete Works.* Translated and edited by E. Allison Peers. London and New York: Sheed & Ward, 1946.

Whitehead, A. N. *Science and the Modern World.* Cambridge: University Press 1932.

INDEX